When Best Doesn't Equal Good

Educational Reform and
Teacher Recruitment

A Longitudinal Study

When Best Doesn't Equal Good

Educational Reform and
Teacher Recruitment

A LONGITUDINAL STUDY

James T. Sears
J. Dan Marshall
Amy Otis-Wilborn

Teachers College, Columbia University
New York and London

Published by Teachers College Press, 1234 Amsterdam Avenue,
New York, NY 10027

Library of Congress Cataloging-in-Publication Data

Sears, James T. (James Thomas), 1951–
    When best doesn't equal good : educational reform and teacher
  recruitment : a longitudinal study / James T. Sears, J. Dan
  Marshall, Amy Otis-Wilborn.
        p.   cm.
    Includes bibliographical references and index.
    ISBN 0-8077-3346-6 (cloth : acid-free paper). — ISBN
  0-8077-3345-8 (paper : acid-free paper)
      1. Teachers—Training of—United States—Longitudinal studies.
    2. Teachers—Recruiting—United States—Longitudinal studies.
    I. Marshall, J. Dan.   II. Otis-Wilborn, Amy K.   III. Title.
    LB1715.S39   1994
    370.71—dc20   94-14176

Printed on acid-free paper

Manufactured in the United States of America

01 00 99 98 97 96 95 94   8 7 6 5 4 3 2 1

To Bob, whose relationship has developed and grown beyond the eight years of research for this book.   *JTS*

To Frank, Joan, and Michael, teacher siblings. To Rita and Frank, the parents of teachers. To John and Cheryl, teacher relatives. To Anna May and Evelyn, departed teachers. And to Tara—who teaches me so much of such importance.   *JDM*

To my mother and father, who shared in the excitement as this research and book project began but didn't live to see its completion; and to Pat, my husband, and Anthony and Aren, my children, who continue to keep me centered on life's priorities.   *AOW*

To those educators, from pre-kindergarten through university, who work directly in the preparation of new teachers as well as those who aspire to become classroom teachers.   *JTS, JDM, AOW*

Contents

Foreword

The first and second waves of educational reform of the 1980s created a common sense among reformers: The success of educational renewal and of teacher education reform are intimately linked to recruiting and retaining high-ability persons in teaching. Smart people, especially ones who know their content areas, make the best teachers, and having smart people in teaching is not only good for students but crucial for achieving professional status and improving teaching's public image. Based on common sense, standards for admission into teacher certification were raised, programs revised, and a great deal of energy spent figuring out ways for luring more smart people into teaching and keeping them in the classroom.

It has been 10 years since *A Nation at Risk* (National Commission on Excellence in Education, 1983) was released and a large number of teachers have been certified through programs inspired by the reports of the second wave, *A Call for Change in Teacher Education* (1985), *A Nation Prepared* (1986), and *Tomorrow's Teachers* (1986). It is now time to check results, which is exactly what the authors of this book set out to do. Although based on a six-year longitudinal of only one program, their findings raise disturbing questions for teacher educators.

Don Wright, an innovative teacher educator at "Central College," recruited 17 high-ability high school students to enter a special program leading to certification and a degree. To lure students into the program, each was offered substantial financial support in the form of forgivable loans—forgiven providing they completed the program in four years and taught in the local area—that would enable attendance at Central, an expensive and respected private college. The authors take us on a journey with five of the "Bridenthal Interns," from their freshman year in college through their second year of teaching.

This book recounts what happened to the interns and explores why it happened in relationship to the claims of reformers, the recent history and politics of reform, and a substantial and far-ranging body of scholarship. The results and the authors' interpretation of them cast a shadow on many cherished beliefs about education reform generally, and teacher education reform specifically, particularly those that find hope in rationalizing teaching and controlling teacher behavior. As the authors argue, such approaches reduce education to training—the learning of techniques—and emphasize external evaluation in quest of a narrow professionalism, one that celebrates the elite professions, law and medicine, as models to emulate and ignores the unique nature of teaching as a caring relationship with young people. This pathway can lead only to disaster.

The Central program is criticized for a good many reasons, but the criticism is not of Central alone. I suspect that Central's failings are widely shared. A sense of community and collegiality never fully develops among the interns. Expert views of knowledge held by the interns were supported, not challenged; the entire college program was driven by what the authors characterize as a "perennialist perspective," in which knowledge is "universalized." Such a view holds that knowledge is received, not constructed; and truth-enduring, not negotiated and reconstructed. Little attention was given to the ethics and politics of teaching. Given that the interns were required to complete the program in four years, there was virtually no time to explore the disciplines or to leisurely consider ideas or career options. Everything was hurried, and initial decisions—about major and minors, for example—became permanent. Induction into public school teaching was haphazard and mentoring of very uneven quality. Don Wright's involvement with the interns dropped considerably as other interns were recruited and as he initiated additional reform projects, including establishing "Alliance Schools" (what others might call "professional development schools").

Wright's story is intriguing, although through most of the book he appears more as a force working behind the scenes than as a central character. He is portrayed as an ambitious and smooth innovator and a bit of a hustler whose initial vision, one heavily influenced by the major reform reports, was to forge the interns into change agents who would go out into the schools and reshape them by the example of their intelligence and dedication. Through the force of his personality and drive he created the program, but he was not fully able to sustain either it or his vision over the long run.

As a teacher educator, I empathized with Don Wright. I know something about the difficulty of getting a new program off the ground. I was impressed with his energy and commitment to reform. Reforming teacher education is hard, frustrating, and seldom appreciated work; and it is little wonder there are so few Don Wrights. As I read, I found myself pondering his actions, and thinking about his work in relationship to my own. Some of the problems with the Central program came because it was the first cycle, and undoubtedly much would later change. But even knowing this, I still felt disappointed. The program should have been more than the Peace Corps that the authors claim it became. I wanted Don Wright to slow down and contain his ambition a bit. I wanted him to take more seriously the importance of community building to education reform and of exploring personally held and deeply imbedded images and beliefs about teaching that form the basis of teacher identity and that so dramatically influenced what the interns learned and did not learn in his program. I wanted him to help the interns develop a collegial vision of teaching and of the responsibility of teachers, one reflecting a profession grounded in a service ideal and ethic that enables teachers to "feel special" because they make a difference and not because they were "Bridenthal Brats," as other students characterized them, and the "best." More than anything, I wanted Don Wright to reconsider the assumptions about reform that underpinned his work, and to attend with greater care to counterevidence, just as I wanted his students to explore their own assumptions about teaching and learning. Without doing this, it is likely that the program results will be about the same for future groups of interns as they were for this one. The problem is in the assumptions. Common sense often leads astray.

And what were the results? The context of teaching, coming to terms with what Gary Fenstermacher calls the "systemics" of teaching, nearly overwhelmed the interns during their first two years of teaching. Generally they found themselves isolated, frustrated with students' lack of interest in content and other teachers' limited interest in teaching, and forced to engage in a variety of compromises that required, for some, setting aside their visions of themselves as teachers developed through the program to embrace more institutionally fitting and conservative roles. A harsh realism set in. All of this sounds familiar, and comes as no surprise to veteran teacher educators. Those interns who continued to believe they could help reform education looked outside the classroom, especially toward educational administration, as the most promising avenue for pursuing change. Despite program claims, the interns, "the best," turned out to be remarkably like other teachers who go through regular certification programs and who similarly often think of teaching as a interim job. One of the interns, Rita, for example, observed: "The people I know in the regular program didn't do any worse or any better than I did in student teaching. I wasn't any more prepared for student teaching, I don't think. I had the same problems they did."

Roberto is the exception. A great deal can be learned from Roberto. He is one of two ethnic-minority interns and felt the pressures associated with being different. Central is a school primarily for wealthy white students. Without the internship, Roberto probably could not have attended

Central, nor would he have entered teaching. Originally he intended to become a child psychologist, a dream he maintained until his senior year. His experience "converted" him to teaching. By the end of his second year of teaching, Roberto was an important member of the King-Jackson elementary school community, a magnet school drawing students from four low-income schools. Throughout his time there he felt supported by his colleagues and, by virtue of landing a job in an Alliance School, the Central faculty. He eagerly sought the feedback of others on his performance and consistently received exceptional formal evaluations. In particular he was recognized for his ability to develop rapport with students, especially poor children, and for gaining insight into and responding appropriately to their educational needs. Drawing on his background as a minority person he reached out to young people, hoping to connect with them and in the process give something back to education. He engaged other faculty members in conversations about teaching and sought to extend the feeling of collegiality that existed within the school. Recognizing the importance of context to his development, he worked hard to improve it. In this respect, his experience illustrates a point well made by the authors: Community is not likely to emerge from reform efforts that have as their centerpiece the creation of a stratified or staged teaching profession. Helping must be seen as every teacher's responsibility, not just someone labeled a "teacher-leader." However, collegiality is not likely to emerge through helping and sharing unless they are tied to significant and meaningful activities such as joint planning and experimentation. Roberto engages in such activities, and is connected with the wider school as a result: "I've been able to be a decision maker. I've had a voice in my school." By the end of his second year of teaching he willingly assumed a leadership position: "I'm looking forward to being team leader; seeing myself take on that role, see how I do. I know they'll [colleagues] be right behind me, helping me out." Perhaps more than any other of the interns, Roberto has the potential to become the "transformative intellectual" the authors value and the change agent Don Wright seeks. The extent of the influence of the Bridenthal program on Roberto is uncertain, however. What is certain is that without it he would not have entered teaching at all. But is one Roberto, and several short-term teachers, worth the tremendous expense? Perhaps. Perhaps not.

The authors wonder if the Bridenthal money might not have been better spent differently, on programs driven by other assumptions—particularly about what counts as "best." For instance, the single-minded pursuit of test-score-driven standards of excellence has the perverse result of excluding from teacher certification programs significant numbers of otherwise very able minority students. Ironically, the same reports that call for the "best" based on test scores also bemoan the shortage of minority teach-

ers. What counts as best must be made problematic. What is best? Best for
what contexts and for what purposes? As the authors argue, there are good
reasons for not tailoring our programs to the best students, as currently we
conceive of that term, despite the obvious public-relations advantages for
doing so. As this book's title asserts, there are situations where best doesn't
equal good: The best students do not necessarily make the best teachers.

The authors present a view of education reform different from the one
put forward by the major reports of the second wave. They invite us to
reconsider assumptions:

> Talk of changing or improving teacher education must . . . be tied to talk of
> changing schools—not simply changing teachers' work but changing the job of
> teaching by restructuring and reevaluating the school culture. Change of this
> sort recognizes the importance of teachers as participants in, not merely recipi-
> ents of, change. Change of this sort recognizes the need to see change within
> its broader historical, social, and political contexts—contexts that have shaped
> the very language and understandings we presently have about education.
> Indeed, change of this sort requires genuine new ideas—not mere variations on
> old and usually bureaucratic ones.
>
> Further, the process of becoming a teacher would change dramatically, as
> the places where teachers are taught experienced cultural change. Preservice
> candidates would learn that their future career is nothing short of a life's
> work that, while rooted in the classroom, requires them to take their energy,
> intelligence, and wisdom as educators well beyond classroom walls. These
> future teachers would recognize the absolute necessity of developing and evolv-
> ing a genuine social vision to guide their work and would learn to see that their
> rewards are to be measured not in test scores and college-bound graduates but
> in the kind of society their students help to shape and build. Most importantly,
> people who enter teaching . . . will come to understand that their work, like
> that of all others, shapes and is shaped by political, social, and economic forces
> at every turn, and that in order to maintain a balance in this cultural dynamic
> they must actively and intelligently participate in representing their profession
> in this exchange.

Throughout this book the authors offer a few hints about how to
engage in what they deem "the difficult work of culture reform," work that
is under way to a degree in Roberto's school. But, they are only hints. They
succeed in challenging on empirical and theoretical grounds the legitimacy
of the four major assumptions on which the Bridenthal program was conceptualized, assumptions common to a good many programs of reform:
"(1) 'the best' students can be matter-of-factly defined and identified;
(2) these students should be recruited into teaching; (3) these recruits 'deserve' more . . . money, more prestige, more opportunities . . . than other
prospective teachers; and (4) these recruits will be better than the average

classroom teachers." In doing so, and through the questions they raise and problems they pose, they illustrate the importance at this moment in our history, when confidence in the power of education to reshape our public world is waning and the future of teacher education is insecure, of reframing the debate over teacher education reform in wider cultural and economic terms. As the authors argue, the significant problems of teacher education are structural, and "symptomatic of a systemic crisis of institutions." They are right, it is time to switch conceptual horses, and break a new trail.

Robert V. Bullough, Jr.
University of Utah

Preface

Why not the best? This is the question we pondered as Central College's Department of Education threw its hat into the arena of educational reform. Central's reform innovation, the Bridenthal Internship in Teaching (BIT) program, began in the fall of 1984 as 17 top high school graduates started a specially designed, six-year teacher preparation program.[1] As one of the first reformed-based programs seeking to recruit, prepare, and retain high-ability students for public school teaching, the Bridenthal program presented a unique opportunity to research a number of questions regarding teacher education, beginning teachers and the context of their work, and educational reform. "When best doesn't equal good" is our response, based on the data generated from these questions, to those who too simplistically ask, "Why not the best?"

The three phases in our six-year study of the Bridenthal program aligned with the program's original goals: acclimation (recruitment), specialization (preparation), and professionalization (retention). During the acclimation phase we looked at recruitment into teaching, career decision making, and the transition into postsecondary education. In years three and four, we focused on developing knowledge bases, student teaching, and job selection. In the final phase, years five and six, we examined aspects of induction into job and career, job satisfaction, performance, and commitment to teaching. Across all phases, three broad themes gave definition to the broader context of our study: career development, professionalization, and educational reform.

Our research design was multifaceted, representing a variety of interrelated qualitative and quantitative data collection and analysis techniques. In-depth individual and group interviews served as our major source of data and created the foundation for the development of other instrumentation. We conducted on-site interviews with the interns at the onset and conclusion of each academic year, and telephone interviews at mid-year. Over the

---

[1] The names of the program, the institution, and the participants have been altered.

years, we periodically interviewed other relevant persons, including interns'
parents; Dr. Don Wright, the program's director and Chair of the Department of Education at Central; faculty members integral to the interns'
teacher preparation program; a selected cohort of preservice students in
Central's traditional teacher education program; cooperating teachers and
university supervisors; and interns' program supervisors and/or building
principals in their first two years of teaching. All of the interviews were
audio- or videotaped for analysis. Additional qualitative data included interns' personal journals, field notes from on-campus participant observation, media coverage, and interns' research and opinion papers from education courses.

Throughout the research study, we developed and employed a number
of paper-and-pencil instruments. The data collected through these instruments helped us establish interpretive reliability and to monitor patterns in
interns' attitudes toward Central College, the Bridenthal program, their
developing knowledge and teaching competence, and their long-term commitment to teaching as a career. The items on these instruments included
open-ended and scaled question formats derived directly from information
that surfaced within the interviews. Interns completed these instruments at
strategic points across the six-year study.

Various standardized data provided us with information that allowed
us to look at the interns within the context of other more general populations. Instruments identifying career development and teaching orientations
included the Self-Directed-Search (Holland, 1985), the Career Maturity
Inventory (Crites, 1978), and the Surveys of Personal Values (Gordon,
1984) and Interpersonal Values (Gordon, 1976). During years five and six,
the interns completed the Curriculum Ideologies Inventory, the Teaching
Style Inventory (Silver & Hanson, 1981), and the Minnesota Teacher Inventory. All standardized instruments were administered in pre- and post-
fashion in order to monitor changes in interns' development and orientations over time.

Several of our most fundamental research questions related to the quality of the interns' teaching performance. For this reason, we collected data
from several sources in order to provide multiple perspectives on their classroom teaching. First, we videotaped episodes of interns' student teaching
and first and second years of teaching. We then analyzed these episodes
ourselves and, in the case of the first-year videotape teaching data, with the
interns themselves. To provide another perspective of these same teaching
episodes, an individual not connected with this research project or Central
College evaluated each of the interns' videotaped teaching samples using
the North Carolina Teacher Assessment (NCTA) and the Compensatory
Remedial Observations Systems (CROSS) (Anderson, Cook, Pellicer, Sears,

& Spradling, 1989). This individual, a veteran school administrator with expertise in curriculum and instruction, regularly evaluates teachers in his own building using the NCTA and completed his dissertation using data drawn from the CROSS. Additionally, we collected evaluations conducted by the interns' area supervisors and/or building principals, who used the state teacher assessment survey as part of a mandated teacher evaluation process. These data, along with perceptions of interns' teaching solicited from those with whom they worked, combined to create our picture of the interns' classroom teaching.

Our data analysis followed a disciplined inquiry: a sequence of steps that includes data collection, data reduction, data display, drawing conclusions, and verification. At the end of each project year, we conducted a preliminary review of all raw data collected during that year. After developing individual working hypotheses, we met to discuss these, and eventually to construct one consensus set of hypotheses. Next, we completed a detailed analysis of all data in order to verify or reject working hypotheses. Quantitative data were treated statistically while qualitative data were subjected to the processes of categorization and analytic induction (Goetz & LeCompte, 1984). All of the various types and sources of data were then triangulated in order to verify findings and interpretations (Lincoln & Guba, 1985). The triangulization of various data pointed toward fruitful avenues for further investigation, challenged theoretical constructs developed from previous analysis, and tested patterns suggested by prior data analyses. Following this, we developed strategies and directions for the coming year; we then created and refined data-collection instruments and established our data-collection schedule. This process was ongoing across the six years of our research study.

Over the course of this six-year study, our research findings and analyses have been documented and reported regularly.[2] In the last three years of this project, we maintained project summaries, publishing several articles using these data. These publications are referred to throughout the text. This book represents a summary of our BIT research in which the lives of five of the interns play out within the context the broad themes of educational reform, teacher career development, and professionalism. The sheer mass of data collected on the experiences of all interns, however, still leaves many issues untouched and stories untold. *When Best Doesn't Equal Good* is both the story of one small group of interns and an analysis of the

---

[2]See, for example: Marshall, Otis-Wilborn, & Sears, 1991; Marshall, Sears, & Otis-Wilborn, 1987; Otis-Wilborn, Marshall, & Sears, 1989; Otis-Wilborn, Marshall, & Sears, 1990; Sears, Marshall, & Otis-Wilborn, 1989; Sears, Marshall, & Otis-Wilborn, 1990; Sears, Moyer, & Marshall, 1986.

effectiveness and wisdom of programs designed to recruit, prepare, and retain high-ability persons in our public schools.

We would like to acknowledge those who have contributed to or shown interest in and support for this project over the years: Phi Delta Kappan and The South Carolina Educational Policy Center; Shannon Hart, Pat Lindler, Deborah McCarthy, Rosemary Schiavi, Phil Moyer, and David DeWitt; the faculty and staff at Central College; the 12 interns whose stories are not a focus of this book yet who invited us to tag along with them as they became teachers and the five interns (Jan, Roberto, Gene, Lucy, and Rita) and, of course, Don Wright; and the reference and interlibrary loan departments at the University of South Carolina.

When Best Doesn't Equal Good

Educational Reform and Teacher Recruitment

A Longitudinal Study

CHAPTER 1

The Reform of Teacher Education in the Decade of the Eighties

In 1983, the year of the first wave of contemporary education reform reports, Don Wright, a visionary education professor, persuaded a local foundation to provide more than $500,000 to "recruit, train, and retain high ability people for the teaching profession." Seventeen 1984 high school graduates became Bridenthal Interns, which, for most, included tuition and allowances at one of the most prestigious institutions of higher education in the region—Central College. In return, they agreed to embrace teaching as a career and to commit themselves to two years of teaching in one of the 15 local public school districts.

At the end of the decade, 16 of these interns completed their two years of teaching. This book is the six-year story of these interns portrayed against the backdrop of two waves of educational reform. How five of these interns—Roberto, Jan, Lucy, Gene, and Rita—developed into teachers under Wright's watchful eye is one of the stories in this book. In the following pages you will see, for example, Roberto transformed from a shy, reticent young man to a thoughtful teacher and an articulate leader, and you will watch as Lucy meets the academic demands of Central and the situational stress of teaching while she struggles as a single parent. Here the stories of these young women and men—representative of the best and the brightest graduates of our nation's high schools—unfold chapter by chapter as they enter into the daily challenge of college life, listen to state and national leaders in educational reform, choose a college major and teaching specialization, speak to the nation through conference appearances, television interviews, and newspaper stories, and enter the classroom as novice teachers. There are, however, other stories.

In an exhaustive review of the teacher education reform literature pub-

1

lished between 1980 and 1987, we identified 45 reform programs (Sears, Marshall, & Otis-Wilborn, 1988). Those programs that altered, improved, or redesigned their professional education component reported doing so for one or more of the following reasons: (1) to increase preservice teachers' knowledge base and teaching skills; (2) to link theory presented in courses with teaching practice; and/or (3) to foster a partnership with local schools. From the myriad articles, papers, and documents discussing these programs, however, only 1 percent incorporated any type of evaluative or research basis. While an increasing number of articles and books cast doubt on the wisdom of particular reform proposals or the value of popular approaches to educational reform, the number of evaluative or research-based studies represents but a fraction of this volume of work. This is one of the first research-based books to systematically examine the effectiveness of a reform program using its stated goals as one benchmark for success. It is the first longitudinal study on the effectiveness of a teacher education program modeled, in part, on the reform reports of the early 1980s.

Throughout this book we examine the six-year educational journey of the 17 Bridenthal Interns in light of the literature of educational reform, the politics of professionalizing the craft of teaching, and the research base of career development. In the rest of this chapter we will consider each of these as critical frameworks for our study.

We have chosen to group the chapters in this book in three parts, each reflecting a distinct phase of the Bridenthal Interns' experience. Part I, the *acclimation phase*, extending through the interns' first three college semesters, reveals their orientation to college life, their familiarization with schools and classrooms, a development of group identity, and an infusion of mission and purpose. Part II, the *specialization phase*, continuing through their student teaching experience and college graduation, marks their entry into formal professional studies and a point of decision making regarding their certification program and content area. Part III, the *professionalization phase*, defined as their first two years in public school teaching, ushers them into the professional world of teaching. Within each of these parts, we will use the research literature of educational reform, teacher professionalism, and career development to articulate chapter-specific themes.

EDUCATIONAL REFORM OF THE 1980S

Prior to 1980, only one state had initiated recent educational reform. Within two years following the publication of *A Nation at Risk* (National Commission on Excellence in Education, 1983), all but four states (Alaska, Nebraska, Utah, and Vermont) had convened commissions or committees to study and recommend state reforms in public education ("Changing

Course," 1985; Goertz & Pitchor, 1985). Several hundred state and national reform reports and proposals followed (Cross, 1984; Robinson, 1985). Between 1980 and 1986, the "first wave" of educational reform, $4.2 billion was allocated by the states and their localities for elementary and secondary education (National Education Association, 1986; for a summary of how states have financed educational reform, see Odden, 1986).

By mid-decade, teacher preparation itself had become a prime focus for reformers. Educational associations, private foundations, and executive and legislative bodies all issued reports (Plank & Ginsberg, 1990), three of which epitomized a "second wave" of educational reform: *Tomorrow's Teachers*, issued by the Holmes Group (1986); *A Nation Prepared*, prepared by the Carnegie Task Force on Teaching as a Profession (1986); and *A Call for Change in Teacher Education*, published by the American Association of Colleges for Teacher Education (1985). (For a critical review of some of the reports written during this period, consult: Cornbleth, 1986; Feinberg, 1987; Finkelstein, 1984; Gideonese, 1984; Passow, 1984; Popkewitz & Pittman, 1986; Weiss, 1985.)

Two Waves of Contemporary Teacher Education Reform

As the Reagan decade began, words like *excellence*, *quality*, and *competence* entered public discussion about schools, teachers, and teacher education. In his inaugural address to the membership of the American Association of Colleges for Teacher Education, for example, Robert Egbert (1980) exhorted his colleagues to "make educational excellence our leadership priority for 1980" (p. 7), and to engage the public in a dialogue about the importance of education.

At the same time, the U.S. Department of Education, despite the Reagan administration's rhetoric about eliminating its cabinet-level rank, was busy selecting 18 members for its National Commission on Excellence in Education, who toiled almost two years to produce *A Nation at Risk*. With its publication, the public debate about educational excellence and teacher competence began in earnest (see, for example, DeYoung, 1986; Greene, 1984; Raywid, 1987).

A Nation at Risk focused on public schools, decrying low achievement scores and short school years, little homework, and the absence of rigorous curriculum. It also championed the need for a renewed teaching profession that attracted top students, prepared them within an academic discipline with a deemphasis on educational methods courses, and awarded them with adequate salaries and the prospect of genuine career advancement.

Most states responded to this report by convening committees or commissions to recommend educational reform. These legislative and institutional policy reform efforts represented the first wave of teacher education reform during the 1980s. Collectively, their most popular directive for policy reform was to raise teacher standards. More stringent state certification procedures, most notably in the Southeast (Anrig, 1986), included mandating the testing of teacher candidates prior to state certification. By mid-decade, all but a handful of states required specific tests for teacher certification. States frequently used national or state proficiency examinations of general knowledge and basic skills, as well as of subject area and professional knowledge (Anrig, 1986; Goertz, Ekstrom, & Coley, 1984; Harvey, Madaus, & Kreitzer, 1987; Sandefur, 1985).

A number of problems accompanied the implementation of reform policies of the early 1980s. Elsewhere (Sears, Marshall, & Otis-Wilborn, 1988) we have documented that most first-wave reform efforts resulted from purely external, political forces or agents (e.g., national reports or state legislative mandates) or some combination of these with internal forces (e.g., declining enrollments or faculty/administrator desires for change). As a result, these early reform efforts were unlikely to receive the types of structural (e.g., financial) and personal (e.g., faculty commitment) support needed to sustain long-lasting change. Consequently, they perpetuated the image of a profession that follows directions mapped out by others. The power of these external forces can be seen in the conceptual frameworks of most reform efforts (traditional, linear, cause-and-effect) and their largely piecemeal approaches—many of which emanated directly from forces outside of the teacher education institutions. We discuss many of these problems here.

Concerns about the failure of these policies to address more profound structural problems in teacher education resulted in a "second wave" of reform reports, which appeared in the mid-1980s. By this time there were signs that the reform "movement" was shifting into a new phase, prompted at times by the architects of the first wave of reform initiatives themselves (Bacharach, Bauer, & Shedd, 1986). New voices were heard, new concerns were raised, new kinds of proposals were advocated, and new coalitions were formed to press for their implementation.

On the heels of *A Nation at Risk*, the National Commission for Excellence in Teacher Education heard testimony from a variety of persons, including the Chair of Central College's Department of Education. In his testimony, Don Wright emphasized the need to devise a teacher education program that would successfully recruit, train, and retain "high-ability" people for *careers* in teaching. His testimony, a sketchy vision of an innovative approach to teacher training, was no less compelling than that offered by the small army of contributors to the American Association of Colleges for Teacher Education (AACTE) data pool—some of which were incorporated into AACTE's *A Call for Change in Teacher Education* (1985). What set Wright's vision apart from the rest was that his idea was already becoming a reality.

A year later, 17 education deans from many of the major research universities met to discuss ways to improve teacher education and to reform the teaching profession. Known as the Holmes Group, in 1986 they distributed *Tomorrow's Teachers*—the benchmark of second-wave reform. A month later the Carnegie Task Force on Teaching as a Profession (1986) issued its report, *A Nation Prepared: Teachers for the 21st Century*, prepared by a diverse group of 14 persons. Stressing the integral relationship between a strong national economy and a premier system of schooling, this report underscored the importance of a "knowledge-based economy." Comparing European and Asian schools with those of the United States, its authors asserted: "In our country, by contrast, real intellectual effort in schools is not often demanded by parents and is generally frowned upon by students' peers." *A Nation Prepared* called for a "fundamental redesign" of the teaching profession, which included establishing rigorous national teaching standards, "recruiting the most able college graduates to teaching," and restructuring the teacher work force and the school's work environment (p. 21).

These three reports expressed many of the same themes as *A Nation at Risk*—the need to attract quality students into teaching, to institute strenuous education courses, and to require a discipline-based, subject-matter-centered degree program for all teachers. They differed, however, on linking reforms made in teacher preparation to reforms in school culture, in the relationship between the school and the university, and in overall professional governance and control.

Three Domains of Reform

Chapters 2, 5, and 8 place the experiences of the interns and their program within three general reform domains: teacher recruitment, liberal arts–based undergraduate curriculum, and induction systems and school/university collaboration. By the mid-1980s teacher recruitment took the form of incentives, scholarships, and forgivable or low-interest loans in more than 20 states for students pursuing degrees in shortage areas, particularly in science and mathematics (Spero, 1986). Alabama, for example, awarded scholarships on a competitive basis to students who agree to teach three years for each academic year the scholarship is provided. In Alaska, students could receive a loan of up to $7,500 a year, which was forgiven after five years of teaching in a rural area. In states such as Pennsylvania and Tennessee, educational loans were provided to experienced teachers in surplus fields who sought "retooling" in a shortage area.

Policies like these were relatively easy to implement and demonstrated a rapid response to the public concern about teacher quality and the dwindling number of well-qualified teachers in content areas identified by the *A Nation at Risk* as particularly critical. They operated under the assumption that improving education required attracting more able persons into teaching (preferably in critical shortage areas) who would, in turn, produce a generation of students able to outscore students of other developed nations.

Schools, colleges, and departments of education were called on to assume a more active role in screening out the less able and recruiting the more able prospective teachers. Raising minimum requirements for admission into the professional program, increasing the rigor of professional educational coursework (particularly in the area of educational methods), and establishing higher professional standards for teacher education graduates also became common strategies. Typically, recruitment efforts were grounded on crude empirical data such as student grades or proficiency tests rather than a more sophisticated interactional process.

By the mid-1980s, some teacher educators were questioning the validity of such measures, even suggesting that employing only data such as grade point averages might eliminate persons who are actually perceived to be successful future teachers (Nelson & Wood, 1985). The Holmes Group (1986) labeled such reform proposals "overly simple solutions" (p. 25). Indeed, most second-wave reform proposals acknowledged this weakness and recognized the complexities of changing teacher education: "Plans to improve teacher education must be inextricably tied to plans to improve the occupation of teaching" (Keith, 1987, p. 26). Instead of asking how we can get "better" students into our "better" programs, "the question . . . becomes: How can teaching *as a profession* attract and retain qualified and capable persons?" (p. 23; emphasis added).

The Bridenthal program was developed in the midst of the first-wave reports and implemented during and following the issuance of the major second-wave reform reports. How this six-year program evolved during these two reform waves is one focus of this book. At the outset, it was clearly influenced by the early 1980s reform milieu. The mandate was clear: Bright people should be recruited into teaching. In order to transform the "poor image" of teaching, to improve the quality of K–12 instruction, and to serve as a catalyst for change in the public schools, a cadre of high-ability students dedicated to teaching and, more importantly, to educational reform was necessary. As we will document in Chapter 2, however, recruiting the brightest and the best was, at its core, an issue of public relations, not public policy; the paramount goal was the *re-presentation* of the image of public school teaching.

The early 1980s also brought renewed calls for colleges to return to a liberal arts–centered curriculum and for educators to embrace a liberal arts–based teacher education curriculum. This curriculum rests on the twin pillars of a broad liberal arts education and an academic major. The three major second-wave reform reports all proposed that prospective teachers be exposed to liberal education requirements that were at least as strenuous as those for noneducation majors. This reform goal has been generally accomplished by decreasing students' exposure to professional education courses to make room for additional university coursework, and / or extending their overall program of professional study beyond the conventional four-year period.

In short, the argument was that the preparation of teachers requires a broad liberal arts core of study that is the responsibility of the entire university faculty. This increased knowledge base results in well-rounded teachers steeped in the subject matter, who will enhance their students' quality of learning. But, as we discuss in Chapter 5, these assumptions raise numerous questions: What is the relationship between subject-matter knowledge and teaching effectiveness? At what cost do we split subject-matter knowledge and pedagogy? Can a biologist teach biology? Can a major in Elizabethan drama help inner-city adolescents bring meaning to Othello? What are the costs to students, particularly those without scholarships or adequate income, in pursuing extended teacher preparation programs? And, can exposure of preservice teachers to liberal arts faculty be counterproductive? At the core of such questions lie epistemological issues about the nature and value of knowledge. Advocates of a knowledge-based curriculum assume a *universalization* of knowledge. From this perspective, a core of knowledge exists, context-independent and common to all students, serving as the basis for human understanding and interaction as well as the foundation for professional study.

As we detail in Chapter 8, a third area of concern for teacher preparation institutions reforming their professional preparation curriculum in the 1980s was forging partnerships and induction systems for novice teachers with local school districts (Levine, 1992). Researchers have long documented the difficulties faced by novice teachers as they make an uneasy transition from teacher preparatory programs to classroom teaching (Fuller, 1969; Ryan, Newman, Mager, Applegate, Lasley, Flora, & Johnston, 1980; Veenman, 1984). Not surprisingly, the major second-wave reform reports stressed the importance of teacher induction programs for beginning teachers. *A Call for Change in Teacher Education* (American Association of

Colleges for Teacher Education, 1985), for example, advocated a one-year, supervised, paid internship for beginning teachers beyond the provisional certification requirement. During this first year, interns would be assigned reduced teaching loads in order to take advantage of special induction activities developed collaboratively by the school district, local educational associations, and nearby colleges of education.

Despite such proposals, the reform most often implemented to integrate new teachers into the profession and the work place has been the induction model, which focuses on *socialization*: fitting the novice into the demands of the workplace. This deficit-based, technically oriented model is evidenced in common topics covered during an induction year: preparing for teacher performance evaluations, classroom management techniques, and understanding district policies, procedures, and personnel. This technical orientation toward teacher induction is not surprising given that the primary impetus during the first wave of the reform movement often resulted from the policy decisions of state legislatures (Hawk & Robards, 1987).

Internship programs such as the Bridenthal program would appear to be at odds with such induction programs given the former's emphasis on transforming the teaching profession and developing teacher-leaders as change agents. Also at odds with this induction model would appear to be those second-wave reform proposals articulating the importance of school restructuring, teacher empowerment, and professionalism commonly associated with professional development schools.

THE PROFESSIONALIZATION OF TEACHING

The need to further professionalize teaching lies at the center of all 1980s teacher education reform—an important need, too, in 1825, when several prominent men, including a New England minister, began a public campaign for normal schools. By 1839 the first normal school had opened, in Lexington, Massachusetts (Harper, 1939). Throughout, as Sears (1981) has noted, the campaign to professionalize teaching was tied to the social, political, and economic transformations under way within the United States itself. With the development of a nationwide system of public schools and the creation of a managerial group to oversee it, the twentieth century delivered a highly bureaucratized operational context for schooling that required professional teachers. The establishment of normal schools, and their later evolution into four-year teachers' colleges, allowed teacher preparation itself to evolve and fill this need (Harper, 1939). Yet the training of teachers remained tied to questions of professionalism itself (Altenbaugh, 1974; Lieberman, 1956).

Basic Characteristics of a Profession

Most contemporary writers discuss professionalism through the use of taxonomies or lists of characteristics that distinguish expert or elite professionals from other workers. We can categorize these often diverse characteristics into five basic or fundamental areas: ideal of service, ethical code, specific body of knowledge, autonomy, and distinctive culture.*

Stemming from the original professions (medicine, ministry, and law), an ideal of service reflects the professional worker's commitment to serve both society as a whole and its individual members and represents a "devotion to the client's interests more than [to] personal or commercial profits" (Macklin, 1981). Such an ideal also suggests the relationship between one's profession and one's "life's work" (Hughes, 1969; Weil & Weil, 1971), or the tendency to see a profession as all-encompassing to such a degree that "to the professional person his [or her] work becomes his [or her] life" (Greenwood, 1957, p. 53). This ideal of service suggests how members of a profession will conduct themselves and, as such, is closely tied to another basic characteristic of every profession — an ethical code.

While each profession's ethical code is distinct, most identify the need to keep an emotional neutrality toward clients; to provide services to whoever requires them, regardless of personal convenience or clients' differences and characteristics; and to provide the highest quality of service possible (Greenwood, 1957).

A specific body of knowledge serves to fundamentally distinguish professionals from laypeople. The body of knowledge held by professionals must be codified, systematic, unique to the profession (i.e., not borrowed from another profession), and able to help solve the problems of everyday living (Goode, 1969; Horton, 1944; Ornstein, 1981). Although often emphasizing intellectual information, most professional knowledge includes specific skills required of the successful practitioner. Attaining this body of knowledge requires lengthy, specialized training (Weil & Weil, 1971), the length and nature of which is unique to each profession.

Wide-ranging and inclusive, autonomy provides the profession with an ability to control the entrance and conduct of its members (Horton, 1944), to encourage and/or require continued education (Weil & Weil, 1971), and to provide a self-governing organizational structure for its members (Lieberman, 1956). At the same time, individuals within the profession remain free to exercise professional judgment and assume responsibility for

---

*Most of our discussion of professionalism borrows heavily from Hart and Marshall (1992).

such judgment. Attainment of professional autonomy for a group and its members indicates society's trust in and acceptance of the profession.

Finally, each profession creates and recreates a distinctive culture(s)—norms, values, and symbols that combine to sustain the profession's own reasons for existence. Through the sharing of culture a unity is formed among members that helps to sustain the structure of the profession as a whole (Langford, 1978). The acculturation of neophytes, a distinctly important function of professional preparation, is typically accomplished through "test situations" that provide graduated exposure to this distinctive culture (Greenwood, 1957) as well as through professional training. Surviving the rigors of training requires future professionals to work together and results in an "all for one" feeling among new entrants. This bonding helps to form the new, desired "professional identity" when survivors become "one of them"—a crucial self-perception in the development of a distinctive professional culture.

Teaching as a Profession

Professionalization is more a process than an outcome, and teaching exists somewhere on a continuum of professions. Second-wave reform agendas aimed to move teaching further along this continuum toward elite status and highlighted the importance of professionalizing teaching. A brief look at teaching in light of the above professional characteristics illuminates this quest for professional status.

As Pullias (1940) noted more than a half century ago, teaching will be considered a profession and "education [will] be adequately and willingly supported when and *only* when it produces a society that understands and appreciates its function and worth" (p. 268). With respect to their service ideal, teachers have again come under heavy attack for their perceived lack of commitment to students and to their school communities. Beginning in the decade of the 1960s, when teachers moved toward greater activism, the public has tended to see them more like self-serving, unionized laborers than as elite professionals.

Coupled with this is the public's doubts about the overall social value of "professional" teachers. Despite more than a century of work to construct a meaningful path toward the professional preparation of teachers, some states have ignored the standards of professional organizations and legislatively reduced the amount of professional coursework required for professional preparation. At the same time, many states now have both tests to assure the "minimum competency" of those who complete professional preparation programs and alternative avenues to enable persons who have no professional preparation to enter classrooms and do teachers' work.

The code of ethics for teaching was first established in 1929 by the National Education Association (NEA) and last revised in 1975 (Smith, Travers, & Yard, 1990). However, between 1959 and 1986 the code had been enforced by the NEA in fewer than 10 instances. Two principles make up this code: commitment to the student and commitment to the profession. The first provides eight specific directives, most focusing on the fair and equal treatment of students. In the second, eight additional directives focus on maintaining high ideals and service standards. Ironically, few teachers know much about this code, few preparation programs include it as an important part of professional knowledge, and little can be found about it in the educational literature.

Although teaching's formal code of ethics receives little notice, the act of teaching has many ethical dimensions (see, for example, Rich, 1985; Sockett, 1990, 1993; Strike, 1990a, 1990b; Strom, 1989). Issues that require ethical judgment and behavior are common in classrooms, schools, and communities, suggesting that "ethical behavior is more complex than following the rules of a code; it involves learning to think, act, and acquire the attitudes of a professional teacher and to be guided by one's own philosophy of education" (Rich, 1985, p. 22).

The question of the existence of a unique body of teaching knowledge remains hotly contested (see, for example, Beyer, Feinberg, Pagano, & Whitson, 1989; Tom & Valli, 1990). Much of this debate is fueled by basic epistemological differences between those who view teaching knowledge as scientifically based, lawlike generalizations and those who understand this knowledge as constructed and reconstructed, practical and site-specific.

Despite epistemological differences, general agreement exists on at least two points. First, teaching is acknowledged to be complex, multidimensional work that calls on different sorts of knowledge, actions, behaviors, and decision-making abilities (see, for example, Ayers, 1990; Barnes, 1989; Feiman-Nemser & Floden, 1986). Second, in response to this complexity, teacher knowledge must include both subject matter and pedagogy as well as the intricate relationships between them (see, for example, Beyer et al., 1989; Dreeben, 1970; Howsam, Corrigan, Denemark, & Nash, 1976; McDiarmid, Ball, & Anderson, 1989; Shulman, 1987).

Currently, these two broad areas of teacher knowledge combine to form what is generally referred to as the knowledge base of teaching. This knowledge base is typically represented within preparation programs as general knowledge (i.e., coursework in the liberal arts, including the discipline-specific focus discussed above) and professional knowledge (i.e., professional pedagogical knowledge, which includes coursework in the foundations of education and methods of teaching, coupled with classroom-based clinical work).

Discussing autonomy, Lieberman (1956) suggests that as a group, teachers should evidence autonomy in decisions regarding factors such as qualifications for entrance into professional preparation; the length, content, and nature of this preparation; standards for entry into and expulsion from teaching; and identification of professional leadership and spokespeople at all levels. As individuals, teachers should have autonomy when making decisions regarding factors such as subject matter and teaching materials; criteria for student admission, retention, and graduation; and format for reporting pupil progress. Few teachers recognize such freedoms in contemporary early childhood, elementary, or secondary educational environments.

Teachers typically exhibit their broad, collective autonomy through membership and participation in either the National Education Association or the American Federation of Teachers, both of which have had representation in the current nationwide reform agendas. Small-group (typically at the building or district level) and individual autonomy is evidenced in teachers' growing interest in the decision-making processes that most directly affect their classroom work, such as those pertaining to curriculum, teaching methods, and the right to judge their own achievement as well as that of their students (Wise, 1989, 1990). At the same time, however, many such decisions continue to be made by administrators, textbook publishers, school boards, and state legislators.

Despite the diversity among teachers, their work, and their work environments, most can recognize the shared aspects of their group that form the framework of a distinctive teaching culture or cultures. Equally recognizable are the inherent and embedded dilemmas that require continuous struggle and attention. These include being authoritative and controlling in the classroom while creating welcoming learning environments and making personal connections with students (Feiman-Nemser & Floden, 1986; Jackson, 1968; Lortie, 1975; Sarason, 1971), and looking to administrators for various forms of professional support while simultaneously seeking autonomy in the making of professional decisions (Feiman-Nemser & Floden, 1986; Lieberman & Miller, 1984; McLaughlin, Pfeifer, Swanson-Owens, & Yee, 1986). How these dilemmas are resolved represents an important facet of the teaching culture.

Many rituals of teaching are embedded in the day-to-day activities of schooling—daily, weekly, or annual activities and events that provide routines and structures to the job. Sarason (1971) refers to these as existing regularities, taken-for-granted rituals whose original rationales were long ago lost in the folklore of the culture.

The culture(s) of teaching can be characterized, too, by a feeling of professional silence and aloneness. For many teachers, the classroom is their "world," one that only they and their students share (Lieberman & Miller, 1984). Time spent with colleagues is seldom used to discuss professional questions, concerns, or triumphs; seeking advice is seen as an admission of failure and offering it as a sign of egotism (see, for example, Dreeben, 1970; Feiman-Nemser & Floden, 1986; Lieberman & Miller, 1984; Zeichner & Gore, 1990). This "norm of silence" and tendency toward isolation represents another aspect of teaching's culture.

Finally, the norms, values, and myths found within the larger society help to create and maintain teaching's culture(s). Teaching as "women's work" is perhaps the strongest example of this—attitudes that tend to undervalue women as competent, able decision makers and negatively affect the personal and professional image of teachers as a whole. This view in particular is held responsible by many for the continued low status and pay of teachers.

To be sure, some enculturation occurs long before one enters a teacher preparation program, for all teachers have spent considerable time within the classroom as students themselves (Florio-Ruane, 1989; Ost, 1989; Zeichner & Gore, 1990). Lortie (1975) describes this unique aspect of the teaching profession as "apprenticeship through observation," where students begin deciphering teaching's norms, symbols, values, and rituals, some actually imagining themselves in the role of teacher. And while preparation programs aim to prepare former students to see the "other side" of teaching, much of teaching culture emanates from hidden messages within these same programs—issues regarding the status and power of teachers, the undervaluing of teachers' knowledge and decision-making ability, and the attempt to present teaching as depoliticized (Ginsberg & Clift, 1990).

Three Problematic Aspects of Teacher Professionalization

Chapters 4, 6, and 9 portray the Bridenthal Interns contending with three specific problems inherent in contemporary teacher education reform agendas: the defeminization of teaching, the intellectualization/rationalization of teaching, and the stratification of teaching. Each of these problems arises from specific attempts to promote greater professionalization of teaching exemplified in the three major second-wave reform calls.

Sociologist Wilbert Moore (1970) once argued that teaching has "no clear claim to professional status" (p. 205). Though one can argue about the degree to which the fundamental characteristics of an elite or expert profession can be found in the role of teacher, the above description suggests that teaching falls somewhere along the professional continuum and might better be seen as a "semi-profession" (Etzioni, 1969), "lesser profession" (Greenwood, 1957), or a craft profession (Pratte & Rury, 1989). A more immediate concern, it seems, would be the question of whether teaching should become more like an elite profession (attention to professionalization) or further enhanced as the sort of profession that it seems to be (attention to professionalism).

Pratte & Rury (1991) argue that teaching can never fit the above-discussed dimensions of an expert profession because teachers work for wages, belong to unions, are in the lower-middle-class economic stratum, and lack control over their own members. Further, teaching is seen as a feminized, low-risk, relatively secure, reasonably financially rewarding job that virtually anyone can do. In their view and ours, educators should strive, instead, to develop their work as a craft-profession and support reforms that would strengthen their professionalism as such, rather than move them toward greater professionalization.

The "concept of craft seems to belong to both the world of skill and the world of a calling or profession," yet given the nature of the job "it is very difficult to treat teaching as a simple aggregate of requisite skills. To develop as a teacher, one must acquire and develop a *sense of craft*" (Pratte & Rury, 1991, p. 64). Because craftspersons are not autonomous experts, they require a deep sense of community—a closeness to others involved in endeavors like themselves from whom they can learn and with whom they can grow and refine their work. Unlike the expert professions, where expertise is technically defined, judgment rests on expert knowledge, members function individually (and often competitively), and little emphasis is placed on shared experience, the craft-profession of teaching should emphasize practitioners' working together.

Focused on how the interns shaped their initial ethical/moral beliefs and service ideals, Chapter 4 discusses how much of the essence underlying this sense of a craft-profession and its concomitant requisite sense of community mirrors the values, beliefs, and practices of what might be called the "feminine" side of teaching (e.g., nurturance, mutual respect, intuitive wisdom, cooperation, and caring). When juxtaposed with reform efforts that devalue or attempt to discard these aspects of teaching, we can begin to see problems with attempts at the *defeminization* of teaching.

In the end, becoming a good teacher requires developing a "conscience of craft" and an ability to judge one's performance according to the collective knowledge and wisdom of other teachers who reflect the craft's highest standards. "This sense of appreciation is developed and sustained by membership in a guild-like community" (Pratte & Rury, 1991, p. 65). Chapter 6 describes the interns' decisions to specialize and the various knowledge bases found in the Bridenthal program. As a reflection of contemporary reform efforts, their program distinguished isolated, expert knowledge from collective, embodied craft knowledge. We argue that agendas such as these to provide teachers with more technical, esoteric knowledge against which teaching is objectively measured represent problematic aspects of the *rationalization* of teaching.

By focusing on the goal of professionalization, we lessen the likelihood of refining teachers' existing sense of professionalism, thus diminishing the knowledge and actions of both the individual and the community. Suggestions to move the definition of teaching closer to that of an expert profession without honoring its craft essence may fundamentally alter the existing culture of teaching in detrimental ways.

In Chapter 9 we follow the Bridenthal Interns through their first two years of classroom teaching in an attempt to discern the ways in which they develop as autonomous contributors to and potential leaders within their new culture. In relating these stories we suggest that current reform attempts to further professionalize teaching through the creation and maintenance of more clearly apparent hierarchies within the field (as well as a more distinct difference between educators and the public at large) create continuing problems associated with the *stratification* of teaching.

CAREER DEVELOPMENT

Between 1963 and 1980, teaching suffered a greater loss in prestige than any other occupation (Sykes, 1983). Linda Darling-Hammond (1990) describes several negative perceptions of teaching that prompted this decline: (1) relatively low beginning salaries and flat wage and career structure; (2) low levels of autonomy and decision-making responsibility; (3) little opportunity for advancement or variability in job functions; (4) low community regard for the occupation of teaching; and (5) relatively unattractive working conditions with respect to physical facilities, access to office space and equipment, and opportunity for collegial exchange. In light of these characterizations, educational reform invested heavily in proposals aimed at increasing the appeal of the occupational organization and structure and the value of rewards in teaching, including compensation. In short, second-wave reform coupled teacher quality with the occupational characteristics of teaching.

General theory on career development also attends to both the individual and the occupation while emphasizing the interaction between the two on the premise that people reflect aspects of themselves in their work, and occupations reflect the people within their ranks. DeLong (1984) suggests that "for years, society has taken issue with public education without focusing enough attention on the multi-faceted nature of the people who lead in the learning process in classrooms" (p. 119). Therefore, if one wants to examine reform in the context of career-development theory, individuals' interaction with teaching as an occupation becomes an important focus.

We use career-development theory as a framework through which reform initiatives are examined in light of the recruitment, preparation, and retention of teachers. We also employ the parameters of career-development theory as a framework for examining the career development of five of the interns. The influence of personal and social factors in their career choice, ongoing decision making, and adjustment to career are considered as they relate to the process of becoming a teacher.

The field of career development has a relatively short history, growing out of what previously was "vocational training" and its shift in emphasis from "filling the needs of a workforce" to "meeting the needs of people" (Bailey, 1982, p. 4). The most comprehensive theory of career development is Donald Super's "Life Space, Life Span" theory. He defines a career as "the combination and sequence of roles played by a person during the course of a lifetime. The roles that constitute the 'Life Space' include child, pupil or student, leisurete, citizen, worker, spouse, homemaker, parent, and pensioner" (1980, p. 282). Factors that influence these roles include expectations (one's own and others'), performance, and control.

The "Life-Span" dimension of Super's theory incorporates career development "stages" that intersect with various life roles. Super (1957, 1980) identifies these five career-development stages, which extend from birth to death, as:

- *Growth* (from conception to age 14) refers to an individual's development of a "realistic self-concept."
- *Exploration* (ages 15–25) is characterized by "self-examination," role tryouts, and occupational exploration.
- *Establishment* (ages 25–45) is when an individual works to make a permanent place for herself/himself in their career.
- *Maintenance* (ages 45–65) occurs as few new ventures are undertaken.
- *Decline* (over 65), the final life stage, marks retirement and change or reduction in work activity.

The ultimate goal of career development in both the life-span and life-space dimensions is to implement one's "self-concept" through work — that is, to develop a viable occupational self-concept. The ability to translate one's image of self into occupational terms is related to the degree of satisfaction one attains from work. While the development of self-concept begins at birth, operationalizing one's occupational self-concept becomes increasingly relevant following high school.

Career Development and Teaching

The career development of teachers has become an important area of study within the last 20 years. Much of this work is reflected in theories that focus on the development of the individual in teaching. Some of the earliest work here was done by Francis Fuller (1969), whose work illustrated how beginning teachers moved through stages of preteaching concerns, early concerns about survival, teaching-situation concerns, and concerns about pupils. Other writers, such as Christensen (1985), later reviewed life-age, life-cycle, and developmental-stage theories and research describing veteran teachers' development. Taken together, this research illustrates individual career changes.

Still other authors, like Fessler (1985), took this work beyond the focus on individuals to note how one's career cycle as a teacher is influenced by environmental and organizational factors whose interactions influence career development: "A supportive, nurturing, reinforcing environment can assist a teacher in the pursuit of a rewarding, positive career progression. Environmental interference and pressures, on the other hand, can impact negatively on the career cycle" (p. 185). Important to this more recent work is the inclusion of situational or contextual forces in our understanding of teachers' understanding of their careers. Clearly, some of these prove detrimental to teachers' successful career development and initially inhibitive for certain sorts of individuals.

Certain aspects of teaching seem unappealing to the very high-ability young people that reformists hope to recruit. A review of research on career retention by Super and Hall (1978) identified job autonomy, job challenge, and financial compensation as three such aspects. Chapman (1983) characterizes the limitations of teaching in these areas: "What at first appears as autonomy is isolation. . . . New tasks, or even new content, does not provide a challenge in teaching. . . . Within the profession, salary does not provide the validation for outstanding performance" (p. 43).

Additionally, the structure of the career of teaching is flat and goalless (McDonald, 1985) because its functions "are basically undifferentiated. The first-year novice and the 40-year veteran perform essentially the same task" (p. 227). Such an "unstaged" career results in restricted job mobility — which conflicts with prevailing notions of "work culture" that value upward mobility (Talbert, 1986). And while this situation benefits those who make teaching a temporary job, individuals who remain in teaching for a number of years find little flexibility in job role, responsibilities, or earning power.

The working conditions of teaching are no less problematic. Common complaints include limited time to plan, inadequate space available for teaching, and lack of respect for teachers in the community. The ever-increasing bureaucratic aspects of teaching also burden teachers.

Educational reform policy responded to these criticisms by recommending the restructuring or "staging" of teaching as a career, increasing teachers' investment in the structure and process of schooling, and increasing financial incentives. These recommendations specifically target a population of more academically able future teachers.

Reform and the Career-development Process

In Chapter 3, portraits of Roberto, Lucy, Rita, Gene, and Jan allow us to consider their initial match with teaching and their motivations for pursuing this career within the context of the Bridenthal program and Central College. We argue that attention to factors that have been shown to have minimal relationship with teaching effectiveness, such as academic ability, ignores the personal motivations that are critical to recruiting individuals with a high probability for long-term commitment to teaching. Additionally, this *depersonalization* of teaching tends to dissuade individuals from investing in their job and in the students they serve.

However, investment in teaching is related to one's self-understanding as well. Most reform recommendations, for example, emphasize the importance of "in-school" experiences throughout the preparation process. These experiences are always mediated, however, by individuals' biographies — which shape the image of teacher they bring with them. As Kagan (1992), in an extensive review of professional growth, writes: "Only after novices resolve their images of self as teacher can they begin to turn their focus outward and concentrate on what pupils are learning from academic tasks" (p. 147).

The Bridenthal program provided the interns with numerous field experiences. Nonetheless, like most preservice teachers, they viewed student teaching as their ultimate test. The contexts of student teaching, including aspects related to the individual (such as the developing image as teacher) and the environment (setting, structure, etc.), greatly influence teachers' ability to "contextualize" themselves in the career. In Chapter 7 we assert that reform's recommendations for student teaching reinforce traditional notions of "model and practice," which *decontextualizes* the practice of teaching, setting it apart from the individual and the broader social milieu.

At various levels, educational reform wielded power toward "excellence" in education. Among a litany of other activities, reform has influenced curricular directions with calls for "back to basics," fostered a penchant for accountability realized through formal systems of student and teacher testing, and generally increased the bureaucratic nature of teaching tenfold. Concurrently, we induct a new generation of teachers each year with hopes of exercising their own power to change traditional educational practice. Yet teacher preparation programs virtually "fail to prepare teachers to cope with the conditions in the schools that erode their sense of efficacy" (Ashton, 1992, p. 83). The result is a feeling of *disempowerment* and apathy toward change and innovation in schooling.

Chapter 10 reflects the interns' adjustment to the various contexts in which they worked as we examine both their own satisfaction with teaching and others' satisfaction with their performance. Achieving satisfaction on the part of the individual and the organization results in a shaping of their expectations and roles.

The success of recruiting and preparing for teaching individuals who otherwise would choose a different career is bleak under conditions that all too often turn these new recruits into what Giroux (1988) calls "clerks of the empire." Schooling may indeed have become one of these empires.

This book tells the stories of five interns—Jan, Rita, Roberto, Lucy, and Gene—against the backdrop of scholarly writings on specific educational reforms, professionalism, and career development and within the educational reform context of the 1980s. As we follow the journeys of these five very different high-ability students, we raise fundamental questions such as: What is the relationship between academic ability and teaching effectiveness? How can professionalization of teachers occur within a highly bureaucratic context of schools? In what ways does early commitment to teaching among high-ability students affect their short- and long-term career development? As we address these and other questions, we encourage the reader to reflect on various facets of a seemingly innocuous question: Why not the best?

Part I

ACCLIMATION

CHAPTER 2

Being Special in an Unspecial Profession

If one assumes that part of the image of teaching is the image of a serious scholar, then it would seem appropriate that recruitment criteria attend to evidence of scholarship. Will students who graduate in the top quarter of their class be given preference over those who graduate in the bottom quarter? Should admission to teacher education programs be limited to those who graduate in the top half of their college class? In answering these questions, it is critical to keep in mind that the question being asked is not simply one of technical competence (i.e., is a C student capable of becoming a good or outstanding teacher?). The question is also one of occupational identity. Do we want teaching to be viewed as an occupation made up of C students? (Schlechty, 1990, p. 10)

"Why not the best?" Don Wright, the visionary chairman of Central College's education department, pondered as he flipped through a national news magazine following the publication of *A Nation at Risk*. The time, he thought, was right to address his question.

There had been, of course, other times in the annals of educational history when the question "Why not the best?" was raised. In his landmark study on teaching published 60 years ago, Willard Waller (1932) observed:

A popular epigram of a few years ago had it that teaching was the refuge of unsaleable men and unmarriageable women. . . . Unjust or not, the low social standing of teachers, and the belief that teaching is a failure belt among the occupations, which is part of that low standing, contribute much to make the personnel of the profession represent a lower grade of the general population that would otherwise be the case. (p. 61)

During another period of teacher education reform, Koerner (1963, p. 96) wrote in *The Miseducation of American Teachers*: "The quality of instruction in education courses is perhaps lower than that of any other department. Only the extraordinary docility or disinterestedness of the education student permits the low level of instruction from being called more often to public, as well as campus, attention."

These concerns, too, had resulted in scores of commissions, committees, and task forces with recommendations to improve the quality of teachers ranging from the Commonwealth Teacher Training Study (Charters & Waples, 1929) and the National Survey of the Education of Teachers (Cooper, 1932) to the reports issued by the National Society of College Teachers of Education (1935; Harap, 1951) and the Carnegie Commission of Higher Education (Bagley & Learned, 1920; Learned & Wood, 1938) as well as several national conferences such as those sponsored by the National Council on Education (Armstrong, 1944), the National Education Association (e.g., Stinnett, 1955; Hodenfield & Stinnett, 1961); and the Fund for the Advancement of Education (Smith, 1962).

Don Wright was an activist. He had departed his brief stint as a schoolteacher to become an education professor, not to write about the world of education, but to transform it. A fellow professor, Barney Friend, remarked:

> The man knows what to say, what to do and how to carry himself so that he comes across as right, and right for the right reasons. . . . He's a thinker. In order to get things done, you first have to envision it. Then you have to set up a plan of action and carry it through. You just don't let things ride by. He definitely doesn't let things roll over. When he wants something to happen he does what is needed to get things done.

In his dozen-odd years as chairman of Central's education department Wright had demonstrated an uncanny ability to sniff out opportunity, translating it into program grants from business and industry. In the process, the stature and reputation of his department—like that of Central— had grown.

Central College is a liberal arts college in a major metropolitan area. Formerly a church-controlled school, Central became a secular institution in the late 1950s. For many years, it was a sleepy undergraduate school principally serving an affluent female student body. Since the late 1970s, fueled from oil-based stock revenues, it has sought to establish itself as a premier coeducational undergraduate establishment. During the past decade, it has moved successfully along this path: Faculty members have been lured away from prestigious colleges; each entering freshmen group has been accompanied by an increase in SAT/ACT scores; and prominent public figures routinely visit and lecture. Recently, Central was named as one of the country's "best buys" for a college education and cited as one of the top small liberal arts colleges.

At his monthly faculty meeting in the fall of 1983, Professor Wright announced his intention to refashion the department's approach to preparing teachers by recruiting higher-caliber students and restructuring the teacher education program. The first step would be to develop a way to recruit, prepare, and retain high-ability students for public school teaching. Inviting immediate faculty collaboration and feedback, he winced when a junior faculty member suggested studying past educational efforts and consulting with scholars in the field *prior* to any action. By December a complete grant application had been submitted to a local charitable trust, the Bridenthal Foundation, proposing what was to become known as the Bridenthal Internship in Teaching (BIT) program.

With the acumen of a successful CEO, Wright saw a window of opportunity to translate public discontent, business concern, and political attentiveness into genuine educational reform with Central College in the forefront. During the decade of the 1980s, educational institutions were to come under increased pressure to produce a more competitive work force in the United States. This drive would result in calls for renewed educational excellence and the restructuring of teacher education. In this decade of emerging school reform, the Bridenthal program represented the teacher image as Central College's Department of Education became one of the first in the country to implement many of these reform proposals premised on an appealing idea.

THE IDEA

"We recruit halfbacks. We recruit oboe players. But we don't recruit teachers. We sit back in our colleges and universities and wait for them to appear," observed Don Wright impatiently. As the first wave of educational reform appeared, Wright developed the idea: *Bright students should be recruited into teaching.* He set out to produce a "new breed" of teacher—one that would transform the classroom, restore the status of a much maligned profession, catalyze educational change, and, in the process, firmly establish Central College as a premier teacher preparation institution: "What we want to do is to become one of the places in the country where bright people who want to teach would want to go. We simply want that reputation."

Throughout the 1970s, Central's education department, like most schools, colleges, and departments of education in the United States, saw a decline in the number of talented women who had traditionally entered teaching. Jane Davenport joined the education faculty in the mid-1970s.

She recalls having long conversations with Don Wright on the importance of recruiting talented persons who were choosing alternative career paths:

> Through the women's movement . . . we lost many of our finest teachers. When women only had the choice of teaching or nursing those were, of course, the fields they entered. Some of these women were just brilliant; some of them were extremely caring. We lost them. They're in business; they're in law. . . . Now women still come into education today, the ones who really want to mother and who bring with them the nurturing urge. But what we lost was a lot of the intellectual women, those who could be physics teachers.

Thus, the first commonsensical assumption underlying the Bridenthal program's idea that the brightest and the best should be recruited into teaching was that *too few bright people enter the profession.*

This assumption appeared justified given a plethora of research studies published prior to issuance of *A Nation at Risk* (see, for example, Borkow & Jordan, 1983; Feistritzer, 1983; Laman & Reeves, 1983; Roberson, Keith, & Page, 1983; Sykes, 1983; Weaver, 1979, 1981). According to these and other researchers, teacher education graduates, particularly those most interested in teaching as a career, were generally less academically talented than those who graduated a decade earlier. By the early 1980s only 5 percent of first-year college students expressed an interest in becoming teachers, and those who demonstrated the greatest academic talent were the least likely to choose teaching as a career, gravitating instead toward technology and medicine. Accepting these data, Professor Davenport believes this decline of "brightness" (i.e., class rank, SAT/ACT/NTE scores, GPA) was due, in part, to the displacement of academically talented women to higher-status fields, which, until recently, had been generally closed to females (Sullivan, 1981).

It should be noted that shortly following the issuance of *A Nation at Risk*, some researchers (e.g., Fisher & Feldman, 1985; Nelli, 1984; Villeme & Hall, 1985) disputed the assumption that too few bright people enter teaching. In a major review of research studies, Lanier and Little (1986) caution on the use of such studies for developing public policy and educational programs: "The research on students of teaching over the past decade tends to be desultory in nature, poorly synthesized, and weakly criticized." They conclude: "As a consequence, misrepresentation and over-generalization of research findings has occurred in response to growing public interest" (p. 535).

Central College is not reflective of the typical teacher education program, since entry requires meeting the school's high admission standards.

In 1984, the year these 17 interns entered Central, their freshmen class averaged 1,120 on the collegiate test scores and its undergraduate student body numbered approximately 2,400 with a student/faculty ratio of 10.5 to 1. Central, prior to the Bridenthal program, did attract more than its share of high-ability persons to teacher education, often placing their graduates in well-to-do suburban and private schools.

Another aspect of this dwindling pool of talent is the loss of interest among persons initially expressing an inclination to teach and the selection of teaching as an alternative career choice by others. The vast majority (80 percent) of high school seniors who note their intention to major in education never follow through with their original plans (Nelson, 1985). Further, academic ability is inversely related to the probability that a student will continue as an education major through graduation, and between one-quarter and one-half of those students who receive certification will not enter the classroom (Bethume, 1981).

Finally, those academically talented young people who do enter the classroom often do so through wealthy school districts or private schools, which routinely take the cream from the top of teaching graduates. School districts such as Virginia's Prince George's County routinely identify and recruit talented individuals into their classrooms. Newspapers have captured the tone of these efforts with headlines like: "Like a Major-League Baseball Scout, Dallas Recruiter Combs the Country in Search of Raw Teaching Talent" (Diegmueller, 1991). Recruitment approaches range from providing red tote bags and glossy brochures at recruitment fairs to offering teaching contracts with provisions for relocation services, subsidized rent, low-interest loans, guaranteed summer employment, or local business discounts.

SEARCHING FOR THE BEST

The Campaign

After securing the support of the Bridenthal Foundation for his teaching-internship program, Professor Wright launched an intensive media campaign throughout the metropolitan area. Touting a scholarship package of $26,000 in forgivable loans at a prestigious college and enjoying positive media coverage, Don Wright began searching for high-ability high school seniors. He personally telephoned each principal of the 35 area high schools asking them to help with recruitment. He tirelessly roamed these schools, speaking with guidance counselors, conferring with Central alumni, and speaking before student assemblies asking, "Why not the best?" As a result, more than 100 high school seniors who ranked in the top 10 percent of their graduating class applied for the original 10 internships.

Nearly one-half of the interns heard of the Bridenthal program through school assemblies or public addresses; almost as many were informed by a teacher. Only two interns learned of the program first through a guidance counselor. Gene remembers: "Dr. Wright soon followed up my counselor's encouragement with a visit to my high school. He cleared up some of my questions. I became aware that teaching would be cost-effective with this type of offer. This was the time when I became attracted to the scholarship."

Most of the interns selected for the program, like Carol and Angie, were influenced to apply by a teacher. Carol was exactly the type of student Wright sought:

> I had never looked into being a teacher until my calculus teacher sent around this Bridenthal information sheet saying, "If anyone's interested in it, just take one of these applications on my desk." The sheet came around—usually you don't read these things or if you do it's just because you don't want to pay attention in class—but I started reading it and I became really interested in it. It hit me deep that I *could* become a teacher. I took a good look at myself and said, "Carol, what do you want to do?" And it was just like, "I'm going to apply and see what happens! You've got the talent and the abilities, you ought to do it." The more I read it the more I wanted to be a teacher.

Unlike Carol, Angie was seriously considering becoming a teacher before she learned about the Bridenthal program from her government teacher—a former Central student: "She told me that she thought that I would do really well at Central and as a Bridenthal Intern. She thought that I would be able to handle everything because of my good personality and the way I interacted with people."

Wright had to take a more active role in recruiting others: "Some of them are here because I recruited them heavily. One person who was nominated by a teacher said she was going elsewhere to school. I twisted her arm a little bit. She's one of the best interns here!" Another intern recalled Wright's recruitment techniques, saying "He grabbed us and pulled us into education. 'Give it a chance,' he pleaded, 'see if you like it. If not, no big deal. Stay in it for a couple of years and get out.'"

The Selection

The screening process was equally rigorous. Following a review of recommendations from educators and student essays on their "interest in teaching as a career," 60 candidates underwent the first set of interviews.

At this stage, Wright was concerned with personal qualities: "You've got to look for tenacity, commitment. Some bright kids don't do well in college. They don't have 'the bottom,' like they say with horses, to see it through." Another member of the interview committee commented:

> We were looking for people who we thought were really committed to teaching for one reason or another. For example, we looked for high school youth-related activities, like peer tutoring, that reflected a personality that would enjoy a lifelong career of teaching. Most of the students were interested in math and sciences—a predominance we also favored. And we looked for persons who could live on campus and who would be involved in a lot of activities on and off campus.

Professor Davenport, a member of the interview team, recalled "Back then I was looking for change agents because of the resources to be spent on these kids. Sure, they would have to make an impact on children, but first they would have to have an impact on the professionals and the system."

Most interns saw their high school success in academics and extracurricular activities as the key to their acceptance into this program, though several added that their commitment to teaching or their performance in the selection process might have created a favorable impression. The interns also recalled their efforts during the interview process:

> In my interviews, I tried to talk about education and all the state legislature's dealing. I read the paper every day so when I went into my interview I could ask questions about education.

> A lot of people who tried at my school were intelligent. They worked hard in school and they'd go home and study all night. But they couldn't handle themselves during the interview. There's going to be a lot of attention paid to the Bridenthal Interns and if they can't handle that they were pretty much scratched out.

Following these interviews, Wright developed a final list of candidates who, with their parents, would visit campus for a final interview with him. Wright remembers: "In that final interview we talked turkey. I just absolutely challenged these kids. 'This is a six-year commitment. If you're not ready to do it, then you better say so right now.' Some of the parents would look at their children. On two or three occasions, I left them to talk it out."

With the exception of one intern, parents served but an advisory role. The decision to enter teaching, to undertake the significant financial obligations, and to commit themselves to the program (and, more importantly for some interns, to Dr. Wright) was a choice for which each intern assumed final responsibility: "My mother didn't help me on this. Sure, she was an influence, but she didn't make the decision. I did this on my own"; "I made the decision. My mom and I got into a few arguments. But it was what I wanted to do with my life. I was going to be living it, and I will have to deal with it." Thus, while most interns had spoken with their parents, friends, and teachers about applying for or accepting this opportunity, the decisions were theirs.

Not surprisingly, more than half the interns disclosed that one or both parents were less than enthusiastic on first learning of their child's interest in the Bridenthal program. Gene's father, a veteran teacher, questioned the wisdom of his son's career choice: "I told him at supper that I had applied. He stopped chewing his food and looked at me. 'Gene,' he said, 'Are you feeling all right?'" Rita's parents were leery of the instant financial burden their daughter (and they) would incur should she decide to leave the program before her six-year commitment but "they're impressed by Dr. Wright."

Other interns encountered people questioning the certainty of their career choice as well as their ability to complete the program. Carol's father challenged her: "Gee, you never said anything about wanting to be a teacher except when you were just a little girl. Besides, how are you going to attend Central, Carol? We don't have the money for you to go to Central and we can't pay back the money if you decide to drop the program." Another intern's parent cautioned, "You better want to teach real bad. . . . You better not fall in love and marry someone." And a best friend told another intern, "You don't want to go into teaching. You deserve better." Some interns reported encountering parental apathy: "I explained the program to my parents before I applied. I don't think they really paid attention to what I was saying."

In the end, Wright could not winnow his list down to a mere 10. With his formidable persuasive skills and graceful style, he quickly received funds for six additional internships. An additional intern position was available when one of the original 10 interns, Nolan, chose to use his National Merit Scholarship award rather than the Bridenthal award. Thus, 17 persons comprised the Bridenthal Interns. Among the mostly middle-class group of 14 women and 3 men were 5 in *Who's Who Among American High School Students*, a national merit scholar, two valedictorians, and 10 National Honor Society members. All earned SAT scores exceeding 1,000, and all graduated in the top 10 percent of their high school class. All but 4 had seriously considered nonteaching careers such as law, medicine, psychology, and engineering and only 2 were ethnic minorities. During the next six years, this cadre of the "brightest and the best" progressed through the academic curriculum at Central and into the local schools. In effect, their teacher preparation began with their first day of classes and continued through their first two years of teaching.

Being an Intern

As winter surrendered to spring and thousands of the city's seniors ceremoniously completed their high school careers, these select 17 took the Central College stage at an induction ceremony marking the beginning of their careers as Bridenthal Interns. The internships were announced at a program meant to recognize the city's two most outstanding teachers. The interns, surrounded by college officials, Bridenthal Foundation trustees, parents, friends, and the local media, were acknowledged alongside these honored teachers and introduced as "a future generation of outstanding teachers." One intern recalling the moment said, "That's when it really made me think, 'Wow! It is really an honor!'" Another noted, "I remember feeling a sense of pride. We were chosen for some special ability we have." Following the ceremony, they shared stories about when each learned of their selection as a Bridenthal Intern.

Lucy was running the music for drill-team tryouts one Saturday when her mom called on the pay phone with the news that Dr. Wright had called to say that Lucy had been selected. Immediately, Lucy sought out and informed her high school principal, vice principal, and guidance counselor, Mr. Romer (who had nominated her), who quickly exclaimed, "We have a Bridenthal Intern at our school!" Two of Lucy's peers also won spots in the program, and for the remainder of the school year the counselor would say to anyone who would listen, "These are Bridenthal Interns—they just got the scholarship at Central for teaching."

Another intern recalled, "I had to stay calm when Dr. Wright called. But I was shaking. I was just thinking, 'I've made a commitment now.'" A third intern commented:

> I hung up the phone and I was screaming. My brothers knew exactly why. They began screaming, too. They started jumping up and down. My neighbors came over. They thought that I'd been attacked or something. I immediately called my grandparents; they screamed. Then my dad and my other grandparents came home. My grandmother was crying. My dad got tears in his eyes. He just hugged me. He immediately called all his relatives long distance. I was walking on clouds, walking on air all day for a week. They announced it at our school over the intercom, and it was in the school paper.

Three months following the ceremony, when these 17 young people took their first journeys up Central Hill overlooking the city's skyline, they were more than just first-year Central students—they were Bridenthal Interns. One intern remembered: "On that first day I felt a real spirit of adventure. As I was introducing myself, I began to say, 'I'm a Bridenthal Intern.' Suddenly, I became very proud." Seventeen high-ability high school seniors, seven of whom had never considered teaching as a serious career option, had been recruited into the Bridenthal program. Now the more difficult task of recruiting them into teaching began.

RECRUITING THE BEST

Wright's recruitment efforts began in earnest when the brightest and best became Bridenthal Interns; he devoted two years to developing them into informed, eager educational change agents committed to the Bridenthal program and ready to declare themselves as education majors midway through their sophomore year.

Once "in the harness," the interns began acquiring a particular vision of educational reform and their role as reformers. Gene observed, "There hopefully is going to be a major movement in the United States to revamp the education system. We are at the forefront." Rita proclaimed, "It's neat that we get a chance to talk to the mayor and to talk to people in the community. We get to *tell* them what we're doing and what our goals are."

The 17 selected echoed these themes during their first interview. When asked for the first thing that comes to mind when hearing the phrase "Bridenthal program," Lucy candidly replied: "Prestige, honor, and meeting lots of neat people—high achievers." Roberto quietly remarked, "We're the hope for education," and Gene categorically asserted that the program "is a valuable starting point for reform of teacher education in the United States." Jan, on the other hand, briefly spoke about its importance in her quest to become a teacher, and Rita uttered two words: "Don Wright."

A forgivable loan coupled with the prestige of attending Central College and the publicity associated with the Bridenthal program had attracted many students. And, given the particular structure of its material incentives (i.e., students accumulated a scholarship debt of $10,000 over the first two years, $12,000 over the second two years, and a $2,000 stipend for each of their first two years of teaching—all of which would be forgiven following the completion of their commitment), it became progressively more difficult for an intern to leave the program. Thus, while one might conclude that the program's recruitment goal was met when the interns "signed on the dotted line," it really extended past the first two years of their program.

As we discuss in Chapter 3, 8 of the 17 interns would probably have entered a teacher education program without these incentives. In a sense, then, it was the remaining 9 who were recruited into the Bridenthal program and who were more likely than their teaching-oriented peers to opt out in its early stages. Under these circumstances, the concept of recruitment can be seen as a process whereby students are enculturated into the world of educational reform and recruited into teaching.

Once the interns were recruited into the program, Wright conceptualized a curriculum to accomplish these goals. Curriculum visions, of course, amount to little without some person or persons with the requisite abilities and resources to translate vision into reality. Wright devoted substantial energy to this end. Using his ability to make things happen, Wright planned and taught the newly created seminars, advised 10 of the interns, secured notable guest speakers, and coordinated interns' access to field sites. Together, these components facilitated the interns' entry into the university, their integration into the program, their introduction to the profession, and their expected role in educational reform. Though common in today's reformed preparation programs, these components (e.g., early field experiences, mentorship programs) were unusual at the time.

Seminars

Wright represented the interns as the vanguard of educational reform to the public as he molded them in his weekly one-hour seminars and individual, "fatherly" chats. Wright thought the seminar was a key ingredient in the interns' first-year experience: "It is a way to keep them together. . . . They get to know each other. They begin to rely on each other. This is going to be the glue that holds them together, particularly after they get out of general education."

Wright led the seminar by probing, prompting, and praising the group of 17 that gathered before him along a sleek chrome table. One intern described the sessions in her journal, saying:

> As I sit in our Monday seminar, I see a group of people around the table that want to say something. Yet, we still don't know enough to say. We've got a lot to learn. We've all got something to say, but it has taken Dr. Wright to challenge us. He'll say, "Okay! Let's talk teaching." He expects us to already know some things about teaching. So we start throwing in the pot. We start sorting out good teaching, the education system, what's wrong with it and is it wrong.

The early seminars focused on criticism of public schooling and praise for current reform efforts. The interns read, reported on, and discussed every major publication on educational reform including the *Paideia Pro-*

posal (Adler, 1982), *A Nation at Risk* (National Commission, 1983), *Horace's Compromise* (Sizer, 1984), and *A Place Called School* (Goodlad, 1984). Each wrote an essay discussing an educational concern and possible strategies for reform. One of the interns, Roberto, described the challenge of their first college seminar: "I never read so many books in such a short span of time. I actually welcome the challenge. I push myself to do the studying. I've learned a great deal about the educational system and its problems. I hope I can use some of this knowledge when I become a teacher."

As the interns' first semester progressed, well-known speakers visited Central to address them on issues ranging from pending state legislation to qualities of a good teacher. Janice Little, a student in one of the college's few graduate programs, served as the interns' first-year mentor. She described the importance of this curricular component:

> These interns didn't have any understanding of the educational system. They only understood it from a student's point of view. They didn't really realize everything that it entailed to teach a class, the knowledge that was needed, or the politics of educational reform. In these seminars, they spent a lot of time discussing the national reports, pending state legislation, and so forth. These seminars also really helped them form a strong base of understanding why they wanted to become teachers and what they were going to have to face in defending their career choice as students and entering the classroom as teachers.

During the last meeting of the semester, Wright asked the interns if they thought they could hold their own with anybody in the community when discussing educational reform. These first-year college students replied in a unanimous voice of certainty: "We know the issues!" Reflecting on that first year's seminar Wright sat behind his bowl of jellybeans. He concluded, "I think it is in their blood."

Field Experiences

During the second and third semesters, visits to selected schools began, and the focus of their on-campus seminar sessions progressively narrowed. At each school, interns listened as community leaders and local educators discussed career ladders, curriculum revision, and teacher evaluation. As interns began to concentrate on single schools, larger philosophical concerns were eclipsed by more discrete, functional ones. Returning to some of the same schools they knew as students, the interns began to see schooling in a new light. Global issues relating to the quality of the teaching force and declining student achievement were seen in juxtaposition to teachers' struggles with curriculum materials, community interests, and student motivation.

Throughout the second semester the interns read about and analyzed the city's diverse communities and the schools that serve them. Midway into the semester, they journeyed into the city, amassing data about a specific community and a specific school. For some, these visits were a "rude awakening. . . . I never thought it was going to be easy, but I didn't think it was going to be like this." For others, the visits confirmed their initial feelings about teaching: "I have read, heard, written, talked about and seen the good and the bad in education. But I never really was a part of it, not until I made myself a part by sitting in the class with Mrs. Brown and her students. I felt what they felt." At the semester's end, each intern presented a paper on community issues and educational reform.

During their second year, the interns spent a minimum of three hours each week at an assigned school. Classroom observing, tutoring, and teaching as well as preparing materials, grading papers, and designing bulletin boards were their principal tasks. One intern prepared student pamphlets on *Beowulf*. Another wrote a profile of a student who was experiencing academic difficulty. Most interns reported benefiting from these second-year experiences: "It was kind of a shock for me, I have to admit. I have always been in an upperclass environment. I thought every elementary school had these things. . . . The school I visited had a part-time counselor, a part-time librarian, part-time secretaries. Until this year they had a part-time principal. I was just really surprised by that."

For many of these interns it was "student teaching without the student teaching label." Given that the interns were only in their sophomore year, it was not surprising that some shared experiences that were less positive:

I felt like these were all the little toys, all the little dolls. "We'll let you play with them once in a while. But we don't want you to break them. Be really careful." I just sort of felt they were reluctant to let me teach. I only got to teach one class. I'm not saying that's too little. They were being very cautious. They didn't want me to do it, but since it was Central and since they wanted to stay in good with the program, they let me teach one lesson.

Mentorship and Group Support

Janice Little, a graduate student selected by Wright, assisted the interns' transition into college life and kept the group on top of its many and varied responsibilities. She worked closely with Wright, serving as a sort of kindred intermediary between him and the interns.

For many interns, particularly the three males, Don Wright assumed a mentorship role that, for Roberto and Gene, would extend beyond their six-year experience. The interns described him as supportive, demanding, and imaginative—"our father here in school." But, perhaps more than anything, Wright served as the interns' professional role model: They observed firsthand the role of a leader in public education reform.

There were, of course, costs to such a relationship: "I'm afraid if I don't do well in a class then I am failing to live up to some expectations. I start feeling overwhelmed and frustrated with myself." The fear of failing the program and Wright was real to the interns: "Dr. Wright seems to expect so much out of us. I would hate to disappoint him." Another intern asked, "What if we don't live up to his expectations or I decide I would rather pursue another career? Is the Bridenthal Internship stripped from my chest?" With concerns such as these it is easy to understand the ambivalent feelings and questions that most interns expressed at one time or another: "Can I make it through the semester?" "Is it a waste of time?" "Could I be a good teacher without going through this program?"

Such pressures intensified the interns' need for "groupness" during their first year as "we're all in this together" became their rallying cry. One intern commented, "I have one little edge over everybody else. I have a group of people that I know that we all have something in common, whereas other freshmen are just coming in by themselves." The importance of the group, for most interns, grew in intensity during the year. "Without the group, I'd just be another student out there," noted one. Another said, "I feel accepted. I made my place. I feel comfortable. These are people who I will talk to for the next 20 years."

While the importance of the group varied among the interns, even for the less needy its support became more personally significant as their first year passed:

> I told another intern that I did not label myself as an intern. Later, though, after thinking about it awhile, I realized the intern program does have more of an effect on me than I credited. Not only am I under a loan-scholarship that might make me think twice about changing my major, but I realize I have something good. The help of others in this program is vital to my success here. I would really be struggling without them.

Speakers and Speaking Engagements

Like the seminars, dialogue with "important people" was a component fostering a hidden agenda for creating educational reform. The interns discussed current issues with the city's nationally prominent mayor, Carnegie Foundation president Ernest Boyer, and the chairperson of the state board of education. Through such dialogues the interns gained insight into the dynamics of educational reform while establishing contact with educational leaders about whom most preservice teachers only study.

From the interns' perspective, Wright was a man who cultivates personal relationships with those holding power, exudes the confidence to influence important decision makers, bypasses bureaucratic constraints, and translates ideas into reality. Accustomed to frank discussions of educational problems with school superintendents and free-wheeling debates with prominent persons, as a sophomore, Lucy observed: "Dr. Wright is in Washington DC on business. Rumor has it that he's going to ask President Reagan to speak at our lecture in April. . . . I hope the Bridenthal Interns will have special privileges like we did last year when Dr. Boyer spoke. We got to sit in the front and go to a special party afterwards at the house of Central's vice-president."

Another important dimension of Wright's two-year extended recruitment strategy was the interns' entry into the public arena in which their vocational choice and role in the reform effort were positively valued. Lucy states, "Dr. Wright was really intent on what he wanted to do. It was obvious that he had certain goals. One of them was to promote the Bridenthal program. He wanted us to be visible. He was always finding somewhere for us to speak or somewhere for us to be written up." Wright acknowledged the importance of these experiences:

They've had opportunities to have exchanges with people from all over the country. I took four interns to Florida after the Chicago trip. We started at eight in the morning and finished about 3:30 in the afternoon. . . . Women were there from the League of Women Voters, the Junior League and the American Association of University Women. The kids had two hours of exchange after their presentations. That is very unusual. How many sophomores have had that opportunity?

Most of the interns spoke publicly at conferences and public forums ranging from the state teachers' association to the American Association of Colleges for Teacher Education. Roberto and Lucy remember speaking before the state teachers association.

I have never been more proud to be an education major — an extremely nervous one but being among teachers and professors was quite an experience. At 1:30 we took the stage. All I remember after that was the earth-shattering applause. After we gave our speeches we were not able to give our final thanks because of more applause. Teachers ex-

pressed their happiness for our career decisions. We were jokingly offered scholarships to attend other schools and even some job offers.
The feeling of satisfaction was overwhelming.

It made me feel good. It was almost like they knew what they used to
be like: excited and enthusiastic. But, now they're older and a lot of
the enthusiasm is gone. I think we helped them. I don't know if we
brought their enthusiasm back, but we sure displayed a lot of our
own.

Frequently featured in the local media, the interns were no strangers to
national reporters representing *Newsweek, The Christian Science Monitor,
Business Week,* CBS' *Good Morning America,* and *The Chronicle of Higher
Education.* Though the coverage was routinely positive, the interns were
sensitive to any message at variance with that projected by Don Wright.
After his first interview with a reporter from a national news magazine,
Gene wrote in his journal:

We are learning how the media operates. We are learning that it specifically focuses on propaganda, sensationalism, and the creation of issues. The media can form issues and set the agenda for the solving of
problems. Ted Koppel, in his address at Central, said that good news
is no news. . . . The media is a bit prone to be overly negative about
everything. I am worried that the internship will be a victim of nega-
tivity.

While their surface curriculum prepared the interns academically, the
hidden curriculum readied them for their ministerial mission in public education. For these interns, the Bridenthal program would produce, in Gene's
words, a "race of super teachers." These competent, dedicated, skilled,
caring, and enthusiastic young people would be "the pacesetters for the new
generation of teachers."

Their particular view of reform is captured well in Rita's account of a
panel discussion for teachers at a school district that she and several other
interns attended. The topic was the forthcoming state bill mandating
teacher competency examinations and more careful monitoring of classroom teachers. Reacting to one of the few times she had heard classroom
teachers formally speak about the profession, Rita wrote in her journal:

The teachers in the audience were out to kill. Dissension and sarcasm
were in their voices as they chattered with others during the presentation. At the question-and-answer period, fire broke lose. The teachers

voiced their complaints and questions in a rude manner and tone. The teachers at the forum seem to be objecting to the proposed reform before even considering its benefits in the long run. With teachers who cannot accept change with its hardship and who cannot go through this change with a professional and rational attitude the reform will have *no* chance! Grow up teachers and use your sense!

Rita, of course, is not representative of every intern. Some, like Gene, were more ambivalent about the bill. "Teaching is not viewed as a profession anymore. You cut down on what the teacher has to decide for himself. That's part of your profession; you get to decide for yourself." On the other hand, Gene noted that "teachers who have seen better, simpler times and less paperwork are the most discontent—and that is understandable. . . . But loads of paperwork is a sign of the times. All occupations have more paperwork. It's called progress."

Meanwhile, the outstretched hand of Professor Wright moved behind the scenes: "They know they are pacesetters in certain ways. They know there is a terrible problem in recruitment of high-ability people. All of them can look back and see they can be helpful." As he talked about the program and the interns, Wright uttered certain words and phrases that the interns themselves had used in describing their visions: catalyst, pacesetter, educational revolution, first-class.

BY ITS VERY NATURE, the program's early curriculum brought the group together. Campus notoriety, national publicity, and numerous speaking engagements before local, state, and national gatherings of educators were among the experiences that served to bring a sense of groupness to the Bridenthal Interns. Structural aspects of the program such as weekly meetings and a specially assigned mentor promoted the same end. At the close of their first year, virtually all of the interns identified closely with the group and saw themselves as more like than unlike the group's other members. All were "special people" sharing the dream of becoming a new breed of better teachers. All understood themselves to be public ambassadors-at-large to the teaching profession.

As the extended recruitment phase progressed, however, this cohesiveness began to decay. During their third semester, weekly meetings disappeared and group activities diminished. By the time the interns had formally declared themselves education majors at the end of the second year, the Bridenthal program had virtually disappeared, and the group was touched by its disintegration. Fewer opportunities to attend and speak at professional gatherings and a fading conspicuousness were interpreted differently by the interns. Those activities that defined the interns as a group and validated their sense of specialness were sorely missed by some, while others recognized the loss of these same phenomena as personally liberating. As we describe in Chapters 5 to 7, the time had arrived for the interns to begin the process of defining themselves—both as individuals and as future teachers.

Adopting this understanding of extended recruitment allows us to see that unlike most teacher education programs, the early Bridenthal curriculum spent considerable time instilling in the interns a strong background for and belief in educational reform and the importance of their role as future teachers and leaders in this reform movement.

Based on their survey of high-ability seniors in the South, Brogdon and Tincher (1986) assert: "If more high aptitude students are to be attracted to teaching, the profession will have to improve salaries, opportunity for advancement, social status, [and] attitudes of students, parents, and the community at large" (p. 14). This recommendation sheds a particularly interesting light when seen in combination with the findings of Byers (1984), who notes that "the image of a particular teacher education program may influence the kinds of students who are attracted to it" (p. 11). In other words, if a particular teacher education program were to represent teaching as a career associated with money, prestige, and positive community attitudes, that program would be particularly attractive to "high-aptitude" students.

In many respects, the program did this. Interns received a tuition scholarship and a salary supplement for their first two years of teaching, were placed in the public spotlight and accorded respect at a prestigious college, and were provided mentors and access to supportive community and professional groups. The nature of the particular program, then, would seem to play an important role in enticing each of these students into the Bridenthal program—an assumption we will explore in Chapter 3.

The Bridenthal program clearly succeeded in creating the belief among its participants that they were indeed the kinds of leaders needed in the classrooms of reform-starved schools. Would the recruitment hype of the program match the day-to-day work when these students entered schools as student teachers and fledgling interns? What is the nature of commitment these students hold toward teaching? How effective would they be in teaching and translating the reform agenda into the schools? These questions will be addressed in subsequent sections of this book.

CHAPTER 3

Living with Created Images

The Bridenthal program presented interns with a serendipitous career opportunity in teaching. Opportunity is an important influence in career development and decision making and is often associated with the availability of external social and economic resources (Super, 1957). The program enhanced this call to teach by offering rewards of a scholarship to Central College, involvement in a special program, and potential power to influence education.

In this chapter we introduce five of the interns and describe their expressed commitment to teaching at the beginning of the Bridenthal program. Here, we explore the interns' motivations for pursuing a career in teaching by identifying personal and situational influences on their decision to "become a teacher." These influences shape an individual's concepts regarding the role of work in his or her life, perceptions of occupational interests and abilities, and personal needs and values. Interns' personal and occupational self-concepts served as the basis for their motivation and commitment to teaching.

THE INTERNS' MATCH WITH TEACHING

At the outset we asked the interns to complete Holland's Self-Directed Search (SDS) (Holland, 1985), a career-counseling instrument that identifies matches between an individual's self-assessed vocational attitudes, interests, and skills and potentially satisfying occupations. Responses to the SDS are summarized by a three-letter code that is keyed to a specific occupation. Occupations are classified according to the characteristics of their work environments (S = social; A = artistic; I = investigative; R = realistic; E = enterprising; and C = conventional). The first letter of the code reflects an individual's match to the general work environment. The second and third letters of the code narrow the match to a specific occupation that matches an individual's self-assessed interests and skills. Each of the interns

41

was assigned a three-letter code based on his or her responses and analyzed regarding the match to teaching.

The primary code that is associated with "teacher" is S (social), A (artistic), E (enterprising). The general work environment for teaching, therefore, is social. Weinrach and Srebalus (1990) characterize an individual who prefers this work environment as one "who enjoys working with and helping others but avoids ordered, systematic activities that involve tools or machinery" (p. 43). The second and third letters of the code place teaching in artistic (expressive, nonconforming, original, and introspective) and enterprising (displaying leadership qualities, adventurous, energetic, domineering) work environments. Every intern was compatible with a social environment (S was in every student's three-letter code), and for 13 interns, a social environment was the most satisfying work environment (S was the first letter in the code).

While SAE is the major teaching code (elementary, secondary, and preschool), there are three other code combinations that are associated with teaching (SAI = special education; SIC = social science teacher; SEI = history teacher) in elementary, secondary, and special education. Nine of the interns generated a three-letter code that matched one of the four code combinations for teaching. When we compared the interns' responses with a group of traditional education majors at Central, the interns matched *more* closely with teaching as a career (Marshall, Sears, & Otis-Wilborn, 1987).

The SDS also requires respondents to list their "occupational daydreams." Fifteen of the interns listed "teacher" as among their top occupational daydreams. Other occupations included physician, airline stewardess, interior decorator, and accountant.

In addition to the match established by the SDS, data from individual interviews provided a more explicit picture of the interns' long-term commitment to a career in teaching as they entered the Bridenthal program.

THE INTERNS' COMMITMENT TO TEACHING

Based on information collected in our initial interviews, the interns were divided into four groups based on their career orientation as a function of the level of expressed commitment to teaching. Data from intern, parent, and staff interviews helped to assess career orientation on two points: explicit long-term commitment to teaching (weak = planned to teach for less than five years; strong = planned to teach for five years or more) and serious consideration of teaching as a career option prior to the Bridenthal program (yes or no) (Sears, Moyer, & Marshall, 1986).

Eight interns who had seriously considered teaching as a career option prior to their induction into the program were identified as Traditionalists, persons typically drawn to teacher education programs. If the program had not existed, these students more than likely would have pursued a degree in education at some college or university. A typical comment from an intern in this category was uttered by Jan: "The need to teach is inside me. It has always been there for as long as I can remember." When asked their probable career at age 30, these interns claimed teaching.

The second largest group was labeled the Mavericks. These interns, if not for the scholarship program, never would have considered teaching as a college area of specialization, and they did not express a long-term commitment to teaching. A typical comment from a student in this category was: "I had not considered teaching a prime option. Even though I'm going to be a teacher for two years, it'll give me a good basis so that I can get a higher degree." Presumably, the attractiveness of the program's scholarship arrangements, the opportunity to attend a small prestigious school, and the chance to take part in this special program had some bearing on these interns' decision to enter a teacher preparation program. Four interns entered the program as Mavericks; Gene and Rita were two of them.

A third group, the Converts, consisted of students who, like the Mavericks, had never considered a career in teaching. Nevertheless, in their initial interviews following their acceptance into the Bridenthal program, they expressed a long-term commitment to this career. These interns apparently realized that some match existed between teaching and other interests they actively had pursued for a number of years. One Convert, Roberto, when asked about the attraction of teaching, stated: "Teaching allows me to combine my interest in working with kids with interests in psychology and counseling." There were three Converts.

One intern, Lucy, fell into a fourth group, Reservationists. She had seriously considered teaching as a career prior to applying for the scholarship program but was uncertain about remaining a classroom teacher for any length of time. "I wanted to be a teacher before I heard about the program, but [now] I am not sure. I have so many choices. What do I choose?"

The Traditionalists and Converts expressed strong commitment to a career in teaching, while the Mavericks and Reservationists exemplified weak levels of commitment. The program recruited seven individuals who had never considered teaching as a career option. As a group, the interns illustrated a diversity of commitment that might be expected of first-year college students who are exploring careers. However, unlike most first-year college students, they had made a six-year commitment to public school teaching.

PORTRAITS OF A NEW BREED

Portraits of five interns—Roberto, Lucy, Rita, Gene, and Jan—illuminate how personal and situational determinants, including program enhancements, played a role in their decisions to teach. As a group, these five interns reflected the diversity of the larger intern group, including gender, socioeconomic status, and minority background, as well as each of the commitment categories (Convert, Traditionalist, Maverick, and Reservationist).

As we introduce each intern, aspects of personal and occupational self-concepts characterizing the strongest and most salient motivations for choosing teaching as a career will emerge. Many of the personal and situational factors influencing these interns are similar to those documented in research as generally affecting prospective and practicing teachers. Some factors, however, are unique to the interns and are directly linked to the Bridenthal enhancements.

Roberto: Culturally Bound

Roberto, one of only three males in the program, is the only man interested in an elementary education major. Family and cultural heritage is most important for Roberto. He is the youngest of four children in a family that in many ways typifies a first-generation Mexican-American immigrant family that has worked hard to move up socially and economically. His mother, staying home to raise the children, managed to finish two years of business school and his father, who barely finished high school before serving in Vietnam, works as a police officer. Education has always has been a priority in Roberto's family. Roberto and his sister are the first members of his family to attend college.

Historically, the teacher work force has been drawn from this pool of working-class families and immigrant groups often representing first-generation college attenders (Darling-Hammond, 1990). As a career, teaching represents upward mobility from blue-collar to professional occupations. It is a job that in many cultures holds a respectful position and represents economic stability.

Before being offered the option of joining the Bridenthal program, Roberto wanted to be a school psychologist; he also hoped to be a coach. Don Wright, however, turned his head in a career direction he had not considered: public school teaching. Convinced by his school counselor and a neighborhood teacher to apply for the internship, Roberto admits that attending Central would not have been possible otherwise, since he lacked the "bucks."

His decision to become a Bridenthal Intern, however, faced opposition by those worried about "wasting my intelligence and talents on the apathetic masses." This opposition was particularly strong within his immediate family. Both he and his sister chose teaching. His sister attends the local, predominantly Latino, community college. Roberto's family approved of his sister's choice of teaching, but expressed concern about Roberto's choice. A male teacher conflicted with a strongly held image of "Man as Breadwinner." Long discussions and wrenching arguments culminated in his decision to teach, and he shares his family's concern: "You've got to be the head of a family. How are you going to support them by being a teacher?"

One of Roberto's "missions" is for his family to be proud of him. Neither his mother nor his grandfather attended his high school graduation because of illness. Roberto expresses disappointment because he could not share "what I had partly done for all my family, but especially for them." He struggles with their concerns about his career choice—maybe being a teacher is not good enough? Roberto, like many men who pursue teaching, voices concerns regarding his ability to support a family on a teaching salary:

> I want a family. I want to raise them and be able to support them and not have to hold down two jobs. I've picked up the troubles teachers have been through, the loans that they have to take. I don't want that. I don't want to be rich; I just want enough to give my kids some kind of simple pleasures of life. As far as teaching goes I know I'm going to have to struggle.

For men, economics alone often eliminates teaching from their list of career possibilities (Darling-Hammond, 1990).

However, Roberto is not sure that his family understands the importance of the Bridenthal program to him personally—over and above the monetary enhancements. "I'm sure that when I do become a teacher, when I get my certificate and all that, they'll still be very proud. But I'm sure it's still going to weigh on their minds, you know, that I can make something of myself more than just that."

Another "mission" of Roberto's is to work with children. If he had not pursued the Bridenthal Internship, his alternative career pursuits might have led him into child psychology. He believes that he was accepted into the program because "I presented a close, sincere manner. I did have a concern for kids. I did want to become a teacher. I wanted to somehow be an influence in the child's life."

Roberto is uncomfortable wearing the label "academically talented." He remembers being called "brain" during elementary school and that his own academic achievements entailed hard work and determination against a constant barrage of low expectations and negative images. This perspective from the barrio is one that the other interns lack: "I don't know if the other interns really understand what it was for somebody to struggle up and pull that grade and have to deal with humiliation. I know a lot of people who really try hard and just can't make the grades. It's *not* like they're dumb or lazy as most people will believe when you're a minority or come from this kind of background."

Roberto knows that barriers he faced in public education will not disappear when he walks onto Central's elitist campus. The Central student body is a privileged group that will never understand his childhood struggles and adult concerns. "You have your high wealthy students getting all the benefits and your minorities down at the bottom. You see whites at the top—they've got all the knowledge. Then you've got your Hispanics, your Blacks, and various colors (the rainbow of kids) who are 'dumb.'"

Even in the midst of these conflicts, Roberto defends his decision to teach. However, he still wonders privately whether teaching will be "good enough." In November of his first year, Roberto writes that he will pursue special education and predicts that he will be a child psychologist by age 30—though still involved in schools. For Roberto, his career fate is far from certain: "I enjoy entertaining the thought of my future, yet I have some deep-seated doubt that I made the wrong decision. I presume it will be overcome in time, but I am afraid of the feeling."

Lucy: Giving Life, Building a Career

Lucy exudes energy and maturity. Smallish, with blond hair framing large-rimmed tortoiseshell glasses, Lucy always smiles. She is the oldest of six children and expresses an intense and sincere interest in her younger siblings. Her mother, a music teacher in a private school, and her father, a tax auditor, are separated and heading for divorce.

In contrast to the other interns, Lucy lives at home with her mother instead of in the dormitory because of a significant life event. Two months prior to the first Bridenthal seminar, Lucy gave birth to a son, Daniel. At age 18 Lucy became a "housewife" and an intern. Because her mother works, she is the "chief housekeeper" but describes her home situation as pandemonium. Within this context and with a two-month-old baby, Lucy seeks identity through her school work.

Lucy has always viewed her life's work within the context of building a family. Now, more than ever, this view dominates. "I wanted to be a teacher before I ever heard about the program, but I wasn't too sure. I thought teaching would give me time to have a family and be a wife. I could have my summers off and I could take a year off and have a baby if I wanted to."

Lucy's assessment of the advantages of teaching are not unique to her. Women often choose teaching because it accommodates family life. Jamar and Ervay (1983), for example, asked junior and senior women studying teaching to project their roles as classroom teacher, wife, and mother in 5 and 10 years. Elementary and secondary teachers alike projected the role of classroom teacher as less important with concurrent increases in the importance of their role as wife and mother. Women at very early stages of their careers, therefore, plan to take advantage of the presumed flexibility that teaching offers to have a family.

Lucy weaves her family goals into career goals. Through membership in the Bridenthal program, she sees numerous "professional" possibilities and imagines that she will quickly move beyond the classroom—despite the program's stated goal of retaining high-ability students in classroom teaching. As Lucy begins the program, she imagines her career life at 30:

> There's got to be some way for me to move up a little bit, the head of the department or maybe curriculum coordinator or something to do with education, something where I can be more influential than just in one classroom . . . a principal or something like that. I know I'd have to spend a few years in the classroom, but I think I'll be happy with that—but not forever.

Lucy also values recognition. Throughout the fall, she discovers that the Bridenthal program holds the potential for personal recognition as a member of a special group. She is excited about her opportunity to "meet big, important people" like Central's President Caster and Carnegie's president, Ernest Boyer. The program will bring her high visibility and opportunity: "I think I'll be in demand . . . I think we're already in demand."

Lucy's bridge for recognition is future students and colleagues. She wants to be the kind of teacher who influences students by "turning them on to learning. . . . They need me as a teacher and I want to be needed." Lucy also hopes to earn her colleagues' respect: "I'd like to be the teacher that everybody comes to for help."

Noting that motivations may have desirable and undesirable potentialities, Beigel and Willcox (1953) warn that many of the emotional needs of teachers, such as the need for recognition by others, do not fit with the traditional altruistic motives associated with service occupations. Lucy, though, is driven by the need for recognition in the context of service to others through teaching.

While Lucy is clear regarding what she values, she is just as clear about what she doesn't value: money. In Lucy's life, difficult as it is at times, money is a complication: "I chose teaching because it is an honorable profession, and I didn't want to be rich because too much money complicates your life." During her first year, Lucy realizes that teachers make over $10.00 an hour, which in her mind refutes the idea that people sacrifice money to become a teacher.

In her endeavor to become a teacher, Lucy, unlike Roberto, has found support from her family with a history of teaching. Both her mother and her mother's sister are teachers. However, she credits her father with her long-standing desire to teach, "because he's always taught me. . . . He talks about learning and about school and teaching." Immediately after Lucy decided to pursue teaching, her father began cutting out articles on teaching and sending them to her.

Lucy's mother describes the Bridenthal program as "a gift from God" paying for her daughter's education. Her father views it in more secular terms as an opportunity for Lucy to do what he was not able to do: finish college. Like Lucy, he was a high-ability student, scoring 1,400 on the SAT. These abilities, however, were not reflected in his grades—too low to take him to the university of his choice—nor were they coupled with determination. According to Lucy: "He went to a good college but he flunked out, and I really think that he's always wanted me to do better. He didn't really push, but he encouraged. I think that he's kind of relieved I've gotten into a program that's going to keep me there the whole time so I don't do what he did—make the same mistake."

Still, as with other interns, Lucy met opposition from those asking "Why the best?" and from others who suspected that bright students might not become good teachers. Other teachers tried to dissuade her from teaching. After a few months in the program, her former English teacher, retiring after 50 years of service, asked Lucy if she was still going to be a teacher. She cautioned, "Don't do it, it's a mess."

As Lucy enters Central, her circumstances are not those of a typical first-year student. She carries with her the responsibility and concerns of parenthood. She witnesses in her own life a family that is falling apart while she struggles to create a new family for herself and her son. The Bridenthal program was an opportunity too attractive for Lucy to resist.

Rita: The New Vocationalism

Rita looks as precise as she is: petite, with dark hair, short and neat; her demeanor exacting and decisive. Her father is American, and her mother, Japanese. Because her father is in the military, Rita, an only child, traveled extensively while growing up. She particularly recalls her stay in Japan, visiting her mother's family, when she was in fourth grade.

Rita approaches her decision to teach with an analytical acumen that reflects a true vocational orientation. Having considered a number of other careers, she discarded them one by one in favor of teaching. Her responses to Holland's Self-Directed Search (SDS) (1985) illustrate her decision making as she listed and evaluated her career "daydreams":

- High school physics or math teacher (allows me to use my knowledge in a favorable environment).
- Electrical engineer (money was first motivation but I would not be happy with the job).
- Flight attendant (enjoy flying and people).
- Dentist (wanted to be a dentist strictly for the money but I don't like biology as much as physics).

Rita's Self-Directed Search Occupational Code corroborated her own conclusion that the job of math or physics teacher matched her interests, attitudes, and skills.

Tymitz-Wolf (1984) describes a "new breed" of students who view college primarily as the training ground for their future job and whose career choice and development eclipse personal development. Prospective teachers, as consumers, search for programs with courses that will give them the technical skills. Tymitz-Wolf suggests that this focus can create "unidimensional persons, lacking connections to the cultural and humanitarian traditions that have preceded them" (p. 22). Rita's career search reflected this "new breed."

As a Maverick, Rita had not seriously considered teaching as a career until she became aware of the Bridenthal program. Her real commitment to the program began "on the day she was accepted." She believes, along with her parents, that this program will have a "positive contribution to society" accepting the simple equation: best students = good teachers. Unlike Roberto and Lucy, Rita had always planned to attend Central. Computers, foreign languages, and physics were her major interests.

Rita has given her new "major" much thought, offering a number of reasons why a teaching career might be a good choice for her. First, she finds encouragement to teach in her own successful school experiences and the enjoyment her teachers expressed from watching Rita succeed: "I want to help someone learn. I like to learn new things every day. I like the classroom atmosphere." Rita also chose teaching because she believes the preparation and the job would not be as strenuous as her other most serious career alternative, engineering, which "would just blow me away."

Another reason for Rita's self-match to teaching focuses on "content." Elementary and secondary preservice teachers often are distinguishable based on their expressed motives to teach. A generation ago, LeFerve (1967) characterized elementary teachers as more person-oriented and secondary teachers as more subject-oriented. While both groups typically are motivated to some extent by the need to provide a service and to work with young people, this characterization is still valid as secondary majors often are drawn to teaching because of an interest in a particular subject matter or area of study (Book, Freeman, & Brousseau, 1985). Rita, having from the very beginning identified herself as a secondary education physics major, follows this tradition. Physics gives her a definable and rigorous area of expertise, close enough to engineering.

Rita also believes that the Bridenthal program itself will be just as challenging and demanding as calculus or business. In Rita's mind, the rigor associated with Bridenthal "brings prestige to teaching." Rita sees that teaching can only enhance other career opportunities. On pondering her future in the fall of her first year, Rita first suggests she might become a professor or go into school administration. After some thought, however, she finally reveals her real aspiration: working in Japan. Her desire to learn more about Japanese culture and language and her own family heritage is strong. For Rita, teaching is considered a likely "stepping stone" (Book, Freeman, & Brousseau, 1985) to her future career plans and as a fallback career should these loftier plans go awry.

Rita credits her parents with being instrumental in her decision to teach. She recalls her father's advice: "You have the ability to succeed in this program and you like children. You like to explain things to people and you like to help them. You can become a good teacher." Others, however, discouraged Rita. One teacher admonished, "You deserve better!"

Through the Bridenthal program, Rita hopes to gain important knowledge and skills leading to sound employment, though not necessarily as a classroom physics teacher. Being a Bridenthal Intern is pivotal in Rita's decision to pursue teaching. The Bridenthal program represented knowledge, rigor, opportunity, and prestige. Participating in the Bridenthal program distinguished Rita from her other Central-bound peers.

Gene: Venue Searching

Gene is a tall young man with rugged features who radiates confidence and embodies the spirit of individualism. An only child of middle-class parents, he negotiates life on his own terms.

Gene did not share with his parents his plans to apply for or to accept the Bridenthal Internship until his decision making was complete. Gene's father, a career social studies teacher at Gene's high school, was less than happy about this decision. Irritated by recent educational reforms that have "taken away a lot of his authority to decide," his father sees little merit or prestige in Gene's most recently acquired award. While his father holds out hope for Gene to enter the seminary or law school, his mother prays for him to be a doctor. Gene strategically worked around their concerns: "At that point I decided to be a doctor—not a doctor spelled M.D. but a doctor spelled Ph.D."

Gene's "Ph.D. versus M.D." strategy highlights the value he places on intellect. While he claims to value "knowledge for knowledge's sake," signs or visible reflections of knowledge and intelligence are important. The Bridenthal Internship was one such symbol.

We can learn a lot about Gene's personality from his sophomore-year study abroad in England. After watching school children in an art museum in England recite the name of the painting, the artist, and the date, for example, he reflects in his journal, "I feel cheated. . . . I never had that kind of opportunity and I wish that I had because my life would be richer." Gene learns a great deal about himself during that semester abroad, too. He acknowledges his intellectual "arrogance" and wonders about how it will affect him as a teacher: "I realized today that I am really arrogant. I demand respect from those around me. In fact, I have a tendency to broadcast about myself. I was having a hard time not talking about myself. This could be a problem when I teach." Another intern also shares Gene's concern: "He's a little above everybody's mentality. . . . I don't think he's compatible with what's necessary in the public schools. You have to be able to empathize with every type of kid and in that area, he lacks."

The Bridenthal Internship is Gene's badge of intellectual honor and his ticket into the "Harvard of the South." Without it, Gene would have studied history at the nearby state university—a prospect that he certainly did not relish: "I intend to take every opportunity that I'm getting at Central. I am a person here. I'm not a number like I would be at State."

The Bridenthal program helps Gene construct a vision of teaching that matches Central's prestige and Gene's sense of self-importance. As a "pace-setter" for a new generation of "super teachers," he will help to transform a profession mired in the bureaucracy and mediocrity of his father's generation. Wright's contention that teaching is changing and will have more respect in the future is reassuring to Gene. Wright is less reassuring about Gene's silenced fear of mediocrity:

> I wonder if he expects too much of me or whether I am too lazy to deliver. Perhaps the most frightening aspect of this dilemma is that I am only going to be a mediocre Central student or education major. This is entirely possible. Although we were the best in our high schools, we were recruited because the quality of teachers has been declining over the past years. If the system is bad, the fact that we were the best in it has little meaning.

Gene offers another argument for becoming a teacher based on a theory of "cost-effectiveness." His analysis begins with baseline information: He likes studying political science, he wants to attend Central, and he needs to be employable. As a Bridenthal Intern he can fulfill these needs. Teaching high school "is the only thing you can do with a degree in political science unless you specialize in it and you start writing books on it and you go the route of a professor."

Gene's analysis is a common one for many secondary teachers. Joseph and Green (1986) identified a similar cost-effectiveness argument in their sample of preservice teachers. The added scholarship, of course, makes teaching even more cost-effective. While others have documented the power of scholarships and loans to entice individuals into a career (see, for example, Behymer & Cockreil, 1986), Gene will be the acid test of the program's ability to retain him in this career.

Jan: A Matter of Convenience

A good, albeit conventional student, Jan always wanted to teach. Hearing the announcement in a school assembly about the Bridenthal Internship in Teaching program, she grasped at an opportunity to finally "do something on her own." Jan's grandmother, with whom she has lived throughout high school, encouraged her to apply.

Jan's parents, both of whom have good jobs, were "excited" about her acceptance into the Bridenthal program but for a very practical reason: "They don't have to pay for my schooling, that's why they're happy. It was never because I did something on my own, or it's never because it was a good opportunity or that it was a good program. It was the money."

While the scholarship money was a significant "boost," Jan's plans prior to her appointment as an intern were to attend Central and pursue teaching. A Traditionalist, like 40 percent of other high school seniors who eventually went into teaching, she made her decision prior to age 15 (Williams, 1988). There were other careers that Jan had a passing interest in when she was younger. It is her interest in psychology, however, that Jan thinks brings her to teaching. She likes to "know why people are the way they are" and relates this to teaching because "teachers need to try to understand how they can help children learn."

Other determinants that influenced Jan's looking toward teaching are related to "role models." First, Jan reports having teachers in her grandmother's family. And, although her grandmother (one of the most significant persons in her life) herself is not a teacher, Jan admires her grandmother's ability to make people want to learn. Jan's description of a good teacher emphasizes close relationships with students. A teacher should "be able to relate to the students. Look at the students individually. Be a role model."

In Jan's life, role models are significant. For all the Traditionalists, family members and former teachers play a significant role in the decision to teach (Williams, 1988).

Interestingly, Jan does not credit her academic record with her selection as an intern, but rather her ability to "convince" Wright that teaching was really important to her. Tears well up in her eyes as she talks about becoming a teacher—something that also occurred during her interview with Dr. Wright. Jan volunteers the fact that she was not one of the original interns selected. Part of a second, "fill-in" round, she sees herself as second-best, an outsider holding little in common with the intern group. She feels she is not as smart as the others. She describes herself as quiet, not as assertive, forceful, or opinionated as other interns who "have a good way with words. I just sit and stutter."

Just the same, the Bridenthal program and her association with the interns is special. Jan predicts that the program will help her become a "better teacher, more responsible." Here, Jan's image of the program and her self-image come into focus: "It's also neat because I was chosen to be in this, and it wasn't that easy to get chosen, I guess. I guess that makes me sound more important. That sounds bad, but it's good for other people, too. I think they're all outstanding people."

Aside from her participation in the Bridenthal program, Jan is the quintessential teacher education student for whom teaching is a "career of convenience." First, her preparation program and her teaching career are "packaged" or "prescribed," leaving few opportunities to make decisions (and mistakes). In reflecting on her future, Jan comments, "I wish I could plan 10 years from now like this 6 years."

Teaching is also a stable career. Jan had planned the rest of her life around teaching before entering the program. At 30 she sees herself "being secure in my teaching career." She wants to marry at the age of 27, combining career with family.

Jan's decision to teach centers on her own needs. While we see some evidence of a desire to "help children learn," the needs she attempts to meet through the Bridenthal program and teaching include parental recognition, predictability and stability, and few decision-making opportunities. The Bridenthal program and teaching provide Jan a convenient way to meet her needs.

A UNIQUE INTERACTION OF DETERMINANTS

Individuals pursue a particular career direction based on a complex and interactive set of personal and social determinants. Determinants are internal or external to the individual and are encountered in a historical or a current context. For Gene, Lucy, Jan, Rita, and Roberto, three of the most salient factors that interacted to influence career directions and eventual decisions to accept the Bridenthal opportunity were (1) personal and occupational self-concepts that were a function of each intern's learning history; (2) the interns' highly promoted personal characteristic of "high ability"; and (3) the Bridenthal program, which presented a unique and, for some interns, a serendipitous career opportunity promoting an alternative image of teacher.

The interns' distinction as high-ability individuals provided them an opportunity not afforded most aspiring college students. However, this distinction created a need for all of the interns, in various contexts, to defend their career decision to parents, peers, and former teachers. Teaching did not match the vocational expectations typically associated with academically talented individuals. However, while teaching may not have fit their image, Central did. The Bridenthal program fulfilled interns' need for a well-respected and rigorous college education constituting the most immediate reward for declaring one's intention to become a teacher.

The Bridenthal enhancements and its acclimation phase of extended recruitment drew each intern closer to a teaching commitment. At the outset the interns reconciled many of their occupational self-concepts to match teaching. For some, including Rita and Gene, the program offered economic and social compensation for a six-year hitch. It was a novel idea that, for the most part, put long-term career decisions on hold while they pursued an expected abbreviated teaching career. For others, like Lucy and Jan, the program made teaching (already a career consideration) appear more attractive. For interns like Roberto, the program tapped into an interest in teaching that had not been identified in previous career explorations, providing a unique opportunity to test this interest.

Some interns found it hard to adjust their personal self-concepts to traditional images of teacher. Of the five interns, Roberto and Lucy reflected personalities that are most typical of preservice and practicing teachers: altruistic and humanistic (Joseph & Green, 1986). Their concept of service along with a desire to work with young people helped them see ways in which teaching could fulfill important personal needs (Bergsma & Chu, 1981).

Goodlad (1984) points out that young people entering teaching are often idealistic in their reasons for teaching, and Rothman (1977) notes that many teachers have little self-awareness of the psychological motivations for their pursuit of teaching. Many teachers do not understand the key role that altruism played in their career selection. Rita, Gene, and Jan reflected some of these concerns in their alternative agendas for choosing teaching as a career. While they spoke of altruistic ideals, their primary motivations rested in psychological and personal needs that focused more on self than on others.

Some interns drew on more prestigious images, grounded in Bridenthal's rewards and rhetoric, to fit their self-concept as unique, academically talented individuals "on the forefront of an educational revolution," as models of intellectualism in a "sea of mediocrity," or as "missionaries" bringing enlightenment to a troubled profession. To some extent, all of the interns adopted these images, although a few internalized them more than others.

We will revisit the factors influencing the interns' decision to teach in Chapter 10. While high ability is an obvious advantage to both teachers and students they serve (Schlechty & Vance, 1983), other characteristics that test the interns' compatibility with the everyday demands of being a teacher will become increasingly important. The perceived contradiction between high ability and teaching will take a back seat to the compatibility between personal self-concepts and teaching as a career.

The internship opportunity arrived at an age when many college students seriously explore specifically targeted career options and others still search for potential careers. The Bridenthal program, however, did not extend an invitation to explore teaching as a possibility but demanded a commitment. At the age of 18, six years is a long-term commitment occurring at a critical point in an individual's career development. The ability of these interns to reconcile occupational self-concepts with teaching will reflect long-term aspects of career development.

DEPERSONALIZATION OF TEACHING

We believe that teacher preparation programs need to develop a "conceptualization of teacher" that guides their selection of teacher candidates as well as the preparation process (Howey & Strom, 1987). Conceptualization is important in that it can address the question "What type of person do we value as a teacher?" However, most preparation programs adopt a unidimensional focus of teacher as technician, leaving to chance the development of the multidimensional nature of teacher as person.

Educational reformers have too often focused on recruitment of teachers who reflect "substantial intellectual accomplishments" (Carnegie Task Force, 1986) while only alluding to the need for individuals who can personally interact with students—many quite different from their teachers. *Tomorrow's Teachers* (Holmes Group, 1986), acknowledging that "teaching is conceived as a responsible and complex activity that is clearly related to both group learning and individual learner success," underscores the need for teachers to work with "those children for whom learning is not easy and for whom lots of help at home is unavailable" (p. 27). However, the very implementation of such reform reports has created gates or "standards" for judging academic ability—not to judge individual's motivations for choosing to teach.

Research and personal experience tell us that one of the most valued qualities of a teacher is the desire to provide a service to young people. This altruistic foundation is a staple in teaching. Numerous accounts by teachers attest to this service-oriented image.

In examining the interns' motivations for teaching we do not wish to exclude or devalue the intellectual needs of teachers. Both intellectual and altruistic needs combine to achieve what Sizer (1984) designates "the process of humanistic knowledge," which includes a teacher's personal attention to and interest in the student and subject matter combined with pedagogical technique that engages students in learning.

The altruistic characteristics of a teacher and the pedagogical traits these create are critical vectors in the teaching and learning context. In classrooms where teachers demonstrate these characteristics and traits students are more engaged in learning, work more collaboratively and interactively with the teacher, and more often describe their teacher as enthusiastic (Sizer, 1984).

The effects of reform on the school context, historically as well as today, have served to create an even more entrenched bureaucracy and technically oriented teacher force (Altenbaugh, 1989). Both relying on quantitative reflections of teacher quality and student achievement and standardizing contexts and curricula only underscore depersonalization of education. Individuals who choose teaching because of the social nature of the job find themselves in an environment that does not match their expectations; in an ironic twist, retaining teachers who were originally motivated by altruistic desires becomes problematic.

This form of depersonalization encouraged by reform is in direct conflict with teaching and learning practices addressing the needs of a diverse population of students. Darling-Hammond and Snyder (1992) describe "learner-centered" schools that assure learning for all students, not just some. Learner-centered schools call for a changed conception of teaching:

> The teacher is responsible not merely for "covering the curriculum" but for connecting with students in ways that actively help them to construct and use their own knowledge. If all students are to learn well, teachers must be able to meet them on their own terms, at their own starting points, and with a wide range of strategies to support their success. (p. 11)

Recruitment, preparation, and retention of teachers for learner-centered schools cannot rely entirely on academic ability. Teachers driven by the desire to interact and relate with diverse students and facilitate the reconstruction of knowledge, however, are critical.

Teaching is a moral craft with social and political consequences. However, developing the necessary dispositions or characteristics like those above in the short period of time available in teacher preparation programs is not possible. Individuals must come to teacher preparation with these dispositions and characteristics.

DURING THE ACCLIMATION PHASE, the Bridenthal program conceptualized an image of "teacher as scholar/reformer," emphasizing intellectual ability, subject-matter knowledge, and educational change. The program enticed high-ability students into teaching based on opportunity and motive. Promising publicity, prestige, power, and preparation while representing a more prestigious image of the profession, the program used traditional recruitment and screening practices, which yielded a predictable, albeit diverse, group of applicants. The result was a loose confederation of 17 disparate individuals, all with high academic qualifications but varying in the degree to which they "personalized" the role of teacher, viewed teaching as a moral craft, embraced the altruistic image of a teacher, and displayed personal self-concepts that reflect their motivations for and commitment to teaching as a career.

CHAPTER 4

The (Unnecessarily) Lonely Road to Teaching

This chapter brings closure to the Bridenthal's acclimation phase with a look at service and ethics—aspects embodied in the teaching profession that are largely ignored within contemporary calls for teacher education reform. When coupled with inattention to the myriad potential benefits of community building and collective spirit, the program actually diminished some of the more human and "feminine" aspects of teaching.

SERVICE AND ETHICS AS ASPECTS OF PROFESSIONALISM

The Bridenthal Interns, as we have just seen, entered teaching for many reasons, including the desire to serve others. Like other professionals, teachers must operate with an ideal to serve their clients (students as well as parents and the community) and their profession, but with an appropriate set of principles or normative beliefs to guide their judgments during this service. Whether one holds such service ideals and ethical/moral principles on entering teaching or develops them along the way, one cannot truly act as a teaching professional without them.

Ideal of Service

The ideal of service is basic to professions and is often manifested in values like altruism and benevolence—strong interpersonal values held by college students who aspire to become teachers. As a group, the interns proved no different from the normative group or their nonintern peers entering Central's department of education in their scores on the Survey of Interpersonal Values (Gordon, 1976). A number of the interns would probably have pursued teaching as a career even without the internship offer. These students are those who "self-select" teacher education programs across the country. Jan was one of these Traditionalists. She shares one important characteristic with almost half of the other interns: a service ideal.

Until the age of 10 Jan thought about becoming a veterinarian, later shifting her interests from animals to people and imagining careers in law and psychology. The connection between her interest in knowing "why people are the way they are" and teachers' need to "try to understand how they can help [children] to learn" is perfectly clear for Jan, who recalls generally good experiences throughout school. Interestingly, she feels that she was least well served as a student in the area of history, and early in the program considers becoming a history teacher.

Traditionalists like Jan help to maintain teaching's apparent service ideal—an important task because when society trusts a profession, its work will be honored and its members respected; otherwise, its status erodes. In more recent times, U.S. society at large has grown increasingly concerned about the service ideal of its teachers. Only four decades ago the public viewed teachers as being concerned with the welfare of their students, highly altruistic, and very committed to their work (Lieberman, 1956). In the 1960s, with the trend toward teacher activism mirroring similar changes throughout our society, this perception began to change as teachers throughout the country sought better wages and benefits and began to take action to get them. As the number of teacher strikes grew, tension between teachers and the public increased (Ornstein, 1979; Sockett, 1989). This tension has remained, and teacher unions themselves have recently begun addressing the problem. Albert Shanker (1985), president of the American Federation of Teachers, characterizes the predicament this way: "We tend to be viewed today as though we are acting only in our own self-interest . . . that image is standing in the way of our achieving professional status, for not only must we act on behalf of our clients, we also must be perceived as acting that way" (p. 15).

Unlike Jan, many of the interns were atypical teacher candidates in that they hadn't spent too much of their past mentally preparing themselves to become public school teachers. Furthermore, they began their trek toward teaching at a time when people within their city and across the whole United States were talking about its problems. Roberto was among them.

Quiet, reflective, one of only three males and two minority members in the group, Roberto found the opportunity to join with the Bridenthal group too good to pass up. He represents an example of how programs that offer incentives to certain people can "convert" them into enthusiastic would-be teachers. This is not to suggest that Roberto was any less qualified than his cohorts but that prior to this opportunity he had never seriously considered teaching as a career for himself. For as long as he can recall, Roberto planned to become a child psychologist and hoped to coach tennis as well. What sets Roberto apart from the other interns is not that his commitment to children or other groups of people was measurably stronger or deeper than theirs, but that his service ideal remained at the center of his vision for the reform of teaching.

Roberto seldom doubts his intellectual standing within the group and feels equally liked and respected by his peers, yet he represents (and occasionally speaks on behalf of) the few for whom the decision to teach is a deeply moral and interpersonal one. He is not easily duped by the premise that employing "brighter" teachers will result in better education for classroom students—especially for students of color, who, too many people (including teachers) believe, "just can't learn." Rather, Roberto believes that the heart of good teaching lies in the gratification of helping students grow. Good teachers are those with an "inner calling" who, like Roberto, feel "inspired to teach."

With respect to the interpersonal imperative of teaching, Roberto's beliefs stand in contrast to those of most other interns. Whereas most recognize themselves as "different" from other teacher education candidates (by virtue of their membership in this program), from most teachers (by virtue of what they have been told about the intellectual mediocrity of the teaching work force), and from the public they will eventually serve (by virtue of their professional status), Roberto manages to hold fast to his belief that being a teacher requires a closeness to others—especially one's students. Beliefs like his move teaching far from the notion of professional disinterest and detachment that, "from the professional's point of view, . . . is indeed necessary to get the job done. From the client's point of view, however, detachment is frustrating and alienating" (Soder, 1990, p. 41). Among the intern group, Roberto is a minority in many respects.

Earlier we referred to this 18-month period as a time of "extended recruitment" during which the interns were psychologically recruited into their new profession and their eventual role as reformers within it. This transformation process worked on no other intern better than it did on Gene, who differs from his intern cohorts in his willingness to admit publicly that he will probably not remain a classroom teacher more than two or three years. He feels certain about this for several reasons, including his desire to eventually pursue doctoral studies and become a writer and the fact that his father has been a high school teacher for many years and does not think highly of the job.

Gene is one of four Mavericks who begin the program. Early on he characterizes the other interns as "more human than me. They are more feeling and caring than I am." As for teaching and the process required for teacher certification, Gene believed that it "wouldn't be cost-effective" until the Bridenthal program offer appeared. Little by little Gene's position softens. Following their initial welcoming into the program, he suspects "that the internship program was going to make me a Super Teacher. Before, I viewed the teaching career with less than anticipation. . . . But as I began to talk about the program I began to want to get it on the road, like an epic adventure."

Quickly, Gene's attitude about being a teacher begins to change. For example, before concluding his first year in the program he recognizes that "teachers, in addition to being helpful on homework, can be good friends of and valuable counselors to [other] teachers." Much of this change in attitude results from Gene's relationship with Don Wright, to whom he grows close early in the program and remains close to this day. Gene visits Wright in his office two or three times a week in the early years of the program, just to talk, and comes to also relish the time he spends in classrooms around the city. Early in his second year he even admits that "going to school each week makes me feel special because I am doing something that no one else is doing. More important, now that I get to lecture I am having more fun. My students came up to me after my lecture this week and complimented me! Who says there are no rewards to teaching?"

By the end of the program's first year, Gene, the Maverick, has begun to express an enthusiasm and service-oriented commitment to teaching no different from those Traditionalists who pictured themselves as teachers prior to entering Central. His perceptions of the teaching profession, however, will revert in time to more closely mirror those of the reform rhetoric driving the Bridenthal program itself.

According to the language of second-wave reform, service can also be interpreted as one's willingness to serve the cause or "do one's part" for educational reform. Several interns entered the program with this form of service in mind. They fit the profile of high-ability high schoolers willing to swap their first two postcollege years working as classroom teachers in exchange for an opportunity to attend an elite school as a member of an elite group with a high-profile mission. As time passed, however, one would hope to see them becoming more comfortable with and committed to their two-year teaching commitment, if not to the profession itself. Some, like Rita, never seemed to warm to it, though.

Unlike many of the interns, Rita had planned (and had a family who could afford for her) to attend Central without the Bridenthal scholarship. And like almost half of the others she had never previously considered teaching as a serious career option. In effect, Rita cuts a deal with the reform movement (and its immediate spokesperson, Professor Wright, who recruited her): She agrees to become a teacher with the understanding that she will play a needed role in the rejuvenation of the teaching profession.

She plans not to become simply a *good* teacher but one of the best—a "promise" of the Bridenthal program—and to enjoy the respect that will follow this achievement and come from having participated in this enterprise.

During the program's earliest months, Rita puts little thought into where she will probably be five years after leaving Central. Her energies are better spent focusing on her studies than imagining her future. She enjoys her status as an intern and all that it brings, and she takes her commitment to the program far more seriously, she suspects, than many other interns. Yet throughout this extended recruitment period she never quite manages to fully develop an image of teaching that goes much beyond the reform rhetoric. Consequently, she never personalizes the role.

Teaching's service ideal also implies commitment to the profession as a life's work. Teaching has historically suffered due to its high turnover rate. For many women (who make up the majority of classroom teachers), teaching appeared to be a stopover before marrying and raising children. In the traditional view of professions, this turnover reflects a lack of commitment on the part of (women) teachers to their work, although the same negative perceptions have never been held for men teachers who have left the classroom in much larger proportions than women to move into school administration and higher-education roles.

Recent changes in the way we view the lives and roles of women provide an alternative understanding to the commitment of women teachers. Feminist scholars illustrate that women are no less committed to teaching than men (Feiman-Nemser & Floden, 1986); the differences lie in perceptions. Many women see motherhood as an extension of teaching, and stay in touch with the field through continued education and professional workshops until they return to the classroom. Furthermore, their length of time away from the classroom is shortening because of economic considerations.

Lucy, who enters teacher preparation as a mother, describes herself as "pretty dependable and responsible." She recalls that in her application, "I wrote about being pregnant . . . I wrote about how I need some kind of secure future for me and for my baby," hoping that sharing this information "would prove that I was dedicated and that I really wanted to do this. . . . It would really mean a lot."

During her first semester Lucy finds herself defending her decision to become a teacher. She believes that certain types of college students, like chemistry or business majors, have a more narrow focus than liberal arts–oriented students, the former "just concerned about making money, getting a good job, and moving up the ladder. And you can't have those goals if you're going to go into teaching."

Lucy describes teaching as "an honorable profession" and identifies a teacher "as the only thing I've ever wanted to be." She too has teachers in her family history and a strong reform-oriented service ideal, believing like most Bridenthal program recruits that "I'm really needed there." Her worst fear about being one of the Bridenthal Interns is that others might think that "it's just a bribe and the people in the program just want the money . . . that we're not really concerned about teaching and education."

Ethical and Moral Principles

In each of the above interpretations the ideal of service reflects certain moral implications unique to the teaching profession. Motivation notwithstanding, teaching transcends the simple provision of service to clients, having at its core "the moral obligation which extends to a responsibility for a person developing to full human moral agency" (Sockett, 1989, p. 100).

Roberto's sense of the moral and ethical aspects of teaching stems from an early experience he had with a neighborhood friend, Patrick, whose life turned out quite differently from Roberto's. Patrick had it tough at home and spent lots of time with Roberto's family. School was no easier for Patrick, who by the age of 16 had been labeled socially and academically at risk. "A coach influenced my life," Roberto writes in his journal, recalling Patrick,

and never have I been able to understand why no one influenced his. Even at this juncture in life I was wanting to help others, but I did not help Patrick. . . . I owe him one and I have promised that never again will I fail a child, in teaching, or anywhere. I guess I am in debt to him in a way, because I am inspired to help children. . . . I wish I could tell him this, but I am afraid he would not understand. Maybe I don't either.

Imbued with this internal understanding of the importance that people, especially teachers, have in the lives of young people, Roberto spends his earliest months as an intern *looking* for examples and role models of this inner conviction. Early in their first semester, for example, the interns meet for several successive weekly seminars in various schools throughout the city. During these gatherings they spend time listening to and talking with area teachers and administrators, mostly about the state's new curriculum reforms. Like his intern peers, Roberto believes that these reforms can lead to positive changes in schools — changes that would prove helpful for teachers and students alike. And, like most preservice teachers generally, he hasn't given much thought to the fact that these were legislative reforms and how this fact affects teachers and their work with students.

Following the second of these school-based seminars Roberto senses a troubling pattern: Teachers are impressed with the new curriculum requirements "but, like the teachers we met last week, were not sure what was happening. They seemed scared and tired. I became a little scared, too, because the way they talked led me to wonder about my decision to teach." The next week, following a third encounter with teachers, he perceives "a pervading negative attitude. A comment was made that the state's new reforms weren't needed. I found that interesting, since without it, changes — be they good or bad — would not have been implemented. Education would have been at a standstill." His specific realizations about how such reforms inevitably collide with ethical matters comes later, during the second semester, when Roberto meets Mrs. White.

Roberto is drawn into a middle-school classroom for emotionally disturbed (ED) students taught by Mrs. Anna White. Through this entirely serendipitous encounter, Roberto finds a teacher who seems to embody all the qualities he has become certain good teachers must possess: "caring, challenging, individually sensitive, and able to help kids grow and mature." As he gets to know her he discovers that like him, Mrs. White believes that "a person has to feel that the job is right. Teaching becomes almost a calling." Near the close of his first year as an intern Roberto meets with Professor Wright, his advisor and friend, to map out a route to special education certification.

For his third term of Bridenthal fieldwork, Roberto requests permission to spend the fall semester in Mrs. White's ED classroom. Her principal, however, decides that having Roberto return is not a good idea. The principal argues that Roberto should instead visit a classroom where creative teaching is not the norm (as it is, apparently, with Mrs. White), where a "standard classroom structure" exists (as opposed to the nonstandard, special education environment), and where "the kids are really expected to pass the standardized tests." Roberto makes connections at hearing this polite if somewhat patronizing rebuff, adding: "Another reason the principal didn't put me with that teacher is that she's outspoken and blunt."

As the program develops so does Roberto's awareness, until he needs no teacher to help him see the moral and ethical dimensions underlying most situations. He learns to suspect anyone, even his intern colleagues, who takes teaching for granted or offers thinly veiled rhetoric about respect and equity for students. Though quick to describe the intern group as compassionate, Roberto is bothered by some of the seminar conversations. Sometimes his compassionate friends seem to take everything at a technical level. You know, like you've got to learn to *teach* these kids; that everybody has to learn and they all have to learn on the same level. The other interns talk about individualism but without realizing the feelings some kids have reacting to having to learn, and the pressure that they have watching someone who's a so-called "brain" while they're over here with the semi-average or low-average group having to learn the same things and having to go through the extra tutoring and the humiliation that the other kids will bring them because they're a little slower and they don't really understand.

Yet unlike those whose attitudes and rhetoric he dislikes, Roberto is always quick to forgive the others in his intern group.

The first principle of the National Education Association's (NEA) Code of Ethics, commitment to the student, provides eight specific directives for fulfilling the job of educator to "help each student realize his or her potential as a worthy and effective member of society." These directives focus mainly on the fair and equal treatment of all students. In the second principle, commitment to the profession, eight more directives combine to help the teacher uphold the "highest ideals of professional service" (Smith, Travers, & Yard, 1990). Ironically, few preservice teachers ever read or discuss the NEA's ethical code, and too few are helped to realize that matters such as fairness in grading, discipline, and testing; questions of faculty dissent and strikes; and relations with parents are but a few examples of the many ethical considerations teachers confront (Sockett, 1990; Strike, 1990b).

A recurring theme throughout the literature on ethics for teaching stresses that adherence to a code of ethics is not enough. Attention to a code of ethics is an issue not only of collective interest but one that reflects the need for clear and consistent moral knowledge to help guide teachers through "dilemmas in which we have either no traditional guides or too many conflicting guides" (Abelson & Friquegnon, 1987, pp. 1–2). Nonetheless, the interns described no time during this important phase of their program when they discussed ethical considerations or moral dilemmas, though these "appropriately regulate what teachers commonly do as teachers in schools" (Strike, 1990b, p. 53).

What the Bridenthal and other reform-oriented programs don't seem to help students see about teaching are the three aspects that, according to Strike (1990b), combine to create teaching's unusual ethical dimension. First, teachers work largely in isolation and have a tendency not to seek advice from peers and administrators. This atmosphere of "aloneness" helps to accentuate a second interesting aspect of teaching: the absence of a "collective wisdom" about its myriad ethical aspects, similar to the collective wisdom available in certain curriculum-content areas. Finally, as noted earlier, teachers work with young people — a clientele more susceptible than adults to unethical practice because young people are less likely to recognize unethical practice, less able to resist it, and much less capable of reporting it (or being believed when they do). In short, when it comes to ethical matters, teachers typically "must decide for themselves. The hope must be that they can decide reasonably and responsibly" (p. 49).

Strike is not suggesting that teacher preparation programs need a course, module, or unit that covers professional ethics for teachers. Rather, "it is in those teacher education courses that are not specifically about ethics that we should try to cultivate a general attitude of respect for students and a recognition that the first duty of teachers is to the welfare of their students" (p. 51). The seminars that spanned the program's acclimation period would have provided a near perfect venue for attention to the ethics of teaching (see Chapter 2). As Rich (1985) suggests, teachers must attend to community ethics (community expectations and teachers' rights as citizens, community misconduct and grounds for dismissal, parent relations, etc.), school ethics (relations with colleagues and administrators; issues surrounding the hiring, evaluation, and tenure of teachers; faculty dissent, strikes, and disobedience; etc.), and classroom ethics (academic freedom, testing and grading, student dishonesty, freedom to learn and rights to privacy, etc.).

THE LIMITING DISCUSSION OF SECOND-WAVE REFORMS

Again the Bridenthal program seems unfortunately representative of recent efforts to reform the education of teachers. Despite general agreement that professionals must exhibit an ideal of service and perform according to some (usually explicit) ethical code or set of norms and standards that guides their professional decisions, none of the three major second-wave reform groups directly or substantively discusses these characteristics.

Although the overall thrust of *Tomorrow's Teachers* (Holmes Group, 1986) is aimed at the professionalization of teaching, none of the Holmes Group's five goals specifically addresses an ideal of service or ethical practice. One result of achieving their fifth goal ("To make schools better places for teachers to work, and to learn") may touch on the service ideal in that such schools will be places "where good teachers will want to work" (p. 24); however, this is an obvious stretch on our part and says nothing about serving people or communities, let alone having to make difficult decisions while doing so.

During their discussion of "competent teachers," the Holmes Group (1986) does outline a host of necessary characteristics, including "broad and deep understanding of children, the subjects [taught], the nature of learning and schooling, and the world around them." Competent teachers will be able to interpret students' understandings, "identify students' misconceptions, and question their surface responses" (p. 29). The report even notes about competent teachers that "students admire and remember them many years after leaving school, since such competence and dedication in teaching is unfortunately not as common as it should be" (p. 29). But nowhere within the discussion of competence are any human qualities (e.g., caring, empathy, or benevolence) mentioned.

The Carnegie Task Force (1986) report of the same time period differs sharply from the Holmes Group report by tying its arguments for the need to professionalize teaching (and education) to the national economy (Feinberg, 1987). Given this perspective, it should come as no surprise that the document is not only silent in its discussion of ethics or a service ideal but cacophonous in its description of professionalized teachers (and schools) as more highly skilled, more competitive, and more productive. The closest *A Nation Prepared: Teachers for the 21st Century* (Carnegie Task Force, 1986) comes to recognizing that teaching encompasses more than intellectual and managerial skills and abilities is when its authors admit that certain working conditions for teachers (e.g., autonomy, respect for expertise, and collective decision making) attract our most able college graduates "at least as much as high salaries that typically accompany [them]" (p. 39).

Finally, like its sibling reform groups, the National Commission for Excellence in Teacher Education's *A Call for Change in Teacher Education* (1985) has virtually nothing to say about teachers' ethical/moral perspectives or their ideal of service. This is true despite the commissioners' belief that their report, when seen in light of others released around this time, helps to fill a gap regarding "how new teachers develop into fully competent professionals" (p. 1). Early on this group acknowledges its belief "that education enables people both to fulfill their personal aspirations and to contribute to the vitality of the democratic society of which they are a part" (p. 3). Here, certainly, is rhetoric that implies an educational ideal beyond technologic knowledge, improved skills, and better test scores. Yet after more than 30 pages of position statements and recommendations, only two of the commission's eight characteristics needed by "a new generation of teachers" have some relationship to our focus in this chapter: "able to work with peers and others in diverse environments, and confident of their roles and contributions [to their students, communities, and society-at-large]" (p. 31).

In short, these hallmarks of contemporary educational reform pay too little attention to the *human* interaction that lies at the heart of teaching. The evidence for this contention is most apparent when we look at what recent second-wave reform efforts neglect to discuss (and what will risk disappearance as the inner character of teaching becomes overwhelmed by its outward, public manifestations). Missing, for example, are the need for teachers

1. To support and proliferate teachers' abilities to create more inviting and nurturing environments for themselves and their students, parents, and other community members
2. To establish a valued sense of voice and feel like equal and important members of a school's community and the community of educators they represent
3. To recognize and appreciate their own ability to make decisions based on their sense of responsibility and caring
4. To place students (and their parents) of every sort at the center of the schooling effort
5. To find balance in all aspects of their work (personal/professional, mind/body, theory/practice, etc.)

Additionally, through their neglect to so much as mention the importance of a service ideal for teachers, as well as the importance of the moral and ethical dimensions inherent in providing this service, recent reformers ignore the fundamental importance of the human interaction that lies at the heart of teaching. What we see instead are plans to "masculinize" this gendered profession so that it becomes more like the "true," elite professions of law, medicine, and the clergy (all of which were developed and continue to be dominated by men).

Why might this be? For many who would have it reformed, teaching is seen as the prototypic form of "women's work," which mimics both the nurturing role of the mother and the subordinate role of the wife. Enhanced professionalization, thus, requires a litany of changes to "toughen up" this feminized profession (greater emphasis on the production aspect of schooling, efforts to create a more economically and intellectually rewarding work environment, etc.).

But the tension and dilemmas inherent in this agenda are obvious. While it seems true that "greater professionalization of the work of teaching makes an important contribution toward realizing a situation in which schools can be characterized as gender-just" (Zeichner, 1991, p. 366), the sort of professionalization promoted in recent reform endeavors suggests otherwise: Rather than a more gender-just profession we will have a "de-feminized," more masculinist profession.

MISSED OPPORTUNITIES TO SERVE EACH OTHER

Few can dismiss the important effects feminist thinking has had on educational theory and practice within recent decades. And although feminist perspectives and arguments vary greatly, all who care about education would "reembed ethics in social life" (Noddings, 1992, p. 676). Doing so would allow teachers to connect their struggles with various existing professional norms (e.g., competition and objectivity) to their desire for a stronger community ethic in the face of teaching's infamous professional isolation.

For too many teachers, isolation remains one of the most problematic aspects of teacher professionalism. This aspect of the teaching culture is learned early, as preservice teachers typically operate in similar isolation from their student peers as they proceed through college coursework and their professional programs. Though "cohort groups" have become more common in recent years, they often serve as little more than administrative groupings or ways to identify new batches of students entering their professional sequence of courses.

Efforts like the Bridenthal Internship in Teaching program have an unusual opportunity to build genuine collegiality among selected groups of students that can go far beyond their name or the fact that they've begun a process at the same point in time. Group members can learn to develop consensus, build from members' experiential knowledge, refine their sense of true democratic process, value diversity, and identify the various "common goods" they share and will work to foster. Sadly, this is seldom the case in teacher education, where students can feel no less isolated during that period than they inevitably will once they reach their first classroom teaching assignment. And while many of the interns got what they could from their group membership, some got little or nothing.

For someone who mused early on about the other interns, "The more I see of them the more I don't know how I ever got in here," it comes as no surprise to find that Jan failed to develop a personal or professional identity with the Bridenthal group. Jan represents a small number of interns who got very little from group experiences during this acclimation period. She never developed new, long-term friendships with any of the others in the group, although she did work with several on occasional seminar-related requirements—usually with Rita or Lucy, both of whom she knew in high school. For her, the group offers no resulting friendships or special feelings whatsoever—simply more work. She quickly finds herself getting behind in her studies, which reinforces her opinion of herself as not as smart as the other interns and makes her more reluctant to place herself in situations where they might learn of her academic struggles. Jan determines that many of the interns are serious about their studies in ways that she is not. Deciding not to join any of the interns' "study-bum groups," she studies alone in order to create time to pursue other activities.

Of course, Jan does recognize some benefit from her membership in the program. She is impressed with one of the seminar exercises, in which she sets up and conducts interviews with central-office personnel in a large school district, because she must carry out this assignment on her own. And though she is invited to speak on behalf of the program at one conference, she does not feel at all comfortable speaking to strangers and worries that she hasn't fulfilled Wright's expectations for illustrating "how great the interns are."

Academically, Jan has problems her first year at Central: "My parents say that it's all right though, because they went through the same sort of thing when they were in college. But I don't think it's all right. I am not very impressed with myself. . . . I think it has a lot to do with nerves, and I don't like it." Janice Little, their graduate student mentor, explains how these problems related to the program:

> I'm sure that Jan is probably the one intern that the others had questions about. She had a tough first year. She was the one that I had the most difficult time finding from time to time. I think that she may
> have come the closest to breaking from the pressures — she didn't know if she could handle it. But she pulled it out by the end of the year. It's been a real maturation process for her.

What makes Jan's situation important is not that she has academic problems, for a number of interns experience similar problems during their first year at Central (some continuing to struggle with academics throughout their college years). In Jan's case, she chooses not to share them with or seek advice or help from Don Wright, the two assigned mentors (who were to make sure that the interns obtained tutors when needed), or any of her intern peers. She is, in effect, alone within the program and isolated from the group.

By the end of year one, Jan seems to have but one foot in the Bridenthal program. Though she interacts with a few of the others on a one-to-one basis, she is a member of no cliques. Yet as an intern, Jan feels a particular responsibility, because of the financial support she receives, to do well, get good grades, and take what she does seriously.

Jan is, in effect, simply "in" the Bridenthal program without undergoing much personal change as a result of her presence there. She copes with the additional Bridenthal work and tries to attend the seminars (though occasionally arriving late or not at all), always doubting the appropriateness of her membership within the group and never really joining it in anything but name only.

Jan, however, wants little from Wright and the others in the Bridenthal program. Even after three long semesters together she still doesn't feel like a part of the group and notes, as their fourth semester begins, that "there isn't much of a group." Finding nothing special in the at-hand availability of a select group of peers, or a continuing stream of noteworthy opportunities for young preservice teachers like her, Jan proceeds alone through the acclimation phase, viewing it as neither good nor bad on balance. Instead, she concentrates on her own independence.

Practically any 17- or 18-year-old high school graduate would find the transition to residential life in college, even a small liberal arts school like Central, personally and socially challenging. And Don Wright knew that adding the pressures of membership in a small experimental group would make "going off to college" even more stressful for the interns. This recognition, together with his own sense of personal and professional responsibility for their (and the program's) early success, prompted Wright to secure a graduate student assistant each of the first two years to work closely with him while serving in a "mentor" role for the interns. As events unfolded, it was the active presence of these persons that made the acclimation phase so effective.

Though different in so many respects, the 17 interns became a group by virtue of their special title and opportunity. During their first three semesters at Central they met together regularly in their special seminars and occasional gatherings (e.g., picnics and formal receptions). Much has been written about the importance of group life as it pertains to the teaching/learning process, from formal learning theory (e.g., Bigge, 1982) to methodological strategies (e.g., Cohen, 1986). As Schmuck and Schmuck (1983) point out through their exhaustive coverage of related literature, attention to group development (i.e., the social process of learning) is directly related to those social aspects of learning that both enhance and transcend the importance of "content." The Bridenthal program earned mixed reviews from its participants concerning the value they found in being a member of this group.

What Worked

As noted in Chapter 2, a female graduate student studying in Central's education department served as the interns' mentor throughout the program's first two years. The mentor provided them with certain sorts of clerical and managerial support (e.g., making travel arrangements and keeping appointment schedules), academic support (e.g., securing tutors and providing scheduling help), and personal help (e.g., helping interns' deal with unwanted roommates and offering a sympathetic ear to anyone who needed one). Their first mentor, Janice Little, explains her job:

> I was in charge of keeping them together and communicating to them and making sure that everything's okay. To me that's fairly ambiguous. . . . After I got to know them I had an open door policy: Come in any time you want. If you have a question or any problems in school, call me. . . . Pretty soon they really became very comfortable with me. One of the guys even started calling me "mom" because I would call if they were five minutes late. . . . I knew them all so well that I knew when one was missing and if they weren't sick that something else was going on, and I could find them before Dr. Wright could a lot of the time. . . . I helped get tutors for them . . . some of them were really having problems with roommates and some were just having people problems. . . . I guess I was sort of really a "mom" figure.

This mentoring role proved especially important during the program's first year as these young college students struggled with their new environment and their new role as Bridenthal participants. In Janice's eyes, one of her most important functions was that of role model and confidante. For despite the importance Wright played in the program and despite his desire to have the interns see him as open and available to their needs, he was, by virtue of his role, "distant" in many important respects.

For some of the interns (and all of the males in the group), the group presence as well as the support and availability of a strong leader and a full-time mentor made an important difference in their feelings about representing a new wave of reform-bred teachers. Gene, for example, ranked those factors highly, though he could never be mistaken for someone who was group oriented. Self-confident, bright, and fiercely independent, Gene might have been voted least likely to value whatever sense of "groupness" and community the Bridenthal interns succeeded in developing. Yet Gene soon welcomes the value of group interaction if only for the opportunity it provides him to work through his ideas. And he takes lasting advantage of the presence of both Wright and the mentors in this respect.

Gene fears losing his unfettered streak of individualism through membership in the program. Consequently, he chooses to see the group and its weekly meetings as important forums for sharpening his ideas and meeting his own self-imposed rigorous standards of excellence. Early on he praises the group as a collection of young people "all exchanging ideas, at least in the seminar." By the end of his first year, Gene finds the seminar meetings and their corresponding visits to schools to be key to the program. Further, Gene recognizes the powerful social forces these meetings can have on his fellow interns who, like him, originally harbored doubts about becoming teachers: "I would also say that some of the feeling that the other interns may get of wanting to stay in education comes from the camaraderie and all of us being together . . . [and] that the camaraderie, combined with the insight we're getting into education from starting in on the schools early, could definitely be a converting factor."

No less important than his place among the group is Gene's relationship with the each of the two program mentors. In Janice he finds "a nice person. She's easy to talk to. She takes care of us and gets everything out on time." But unlike many of his intern peers, Gene also finds in Janice (and her year-two replacement, Laura Rose) an older peer and a former teacher with whom he can do what he likes to do best with people: talk through ideas. Each of these mentors gets to know Gene well because of the amount of time he spends with them, Laura recalling that during his second year in the program Gene "visited almost daily during fall term."

But Gene's valuing of his peer and mentor interactions pales in light of his almost immediate sense of kinship to Don Wright; it's difficult to imagine Gene remaining in the program or maintaining his commitment to becoming a teacher without Wright's presence. The Bridenthal program and its personnel become a second family for Gene, and with it he gains a new father figure: "A lot of this program's success is due to Dr. Wright. He has a certain type of magnetism and I feel like I'm a family member here. I think you learn a lot in that way. You become a member of this department and start working with the crew."

Gene develops a close, personal friendship with Wright, who seems—in the eyes of the interns and mentors alike—to favor the three young men in the intern group. "Dr. Wright is very concerned about us and our problems," Gene notes early in his first year, "and he wants to be sure that all of our problems are cleared up so that we can keep our mind more on the program. I'm quite impressed." He is also impressed with Wright's role within the program, which Gene assesses as that of "guide":

> He has an incredible store of knowledge. He is also caring and compassionate and very friendly. . . . His role, of course, is important. If he were merely a teacher, we would not have been as motivated to try for the scholarship . . . [and] he would not be as convincing when he tells us to try diverse activities. . . . The most important quality he possesses, however, is his accessibility. He does not seem to be aloof and apart from or us. We can easily talk to him about whatever problem we have and he usually has time to talk to us.

Most of all, Gene finds in Wright someone with whom he feels comfortable. For Gene, becoming a teacher is anything but a natural fit with his self-image, yet Don Wright had been a classroom teacher, too, working his way to a point similar to that to which Gene aspires. In Wright, Gene locates someone who, unlike his own father, has not given up on what can be done in schools and classrooms—someone who makes him feel comfortable with the mission he has accepted.

What Did Not Work

Eventually most interns came to miss "the group," which had ceased its regularly scheduled meetings by the second semester of year two. But what was it they missed?

Throughout their first three semesters of acclimation the interns never developed a common set of goals or shared purpose beyond the Bridenthal rhetoric. Despite dozens of special seminars and unique opportunities, they never came to any understanding of the potential strength they had as a "revolutionary" group, never developed a sense of ownership for their group, and never capitalized on the potential collective support they could provide to each other then or in the future. Instead, the group remained a group in name only, to be directed by its de facto leader Don Wright, supported by its assigned mentor, and valued by each intern in whatever way she or he sought.

Several examples provide evidence for these conclusions. The first pertains to the numerous public-speaking engagements undertaken by the interns. Wright always chose interns to accompany him to gatherings where the Bridenthal program would be presented and discussed, among them almost always one of the three men in the program. In time, the selection of these intern speakers became an issue for many in the group, who couldn't understand Wright's methods of selection and who became increasingly convinced that Wright favored "the guys" over others in the group.

Eventually, the 14 women interns came to believe that Wright's selections stemmed from the fact that some interns were better public speakers than others (and that the program should be represented by its best speakers) and that the males in the group served as models for a profession that had too few male classroom teachers. A few even guessed that the reason some of them only attended one such engagement was because they had not performed well enough to merit an encore appearance.

In fact, Wright did spend considerable time selecting his traveling companions and did feel that having a young man represent the group was a good idea. He also recognized that some interns were more comfortable (and successful) at public speaking than others. However, questions surrounding this "mystery" were never raised or discussed as a group, nor did anyone make any efforts to develop the public-speaking abilities of the interns as a group. Being selected for these and other special opportunities remained the individual concerns of some interns and the private decisions of Wright.

Another problem felt by a majority of interns was the cliquishness that quickly developed within the group. While the presence of subgroups need not be inherently negative, the existence of these cliques, established along personal friendship lines most typically, bothered many interns. Even the mentors recognized how these small groups of three or four interns could color the mood of a seminar meeting or "freeze out" a less popular intern. Yet without any overt effort to develop a genuine sense of sustained camaraderie or compelling whole-group purpose among the 17, most interns naturally gravitated toward others with whom they found commonalties. And a few would always remain outside of all cliques.

In short, the interns never openly or collectively took direct responsibility for what was happening to them within the program, choosing rather to find what good they could from their relationship to this group, its leader, and the mentors assigned to them. Essentially, membership in the Bridenthal group naturally evolved to the point where for many, it came to mean nothing more than membership in the Bridenthal program. The interns never managed to construct or interpret a collective meaning of this specialness, nor did they come to realize that doing so might have significantly altered their development as teachers. Instead, the group was special because the program was special, and the program was special because it was perceived to be special.

This is Rita's constructed meaning. For her, the group is 17 special people in a special program—not simply a collection of preservice teacher education students with a fancy name. In her first semester she notes that this program will certainly be no less challenging or demanding than those for calculus or business students. She describes the special seminars as "most thought-provoking" and compares the rigor and challenge of classroom teaching with other fields that are typically thought of as challenging or rigorous—an argument she uses throughout the acclimation phase to support her decision to join the teaching ranks.

Membership in the Bridenthal group represents prestige for Rita, an academically strong student who finds the formal curriculum of the seminars no less demanding than it should be for people of her academic caliber. During their second semester several interns grow disturbed with the amount of work the seminars require (especially the amount of time spent in schools each week) relative to the single credit students earn. Rita discusses this concern with Professor Wright, who suggests that she and the others see this additional time and effort as similar to the laboratory requirement in a science course. "You are all bright," he adds, which reminds Rita that if anyone can manage the extra work, the interns certainly are the ones to do it.

When her turn arrives, Rita proves to be a confident and articulate spokesperson for the group at speaking engagements. She is living proof that bright young people can be recruited into teaching and believes that her presence, as the program suggests, will make a difference in the classroom. At the same time, Rita never actually develops any sort of deep understanding of what teaching means to her, or what it is beyond her mere presence that will improve the eventual teaching and learning that take place in her classroom. In part this is due to the Bridenthal curriculum, which, like too many reform-oriented endeavors, neglects to uncover and explore such questions. Rita can easily describe all the work and time the interns spend in schools, all the books they read, and all the assignments they complete in their seminars, yet what she "learns" from all this remains at the level of content acquisition and has no apparent effect on her inner conceptualization of teaching (as we will illustrate in Chapters 9 and 10). All she knows for sure is that being an intern is not easy and that she and her fellow interns do more and work harder than other would-be teachers at Central.

ACCLIMATION: TOUGHING IT OUT AS DIRECTED

In its three long semesters designed to situate the interns within the world of teaching and schooling, the Bridenthal program, according to our data, consistently took the academic "high ground"—adopting the views and critiques of researchers, scholars, and policymakers rather than those of teachers when it came to reforming the face of teaching. In so doing, this program neglected to highlight and explore the very heart of teachers' work, which centers on service and moral/ethical judgments. This is not to suggest that the interns did not confront and deal with such matters. Several, like Roberto, participated in Central College's "Saturday Morning Experience," which brings gifted and talented youngsters to the campus each Saturday for planned activities. And matters of ethics were confronted by other interns like Lucy, who continuously made decisions concerning balancing her life as mother, daughter, and student. Our point, simply, is that the program offered virtually nothing in the way of intentional attention to these aspects of teacher professionalism.

A second irony witnessed during the program's acclimation phase resulted from its own construction. The interns spent more than 18 months meeting together routinely, yet no efforts were made to develop any sort of shared "spirit" or interpersonal reliance among group members. Further, although the interns easily recognized and came to depend on the obvious and sincere commitment to service reflected by both Don Wright and their two mentors, none of this was ever personally articulated anew by the interns themselves. While some interns, like Gene, were integral to the group and grew to rely on it, others, like Jan and Lucy, never gained full membership. The interns found little opportunity to learn how collegiality might work to their benefit as future classroom teachers because they were not expected to develop this sort of collective awareness or to learn about its potential value (or the isolation that exists without it) from the mouths of teachers.

The most powerful result of this situation is evident when we peer beyond the program's acclimation period. While most interns valued their time together as a group, none assumed responsibility to reassemble the group or propose additional future meetings to Wright or each other. Later, each will enter a teaching environment where little or no value is placed on teachers' collegial interaction or collective support. As Duke (1984) notes, although teachers learn best from other teachers, genuine collegiality is seldom seen in schools where they work. Although numerous efforts to promote such teacher collegial support are tried (e.g., peer evaluation and supervision, team teaching, team projects for curriculum and staff development, and peer support groups), such efforts never seem to take hold in ways that might alter the culture of teaching. Though Duke suggests several obstacles to the success of such efforts, he neglects to note that teacher education programs—even model ones like the Bridenthal program—do little themselves to promote the importance of collective work and the value of community among preservice teachers.

Finally, the Bridenthal program's acclimation phase shed little light on teachers' ideal of service to students, community, or the profession itself. Most interns (Roberto represents the exception here) came away from their first 18 months with a commitment to serve educational reform generally (like Rita), or their specific preparation program (like Gene), or their developing selves (like Lucy or Jan), while never exploring questions of professional service or ethics. Even while completing their third-semester assignment to learn about a single student, few interns ever actually spoke with that student, completing the assignment by reviewing the student's school file, talking with the student's teacher(s), and "shadowing" the student through her or his school day.

Efforts to professionalize teaching that ignore aspects of service and ethics/morality result in a developing teacher's need to define her or his role differently. By presenting and treating these interns as special, focusing exclusively on their mission to reform classroom teaching, and sustaining the belief that teachers themselves are a significant part of the problem in the education system, the Bridenthal program and others like it underscore the image of a professional as someone in a detached (expert) role that should be understood as competitive, rationalistic, task-oriented, and decontextualized. In so doing these programs diminish the more humane aspects of teaching (nurturing, emotionally supportive, person-centered, and context focused) — those most readily associated with women.

Part II

SPECIALIZATION

CHAPTER 5

The Universal Soldier: Liberally Educating Our Country's Best

During their specialization phase, which began with admission into Central's teacher education program as second-semester sophomores and ended with completion of student teaching, the interns' thinking was redirected from reforming the profession to becoming teachers. In the next three chapters we chronicle the journeys of Jan, Gene, Rita, Roberto, and Lucy as they continue their liberal arts education, pursue their academic majors, choose their certification areas, engage in professional coursework, and complete student teaching with an eye on permanent teaching jobs. What were the assumptions underlying Central's liberal arts–based curriculum? How did their liberal arts knowledge transfer to the interns' professional preparation and classroom teaching? How did the interns' first three semesters of early field experiences, seminars, and speaking engagements impact their understanding of professional knowledge and their career decisions? In addressing the first question in this chapter, we will explore how the Central curriculum shaped the interns' understanding of the nature of knowledge and coincided with their previously held beliefs about teaching, learning, learners, and subject matter.

DISENGAGEMENT

As we described in Part I, the acclimation phase of the Bridenthal program served several important functions. Particularly significant was the fact that the program's early curriculum brought 17 disparate individuals together into a special group known as the "Bridenthal Interns." As the acclimation phase progressed, however, this cohesiveness and specialness began to wane. Rita noted, "We aren't in constant contact like we were those first two semesters," and Gene observed: "It's reaching a point where we are more indistinguishable [from the other education students]. Part of that is because we are not in the spotlight. Part of that is we've started splitting up and going our separate ways." The program's uniqueness also began to fade. One education faculty member at Central, Professor Watson, noted:

> It was unique when they first came here. They were the only ones taking those freshman seminars. They were the only identified group of special students. Since they entered last year we have had another group of scholarship people. This year we have three sections of the freshman seminar that include both those on scholarship and a lot who are not on scholarships.

As they neared the conclusion of their second year, the interns noted annoyances with the decreasing amount of attention being paid to them by Dr. Wright and the public-at-large. Several who reported "jealous overtones" described acts of favoritism on the part of Wright. Other interns were annoyed with the elitist attitudes held by Central's students and faculty — attitudes reflected in their own campus label, "Bridenthal Brats." Finally, some began for the first time to openly express concern about the degree of commitment evidenced by their intern peers to the Bridenthal mission or to teaching as a career.

The interns adopted a variety of strategies to cope with these changes. Several took it on themselves to promote group activities designed to resuscitate the group's identity, like celebrating birthdays, meeting for lunch, studying together, and printing T-shirts. Such activities often resulted in the regular participation of a group-within-a-group. As Jan commented, "They kind of plan them, like little luncheons at the end of the semester and stuff. I haven't really done anything with all the interns." Another strategy adopted by some was viewing the group as uniquely committed to reform in teacher education. Rita stated, "You feel special, you feel like there's a reason why you're going to school and killing yourself trying to study and do well in all of your classes. There's a reason for it."

Other interns, however, did not share their classmates' alarm over the perceived loss of group identity and "groupness." As Roberto concluded, "I think it has changed more from the fact that we've grown. The program has itself grown."

Regardless of the interns' reactions, one thing was clear: By the end of the second year, the Bridenthal program had virtually disappeared. The time had arrived for the interns to begin the process of defining themselves — both as individual students and as future teachers. The spring semester of their second year, marking the beginning of the specialization phase for the interns, initiated a host of questions with long-term consequences: Will I pursue my teaching certificate? If so, in what specialized area? What academic major will I choose? How important are the feelings of solidarity and specialness generated through the Bridenthal program to me? How do I identify myself: Intern? Special Ed major? Central student? Mother? Fraternity president?

As the interns progressed through their final two and one-half years of college, most viewed themselves as Central students attending a prestigious liberal arts institution with an academic scholarship. The source of that scholarship, the Bridenthal program, grew distant in the minds of many interns.

By the end of their sophomore year, most interns reported that organized student activities such as sororities/fraternities, sports, student government, and volunteer groups had more impact on their lives than did the Bridenthal program. Only one out of three interns related Bridenthal activities, such as participating in early practicum experiences and meeting important people, as still playing an important role in their growth. Being involved in the program had become less important to the interns than their work in formal student activities and their pursuit of their academic studies.

This disengagement is well illustrated in Gene's semester departure to attend the London School of Economics in the spring of his sophomore year. The changed nature of the group was obvious to Gene on his return to Central the following fall:

> We're not doing anything as a group anymore! We're split off into elementary and secondary. We're not doing speeches. I would have preferred to stay together with the group. I guess that's only natural because it provides that sense of identity. It certainly would have helped me out if I had a group to come back to when I returned from England.

Thus as the interns completed their sophomore year, the Central curriculum — not the Bridenthal program — became their defining experience. It was by design, not default, that the core of their teacher preparation program was Central's liberal arts curriculum and its extracurricular activities.

PROVIDING A KNOWLEDGE-BASED CURRICULUM FOR PROSPECTIVE TEACHERS

In the 1980s, American society, undergoing a Reaganesque return of traditional values and educational standards, premised school reform on two educational equations. First, higher educational standards = bright teach-

ers = smart students = higher standardized test scores = higher GNP.
Second, truth = traditional values = Western cultural heritage = liberal
arts education. Having discussed the first equation in Chapter 2, we now
turn our attention to the second equation.

By the mid-1980s, school reform shifted from a concern about K–12
education and declining test scores to higher education and the declining
importance of Western culture in the collegiate curriculum. Scholars such
as Allan Bloom (1987) and William Bennett (1983) criticized liberal arts
studies that substituted dogma and Socratic social criticism for the Great
Books and Platonic asceticism. Advocating the return to a liberal arts education rooted in Western culture, leading conservative intellectuals such as
William Buckley scoffed at revisions such as the Stanford core curriculum,
which sacrificed cultural universals at the altar of "political correctness."

At the same time, the second wave of educational reform reports, stressing the need to change teacher preparation, envisioned a cadre of teachers
skilled in pedagogy and schooled in the liberal arts. The Holmes, Carnegie,
and National Commission for Excellence reports all underscored the importance of a knowledge-base component in the preparation of teachers, each
proposing university requirements for preservice students at least as strenuous as those for noneducation majors and asserting that teachers be masters
of their subject matter. Toward these ends, the reports recommended re-
ducing the number of education methods courses, extending the length of
study for professional certification, increasing arts and sciences requirements, and requiring a demonstration of mastery of teaching content.

While all stressed the importance of the liberal arts, they differed on
whether teacher preparation should be an undergraduate or graduate
school experience. *A Call for Change in Teacher Education* (National Commission for Excellence, 1985) called for superb and longer teacher preparation programs, although not recommending the elimination of undergraduate teacher education.

In contrast, *A Nation Prepared* (Carnegie Task Force, 1986) recommended that students receive an undergraduate degree in an arts and science
discipline *prior* to entering a graduate-level teacher preparation program.
Tomorrow's Teachers (Holmes Group, 1986) also advocated the placement
of teacher preparation at the graduate level, reserving undergraduate studies for pursuit of an academic major and a program of liberal arts studies.
Chiding university faculty for their failure to assume responsibility for baccalaureate programs and their "premature rush to specialization and vocational preparation" (p. 48), the Holmes Group envisioned a "coherent
undergraduate liberal arts education" that would benefit all students, including those intending to teach. The Holmes teacher was first and fore-

most a subject-matter specialist with an intellectual's penchant for critical thinking and reflectiveness; the Holmes curriculum was the liberal arts.

Despite the call from all three of the major second-wave reform reports for a renewed emphasis on liberal arts education in the preparation of teachers, these reports received surprisingly little enthusiasm from those working in liberal arts colleges (e.g., Shaker & Ullrich, 1987; Stoltzfus, 1990; Warren, 1990). Leaders of the Association of Independent Liberal-arts Colleges of Teacher Education, for example, were critical of the Holmes Group for its lack of representation of the small liberal arts college. Many thought the group and its reports reflected an institutional insularity among universities and a lack of appreciation for the contributions made by small liberal arts colleges. There was also the question of whether placing teacher education under the mantle of liberal arts was wise in that the academy would "shape the explicit and implicit criteria for selecting teachers" (Schlechty, 1990, p. 13).

COMPETING CONCEPTIONS OF A LIBERAL ARTS EDUCATION

Beyond the squabble noted above lay a more substantive debate as to what formally constituted a liberal education. Different perspectives on what constitutes "liberal arts education" are particularly relevant in understanding the role of the liberal arts in teacher preparation. Three curriculum perspectives merit particular attention: discipline, progressive, and perennialist (Kellams, 1985; Kimball, 1986).

The Discipline Perspective

In the late 1950s and early 1960s, as a reaction to meeting the economic and technological needs of a post-Sputnik world, the liberal arts component in many colleges and secondary schools began to emphasize the structure of the subject matter itself, with particular emphasis in the sciences (Bell, 1966; Bloom, 1967). The discipline approach, advocated by scholars such as Philip Phenix (1962), Jerome Bruner (1960), and Daniel Bell (1966), exerted enormous impact on the public school curriculum (e.g., Biological Science Curriculum Study [BSCS], the "New Math," Man: A Course of Study) as educators were urged to focus on the conceptual, methodological, and logical aspects of the different disciplines of knowledge rather than pursuing "permanent truths" from the "great texts." From the discipline perspective, prospective teachers study "the nature, philosophy, 'structure,' and characteristics of the discipline . . . as it is known by its practitioners" (King & Brownell, 1966, p. 160) while mastering instructional and evaluational strategies that would enable them to teach at age-appropriate levels.

The discipline perspective on liberal arts had a direct impact on teacher education as evidenced in the development of the Harvard-inspired, Ford-funded Master of Arts in Teaching (MAT) program, emphasizing advanced study within a scholarly discipline and reliance on a disciplinary approach in educational foundations (Stone, 1968; Woodring, 1957). In more recent years, educators seeking to marry a liberal arts education with professional preparation have turned to a discipline-based approach (see, for example, Ball, 1990; Kennedy, 1990; Shulman, 1987). Of critical importance is for prospective teachers to go beyond a knowledge level of the arts and sciences:

> Prospective teachers must know some basic facts, definitions, and procedures in the subjects that they teach; prospective elementary teachers, in particular, often lack knowledge at this level. . . . However, even prospective secondary teachers who are familiar with the facts, definitions, and procedures that they are teaching are often poorly prepared to transform their disciplinary knowledge into a form that is meaningful to learners. . . . Teachers must comprehend the *structure of knowledge*, or relationships among facts, concepts, and procedures in the disciplines, *functions of knowledge*, or how disciplinary knowledge is used for personally or socially significant activities, and the *development of knowledge* in the disciplines. (Anderson, 1989, p. 98, emphasis added)

Problems in transforming subject matter into student understanding extend across the range of curriculum areas and often stem from deficiencies in teachers' own collegiate experiences (Grossman, Wilson, & Shulman, 1989; McDiarmid, Ball, & Anderson, 1989; Shulman, 1987; Wilson, Shulman, & Richert, 1987).

The Progressive Perspective

The progressive view is evidenced in the philosophy of John Dewey and Boyd Bode, the curriculum work of Laura Zirbes and Harold Alberty, and the institutional leadership of Harold Taylor, and represented in the Depression-era curriculum at Black Mountain and Goddard colleges and the current Stanford curriculum. This perspective underscores the importance of "individualism and individual freedom" (Taylor, 1969, p. 9), while stressing the needs and interests of individual learners rather than the idiosyncratic structure of particular academic disciplines. Consistent with this framework are four instructional principles (Olendorf, 1989):

1. Learning occurs primarily through dialogue between student and environment rather than transmission from the environment to the student.
2. Students must actively participate in the learning process.
3. Structures of the mind develop and reorganize in a process of interaction with the environment.
4. Values acquisition occurs through a reasoning process that progresses through successively more adequate stages of maturity.

This perspective also embraces multiple cultures. Rather than requiring a common core curriculum of standard Western works such as Quintilian, Aquinas, and Mozart, the progressive approach permits students to choose courses from a variety of options that include nonstandard Western works by Martin Luther King, Jr., and James Baldwin, as well as non-Western works by Gabriel Marquez and Nuruddin Farah. This component is particularly relevant given the flawed history of teacher education programs using a discipline or perennial liberal arts orientation that "prepared teachers to work primarily with white middle-class students who attend suburban schools" (Zeichner, 1989, p. 25).

The Perennialist Perspective

Evidenced in the writings of Jacques Maritain (1943), Robert Hutchins (1953), and John Cardinal Newman (1959), the perennialist approach asserts a common Western culture with an interdisciplinary emphasis and a commitment to democracy. The goal is social integration, the means is general education. Columbia University's contemporary civilization curriculum implemented in the 1920s, the University of Chicago's Aristotelian-based curriculum implemented in the 1940s, and the general education curriculum developed at Harvard following World War II reflected this approach. For example, *General Education in a Free Society* (1945), commonly referred to as the "Redbook," proposed a shared common experience for every Harvard student: three or four lower-level courses in the humanities, social sciences, and the natural sciences, and three upper-level general education courses. This core curriculum was neither elective nor departmental-based, but rooted in core fundamental themes that cut across a variety of fields.

Most liberal arts colleges of today reflect the perennialist approach — a perspective evident in the assertion that all teachers are better prepared through the universal knowledge of the liberal arts. "At the heart of that curriculum is a well-defined core," writes the president of one liberal arts college, "a central educational experience rooted in the cultural tradition of the society" (Dahlquist, 1990, pp. 9–10).

THE LIBERAL ARTS AND TEACHER PREPARATION: THE BRIDENTHAL EXPERIENCE

Central College's reputation as an outstanding liberal arts undergraduate institution and Don Wright's department's role in its institutional pecking order weighed heavily on his mind as he rethought the preparation of teachers during the early 1980s. For decades, hostility had festered between professors of education and those in the arts and sciences due, in part, to the rise of normal schools and the subsequent decline of academic respectability, ideological disagreements, social standing, and the relative preponderance of practical application in lieu of conceptual analysis (Borrowman, 1956; Conant, 1963; Mattingly, 1975; Powell, 1980). This hostility and teaching's lower esteem were perennial problems on most college campuses, including Central.

For Wright, the solution was simple: stop preparing "education majors" at Central. The Bridenthal Internship in Teaching program would be the vehicle for this curricular transformation. Courses in education, particularly methods, were reduced to a minimum: Interns planning to teach at the secondary level would take one foundations course along with courses in educational psychology, curriculum, and general secondary methods. Their major focus, however, would be their academic major and Central's core curriculum. For elementary education students, the major became the humanities with 36 hours of concentrated courses.

Wright used the Bridenthal program to build the new teacher education program on the bedrock of Central's humanities curriculum, funded in part by the National Endowment for the Humanities. A document prepared by the Central administration succinctly states its purpose: "[A] major in education requires a coherent underlying plan, and a relevant, unitary intellectual anchorage that emphasizes content, not methods." Professor Watson, one education faculty member who shared Wright's vision, noted: "We've stretched ourselves at Central to say, 'How can we provide an exceptionally broad-based, well-rounded program to these students?'"

The Bridenthal program initiated a series of changes in curriculum offerings and graduation requirements. As the interns progressed through their four years at Central, they and their fellow education students were "guinea pigs" for a new array of core education courses and a greater emphasis on the liberally educated student with an academic specialty. By the fall of 1991, following a 20-month college-wide collaboration, Wright unveiled Central's new five-year B.A./M.A.T. program for prospective teachers, which included 12 new humanities courses from departments such as English, history, art history, economics, philosophy, and sociology.

Wright and many other architects of educational reform assume that increased exposure to the liberal arts

1. Enhances commitment to learning in a variety of content areas
2. Facilitates classroom teaching
3. Enhances higher-order thinking skills such as reasoning and problem solving
4. Develops appropriate attitudes for scholarly inquiry

These four interrelated reform assumptions provided Central educators ample justification for requiring a liberal arts education for all prospective teachers. Implementing this reform through a perennialist curriculum placed Central squarely at the forefront of educational reform and in the mainstream of the Reagan-Bennett educational revolution. As Gene commented following his graduation from Central, "It's harder to distinguish Central from other programs. Everybody else is cashing in on it now!"

How were these assumptions manifested in the everyday collegiate experiences, professional preparation, and clinical experiences of the interns? How do these assumptions and the interns' experiences correspond to related educational research? While Chapters 6 and 7 deal more specifically with the interns' professional and clinical experiences, here we highlight some of these experiences as we discuss each assumption.

Exposure to the Liberal Arts Enhances Learning in a Variety of Content Areas

While some liberal arts teacher educators have wondered whether "freeing more time in the undergraduate curriculum [will] foster better preparation of teachers or merely expose them to a different set of disparate courses, taught with little integration" (Shaker & Ullrich, 1987, p. 12), Lucy's experiences at Central suggest the importance of learning in a variety of content areas. Reflecting on her high school education, she laments: "Each subject is isolated from the other and a student never realizes that a biologist must understand chemistry and a geologist must know physics. Ninety-nine percent of teachers know *only* their specific subject matter. This needs to change." Gene also held the belief that "teachers should be very well-rounded individuals" and commended Central for doing a "very good job at rounding out teachers in that way." Paradoxically, while exposure to the liberal arts broadened many of the interns' subject-matter knowledge, the academic challenges of Central and the constraints of the Bridenthal scholarship ultimately resulted in narrowing rather than broadening their content focus.

Exposed to a variety of content areas, Roberto, Lucy, and Rita planned to pursue double majors. By the end of her first year at Central, Lucy, recognizing that she "couldn't teach liberal arts," couldn't decide whether to major in mathematics or science. At Wright's urging, Lucy decided to pursue both. As she took additional courses in mathematics she experienced boredom and a declining GPA. By the end of her sophomore year, Lucy dropped her pursuit of a double major, choosing science as her focus: "I decided to choose science to take advantage of all of the hours I had taken. I could just as easily teach English, but I have a lot more hours in the sciences."

Rita also decided early to pursue a double major: mathematics and physics. By the summer of her sophomore year, however, she too had second thoughts. Not enjoying her upper-division physics courses, Rita decided to complete her mathematics major while taking an "occasional" physics course with the goal of wrapping up her second major at a later time but acquiring enough physics courses for a teaching concentration. From Rita's perspective, she was quite capable of teaching mathematics because "I did okay in high school. It's something I can do. I'm really interested in foreign languages but I can't stop and change majors at this point." A semester later, after completing a practicum in a high school physics classroom and receiving a C in another upper-division physics class, Rita abandoned her idea of an eventual double major.

In addition to these difficulties, all of the interns faced the constraint of time—evidenced in both Rita's and Lucy's decision to pursue a teaching area on the basis of accumulated hours, not expanded interest. Wright implemented the Bridenthal program as a transitional pilot project within the confines of a traditional four-year baccalaureate program. Caught in the transition, many of the interns suffered.

In order to meet the condition of the Bridenthal scholarship, the interns needed to complete the bachelor's degree at the end of their fourth year at Central and to take a minimum of 12 hours each semester. In addition to the 15 hours of education courses secondary certification students needed, for example, the interns participated in a three-semester sequence of Bridenthal seminars (totaling 3 credit hours), did student teaching (6 credit hours), completed their liberal arts courses, and pursued their academic major.

Given these demands, the interns enrolled in as many as 19 credit hours each semester and additional hours during summers. Every intern took a full load (and, like Roberto, an occasional overload), spending three hours more a week attending classes than other Central students seeking a teaching certificate, and devoting nearly double their time to studying. While some were forced to drop their plans for double majors, none of the interns enjoyed the luxury of "changing majors" beyond their first year.

When Roberto completed his first year at Central, he was pursuing a major in child psychology with an endorsement in special education. By the second semester of his junior year, however, Roberto worried about completing his psychology major because of his special education certification requirements. By his senior year, while student teaching fall term, Roberto enrolled in a three-credit-hour psychopathology course at Central meeting one evening a week. He was exhausted and "emotionally consumed" with his schedule and with too many late and sleepless nights. Eventually Roberto dropped the course, along with his major in psychology.

The problem of "fitting courses in" plagued even Gene, the quintessential Central student. At the time of his student teaching, Gene completed his senior thesis and took a French Enlightenment History Class requiring substantial reading. Gene lamented that "to be on Bridenthal scholarship means I have to take a minimum of 12 hours. In education, student teaching is 6 hours, which means that I had to fill it up with two courses. Those were really the only two night courses I could take to fill requirements that I needed. I didn't really have much choice in the matter."

Throughout their Central years, the strain of the scholarship expectations, the general stress of being an intern, and the heightened competition of working within an academically challenging environment took their toll. Although each handled the strain and stress differently, none of the interns felt the luxury of exploring (and certainly not pursuing) other areas of interest introduced to them through their liberal arts curriculum. Like their career decision to become a teacher, their decisions of academic majors were made early and became increasingly difficult to change.

Increased Exposure to Content Facilitates Classroom Teaching

Recent research suggests that most students experiencing problems in teaching have difficulty with problems in classroom techniques, not a poor understanding of subject knowledge (Ashton & Crocker, 1987; Murray, 1986). Drawing from research at the National Center for Research on Teacher Education, Mary Kennedy (1989) writes:

> When asked to illustrate the mathematical sentences, 1 3/4 divided by 1/2 with a story problem, many prospective teachers and even many mathematics majors provide a story that required division by two, rather than by 1/2. Similarly, when given a problem that requires selecting a singular or plural verb, many prospective teachers, as well as many English majors, were unable to explain the concept of subject/verb agreement and how it applied to the sentences. These findings indicate that *possession of a baccalaureate degree, and even a major in a particular subject, do not assure that a person can explain concepts.* (p. 6, emphasis added)

The importance of subject-specific pedagogy will be discussed in Chapter 6. Suffice to say that a variety of studies have documented the inadequacy of the equation: knowledgeable students = competent teachers. For example, studies of undergraduate science and mathematics majors reveal that while students may demonstrate mastery of the subject matter, they often lack the conceptual framework and pedagogical skills to adequately present subject-specific knowledge to the nonexpert (Schoenfeld, 1985).

Some of the interns, like Lucy, recognized this gap in their education at Central. In a paper prepared for Dr. Wright's secondary curriculum course, Lucy wrote: "High school is a totally different situation than college and the skills, techniques, books, methods, and resources need to be different. College professors do not need to tell teachers how to teach but professors can help teachers keep on top of the subject matter they will teach." Concerned about the absent relationship between their major content areas and their professional studies, several interns, including Lucy, approached one mathematics professor to teach a special class on the teaching of math and a science professor, on the teaching of science. Given the interest of these particular professors in issues of pedagogy, these course were eventually offered. Nevertheless, the interns—as a group—found little support for their career choice among their liberal arts professors. Only one out of two of the interns felt that the reactions of other Central professors to the interns' career choices were positive; another quarter found them negative.

The absence of a history of collaboration among college departments in the teacher preparation enterprise, as noted earlier, is a major obstacle in the development of an effective humanities-based program for prospective teachers. Prior to the National Endowment for the Humanities grant that established some collaborative relationships between Central's education department and those in the arts and sciences, Central's professors rarely contributed their expertise to public school teaching. Collaborations funded by this grant resulted in greater communication among Central's faculty and some recognition of teacher preparation being an all-college responsibility. The impact, if any, of these collaborations on the teaching effectiveness of Central education students, however, occurred after the interns' departure.

Since, as Roth and Pipho (1990) note, "there is little evidence to support [the belief that] knowing the subject one is to teach in depth will make one a better teacher" (p. 120), the importance of professional educational coursework should not be underestimated. Roberto observed, for example, that "I have Central's reputation behind me—its departments, professors, and the Bridenthal program itself—but I don't know that I have a philosophy of education," and Rita confessed, "I'm having trouble making math interesting."

Colorado State University researchers (Nelson & Wood, 1985) also found that the only significant difference between student teachers identified as highly successful and those least successful was their performance in professional education courses. In their words, "It would appear that as the content of coursework more closely relates to the knowledge and skills required in teaching, performance in that coursework can more readily predict success" (p. 56). Using pupil cognitive attainment data, a comparative teacher study of "regular" education graduates and those graduating from the arts and sciences enrolled in an alternative certification program found that the education graduates scored 10 percent higher on measures of teaching performance (Denton & Smith, 1983). Additionally, a study comparing "regular" student teachers from four-year and five-year programs at the University of Tennessee at Knoxville with the Lyndhurst Fellows—academically talented graduates of liberal arts colleges completing a special fifth-year program—found that the Fellows significantly outscored the members of the other groups on the National Teacher Examination General Knowledge Test. However, responses from school superintendents, principals, and teacher/mentors were *not* suggestive of the student teaching superiority of Lyndhurst Fellows over traditionally prepared teachers (Boser, Wiley, & Pettibone, 1986).

There is a related problem with the assumption that increased exposure to content will facilitate students' classroom teaching. As Ball & McDiarmid (1990) note, adequate preparation in discipline-specific areas such as physics or history often fails to correspond to the work demands faced by teachers:

> Science and social studies teachers face a common problem. . . . [B]ecause of the way in which school subjects are organized, the courses these teachers become responsible to teach are frequently well beyond the scope of their college disciplinary specialization. Science teachers teach earth science, physical science, biology, health; social studies teachers teach civics, geography, economics, sociology, and history. Yet, as university students, prospective science and social studies teachers major in a single science. (p. 442)

The interns knew this problem well. Lucy, a science major, completed one practicum in a high school physics class with a noncertified physics teacher. In subsequent chapters we will describe Gene's and Jan's teaching experiences, both of whom would be certified in composite social science. Though Gene's academic *focus* was world history and world geography, his student teaching assignment included American history. Jan was assigned in world history, despite her focused study of American history. We will also learn about Rita, who had dropped her physics/mathematics double major in favor of the latter yet found herself student teaching in physics and eventually teaching *basic* mathematics.

Exposure to the Liberal Arts Enhances Higher-Order Thinking Skills Such as Reasoning and Problem Solving

Liberal education has long been hailed for its effectiveness in enhancing intellectual acumen (King & Brownell, 1966). Given the importance of mastering and conveying intellectual skills in teaching, the embrace of the liberal arts curriculum by teacher educators is understandable. As the president of Occidental College wrote, because "a good liberal arts education will liberate the mind of the recipient, it is hoped that our colleges will assist students to think critically about education and the ways in which it can be improved" (Slaughter, 1990, p. 125). Nevertheless, "studies of the changes in student attitudes or ability to reason resulting from variations in their college experiences are few in number and are inconclusive" (Roth & Pipho, 1990, p. 120).

Though the relationship between reasoning and problem-solving abilities and the liberal arts curriculum may be inconclusive, the interns reported that one aspect of their Central College experience that contributed to their growth was "intellectual stimulation." At the end of their junior year, more than half of the interns cited getting a liberal arts education, attending stimulating classes, and sharing ideas with faculty and peers as valuable. In sharp contrast, the interns were not satisfied with the intellectual challenge presented by the Bridenthal program or its assistance in developing critical-thinking skills. They were more likely to comment on these expectations' being fulfilled through their arts and sciences coursework.

Following their graduation from Central, the five interns generally expressed satisfaction with their critical-thinking abilities developed during college. Lucy and Gene were the most satisfied in this area, while Jan and Rita were the least. Lucy noted, "A liberal arts education forces you to examine the fundamental tenets upon which your life has been based in order that you may ask yourself whether these ideas are truly worthwhile." In Chapters 6 and 7 we will juxtapose such positive self-reports with classroom situations demanding these very qualities.

Exposure to the Liberal Arts Develops Appropriate Attitudes for Scholarly Inquiry

At the outset of the first-wave reform efforts, three teacher educators highlighted the need for prospective teachers to develop habits of scholarly inquiry:

If high quality students are recruited, colleges will have to structure learning experiences that foster . . . scholar teachers. . . . Our inability to attract quality may be due, in part, to the "puffed wheat" curriculum we tend to offer. We spend more time giving tips for practice (often in response to demands for relevance) than we do in educating teacher candidates to the importance of seeking knowledge on their own. (Hopfengardner, Lasley, & Joseph, 1983, p. 11)

As we noted earlier, various factors kept the interns from following the less frenzied path of academic studies taken by many of their fellow Central students. These factors—scholarship requirements, time constraints, Bridenthal expectations—also left little room for scholarly reflection as the interns found themselves in a highly competitive academic environment. For many of the interns, protecting and enhancing their GPA, not developing attitudes for scholarly inquiry, was paramount.

Overloaded with credit hours, haunted by fears of failing Wright, driven by expectations of family, and observed by the research team, Roberto, like the other interns, felt "a lot of outside pressures" with respect to grades. Throughout his Central career, Roberto reported serious "headaches" trying to survive his classes and talking himself into believing that getting a B is not bad—"as long as you learned." Another intern revealed, "My mom just never really realizes. I've always been smart, and I never needed to study in high school. She doesn't realize the pressure." Janice Little, their first mentor, described this pressure:

Most of them have never been challenged to the point where they have had to spend two hours a night doing their studies. We put pressure on them because we definitely expect a great deal out of them. . . . There was a great deal of frustration due to this pressure and the time element. . . . There were always a couple of them in my office once a day saying, "Oh, I don't understand. Help me." A lot of them were shocked with their first B's.

Perhaps these pressures were best articulated by Carol, an intern who was held in high esteem among the interns for her intellect and commitment. In her journal, Carol writes:

At the beginning of the semester I found I was trying to be too involved in too many different organizations. In early October I dropped my participation in several of them. Now, I don't feel as pressured or frustrated. . . . This semester I was really ready to come back to school. . . . I thought I could raise my GPA this semester with little, if any, problem. Wrong!

Spanish started off as a challenging class. Then it got frustrating
. . . mostly because my professor spoke Spanish nearly the entire class
period. . . . I ended up missing about six class periods, and I didn't
study as much as I should have. I ended up with a B+.

Another class I had trouble in was Applied Linear Algebra. It
started off as an easy class but only got progressively worse and more
difficult. I ended up with a fortunate C− in the class. . . . I also had a
lot of trouble in my history class making "good" grades (at least a B).
. . . I was incredibly bored with my Computers and Society class and
ended up not attending over one-half of the class periods. Ironically, it
was the only class I received an A in.

Emphasis on grades and the academic difficulties faced by some of the
interns dominated their discussions about Central's intellectual environment. From their first semester until commencement ceremonies, the interns
worried about grades. Their overall performance was less than stellar. Most
interns ended their first year with a solid B average, although 4 of the 17
saw their GPAs drop below 2.5 (B−/C+). While those on the lowest
end—with significant tutoring and other assistance provided by the Bridenthal program—eventually improved their overall academic performance,
few interns distinguished themselves in Central's elite academic environment. At the end of their senior year, three interns graduated with a GPA of
less than 3.0 and two with a GPA of more than 3.5. Thus most of the
interns ended their Central career much as they ended their first year: solid
B students within a highly academically competitive environment.

Membership in honor societies provides some evidence of the interns'
commitment to scholarly inquiry. In their junior year, for example, the
Annual Honors Awards Convocation honored 9 of the 17 interns for
involvement in Kappa Delta Pi, the international education honor society
composed of outstanding upperclass education students. Among our 5 interns, only Jan was absent. Only 2 interns, however, had been elected to
honor societies in their fields of academic specialization: Gene belonged to
Phi Alpha Theta, the national history honors society, and Pi Sigma Alpha,
the national political science honor society; Rita joined Sigma Pi Sigma, the
national physics honor society. None of the 16 graduating interns belonged
to Alpha Chi, the national honor society composed of upperclass students
of superior academic achievement.

THE UNIVERSALIZATION OF KNOWLEDGE:
PREPARING CHALKBOARD SOLDIERS

The perennialist Central liberal arts curriculum assumed that knowledge is,
in fact, universal: What is true and relevant for an Ivy League–bound subur-

ban high school student is also true and relevant — or at least ought to be — for a barrio-bred student headed for a state college education. Although students come to Central from different backgrounds, all are expected to drink and grow from a common fountain of intellectual knowledge: Aristotelian and Euro-American.

Young people who reside in the upper portion of the socioeconomic pyramid complete secondary school with higher grades, attend more prestigious colleges, and generate greater earnings than equally talented students from the lowest economic strata (Folger, Astin, & Bayer, 1970; Lewis & Kingston, 1989; Sewell, 1971). Nearly one-quarter of students entering elite undergraduate institutions report family income exceeding $100,000, yet this income bracket accounts for less than 5 percent of the general population. Further, the probability of a family member who is in this income bracket enrolling at a selective private institution is 10 times greater than it is for a young man or woman whose family net income is less than $20,000 (Lewis & Kingston, 1989). In short, "good" students are those who have the cultural capital — the knowledge base, values, and language — most compatible with schooling; "good" teachers are those who efficiently transmit this cultural capital and effectively manage the classroom; "good" schools are those that evidence this transmission in above-average test scores.

The universalization of knowledge reflected in the Central College curriculum reflects a reification of a particular type of knowledge (upper-middle class, Euro-American) and a specific form of understanding (linear and rational). Yet this form of cultural capital, as McLaren (1991) eloquently describes, is far from universal:

> Has it ever occurred to these marshals of identity that our schools are failing large numbers of minority students precisely because too much emphasis and significance is already being placed on trading in on the status of one's cultural capital? Think about those students who populate urban settings such as Howard Beach, Ozone Park, El Barrio, or the *carnales* of barrios such as Maravilla I and White Fence. They are more likely to learn about Eastern Europe in ways set forth by the neo-conservative multiculturalists than they are about the Harlem Renaissance, Mexico, Africa, the Caribbean, or Aztec or Zulu culture. . . . The crippling irony is that test scores based on the information filtered from the Western canon and bourgeois cultural capital are used to justify school district and state funding initiatives. It is this kind of ideology . . . [that] is undergirding dominant forms of schooling that function and legitimate Anglocentric values and meaning and at the same time negate the history, culture, and language practices of minority students. (pp. 12–13)

It was the currency of this cultural capital (and the largesse of the Bridenthal Foundation) that enabled middle-class students like Gene, Lucy, and Jan as well as Latino students like Roberto to attend Central. As we discuss elsewhere (Sears, Marshall, & Otis-Wilborn, 1989), these interns were able to transform their modest cultural investment into a "first-rate" education generally reserved for their fellow Central students driving Jaguars and vacationing in Vail.

Central, with its matching red-brick buildings contoured over red rock cliffs, was truly a city on the hill. Overlooking the urban sprawl, Central students discussed macroeconomic theories of Friedman and Galbraith without ever experiencing barrio economics; they read the Greek fathers of philosophy, science, and mathematics without ever exploring their African roots. As Central's chapel bell tower rang leisurely every quarter hour, these students of privilege learned their history, culture, and language without ever experiencing the Other.

Gene, Roberto, Rita, Jan, and Lucy dwelled in this insular community of social domesticity and intellectual xenophobia for four years. On occasion some rebelled—Gene writing a letter to the student newspaper chastising the administration for failing to recruit more minority students; Rita questioning Wright about the value of the seminars. These were respectable rebellions—short-lived and uneventful—that failed to develop around "coordinates of difference and power" (high test scores for admissions, a special group with special privileges).

Within the institutional ethos of Central, few professors staked out intellectually free territories of discourse, pedagogy, or politics. Those who did, like a long-tenured leftist sociology professor or a discipline-oriented science instructor, did so outside the institutional mainstream. With such marginalized professors, few Central students crossed over into their "border pedagogy," which Giroux (1992) describes as assuming

> the dual task of not only creating new objects of knowledge but also addressing how inequalities, power, and human suffering are rooted in basic institutional structures. . . . Border pedagogy offers the opportunity for students to engage the multiple references that constitute different cultural codes, experiences, and languages. This means educating students to both read these codes historically and critically while simultaneously learning the limits of such codes, including the ones they use to construct their own narratives and histories. . . . Within this discourse, students should engage knowledge as border-crossers, as people moving in and out of borders constructed around coordinates of difference and power. (p. 29)

During their four years of elite education, no interns crossed Central's liberal arts borders or seriously questioned its canon, the universalization of knowledge. While most interns believed these four years had a great impact on their abilities to make intelligent decisions and to engage in critical thinking, only Rita believed that her liberal arts education helped enable her to respond positively to ethnic diversity, and only Jan and Rita thought it had at least some effect on expanding their tolerance for different people and ideas. Further, with the exception of Rita, the emphases on diversity and tolerance were not seen by the interns as critical or realistic goals to pursue. Like that of other education students (Sears, 1984), the interns' emphasis was, instead, vocational (e.g., meeting certification requirements, preparing to cope in the classroom, having worthwhile field experiences, acquiring instructional strategies).

Even when the interns stumbled over issues of privilege, they lacked the necessary cultural, political, and economic insights to identify and challenge these instances and, in the process, to reconstruct their own narratives within Central's dominant intellectual discourse. In addition to Gene's public but acritical condemnation of the college's failure to recruit more minorities, we can cite Rita's comparative judgment of the types of knowledge available to area students:

> When I first came to Central, I was impressed with the quality of the courses. But I was more impressed after I started talking to Ben over at the Barnard Community College. In English he was learning nouns and verbs; in our language class we were studying thesis statements. It's much deeper. It's such a higher level; it's the right level for me.

The attribution of school success to individual talent, merit, and ability veils pervasive structural, economic, and social relations that reproduce and reify this hierarchical differentiation. Reconciled to her position within this hierarchy, Rita believed she had earned matriculation to Central and deserved the benefits graduation from Central would provide. Why she had access to a Central education and Ben did not or why a degree from Barnard Community College was worth less than one from Central were questions easily explained through a meritocratic ideology; why low-status groups had little access to high-status knowledge and the validity of such knowledge itself were not questioned.

The choice of teaching roles reflects the interns' pursuit of high-status knowledge. Nearly one-half of the group chose to enter into the special education program and all but one of the remaining interns sought secondary certification, primarily in the fields of mathematics and science. No intern chose to pursue a general elementary certificate. Wright's position reflected support for these decisions:

> I've had students tell me over the years, "I'm damn sick and tired of going home to my dorm room with my roommate writing a paper and

I'm cutting and pasting on the floor for elementary education." I know there is some methodology necessary, but good kids can pick that up reasonably fast. You don't have to have five methods courses in an elementary education program for them to get the point. . . . I mean, how many damn times can you talk about the discovery technique?

TEACHING CHOICES AND ORIENTATIONS: LEGACIES OF A LIBERAL ARTS EDUCATION

The impact of this perennialist perspective on the interns is evident not only in their inability to pose such questions but in their decisions regarding where to teach and in the degree to which their personal teaching orientation model corresponded with the dominant intellectualist model at Central.

As we detail later in this book, these interns generally found themselves teaching in the affluent school districts of the city's northside. Among the 16 interns, when they began their careers as first-year teachers, 11 were working in the more affluent northside districts. Although Wright placed emphasis on those 5 who did work in other districts, 3 of those interns were returning to their old downtown or southside school districts. In fact, there was a strong relationship between where the interns ultimately taught and their home school districts. This pattern, though, according to Wright, was not his responsibility:

> I can't tell them where to go. That's their own business. I have actively tried to recruit several people to William Casey middle school which has lots of problems with drugs, achievement, violence, drop-outs. The interns I talked to decided—after some soul searching—that they could not be as successful in a school like that. I suspect that they are right.

Although Wright could have structured the Bridenthal program to have emphasized or required inner-city teaching, after the interns accepted the conditions of their scholarship Wright, of course, could not "tell them where to go." However, Central's hidden curriculum inched them along the intellectually conservative and socially sheltered path semester after semester: the orientation of its liberal arts curriculum; the composition of its student body; their special experiences. Even in those cases where some of the interns were placed in an inner-city school for a clinical practicum during their sophomore year, the experiences tended to reinforce their predispositions without challenging them to ask fundamental questions about power, authority, and control and their role in legitimizing or challenging it. For example, Rita, anticipating her weekly classroom visit to a metro technical high school, stated: "It's going to be a lot different than the one we went to last semester. I can already tell the difference. I'm sort of scared. I've heard all these stories about inner-city school and the minority groups. It's right in the middle of downtown! The faculty isn't enthusiastic and the students are less motivated." Another intern accompanying Rita to the technical school wrote:

> At the northside school the kids had every opportunity. Tech is almost at the other end of the spectrum. Most of the kids here are lucky if they even get to go to school on a regular basis. A lot of them must stay home to watch younger sisters and brothers while their parents work. . . . I think it is really sad that the parents aren't giving their children any kind of support. On the northside the kids are little adults and they can handle all the information we give them. At Tech we just try to get them into the classroom and teach them something.

Returning to his southside school for practicum experience, Roberto observed that "something" was often very little: "The teachers have fallen into that groove: everything is on the mimeograph. . . . They really don't hold any expectations any more for the kids. . . . Everything is revolving around basic skills and teaching for the test. The kids aren't reflecting on what they're actually learning."

While Central's curriculum sculpted the interns' intellectual understanding, it had less impact on their teaching orientations. While it paralleled the pedagogical predispositions of many of the interns like Gene and Rita, who emphasized this universal dimension of knowledge in their teaching, it fit less well with other participants. Lucy, for example, throughout her four years at Central tended to focus on the structure of the knowledge discipline rather than the subject matter itself. Too few arts and sciences professors emphasizing this approach and its absence in her professional studies disabled her ability but did not dissuade her interest. Similarly, for Roberto, who emphasized the affective and empathic dimensions of teaching, good teachers were thought to be those who demonstrated caring relationships within the classroom and who understood the problems of students on the academic or social margin of school life. Finally, there were students like Jan who tended to focus on the technical and social efficiency aspects of teaching.

Though no interns would exclude any of these elements from their conceptions of a "good teacher and good teaching," the degree of emphasis placed on these qualities and the manner of their acquisition differed indeed. The differences in their orientations reveal both the diversity among these high-ability students and the inability of any one teacher education curriculum, no matter how well designed and executed, to meet effectively these different conceptions of what it means to be a good teacher and to demonstrate good teaching.

The Intellectual Orientation: Teacher as Knowledge Dispenser

As the interns completed their professional studies and entered the classroom as novice teachers, some adopted a teaching philosophy similar to that experienced at Central and advanced by Don Wright. All of the interns completed the Teaching Style Inventory Questionnaire, a simple self-descriptive test of psychological types. Following student teaching, Gene's dominant teaching style was that of the "intuitive-thinking" teacher. As described by Silver & Hanson (1981), this teacher "is intellectually oriented. The teacher places primary importance on students' intellectual development" (p. 5).

Gene's preferred classroom atmosphere was one in which "students are provided with a variety of resources and activities designed to develop their critical thinking skills." Using instructional strategies such an independent research, reading assignments, and debating issues, Gene's preferred lesson plans "focus on conceptual objectives rather than measured results" (p. 2). For Gene, learning is characterized as "logical, intellectual, and knowledge-oriented." Unlike Rita, who also shared this dominant intellectual orientation, Gene preferred students who demonstrated insights and original ideas, who were not confined by convention — traits remarkably similar to Gene's self-image.

This intellectualist orientation is not a student-oriented perspective; Gene's focus is cerebral, not heartfelt. As Professor Roberts of Central's education department underscores, this orientation is not inimical to teaching:

I think that if you have a person who is brilliant in physics or European history and that person had difficulty in relating to other people, if the person was teaching honors courses in a competitive high school or teaching at a prep school, you might be able to really make an important contribution in the lives of the young people through the information that's given.

Gene eventually would teach honors courses. While we detail such experiences in the next two chapters, it is important to emphasize the correlation between interns' teaching orientations vis-à-vis their classroom effectiveness and career satisfaction. This will become even more evident as we follow Gene into his first two years of teaching primarily upper-level students.

Transmitting her love for knowledge acquisition was an important goal for Rita, who also scored high as an intuitive-thinking teacher. Rita, excited about teaching, noted "I picked teaching because I wanted to be somewhere I could influence other people's lives. I just got so caught up in learning." Unlike Gene, however, an equally strong emphasis for Rita was a technical/outcomes orientation — an orientation that best fits Jan, whom we will discuss shortly. While Rita wanted an intellectually stimulating classroom atmosphere with students who work independently and strive for perfection, she preferred teaching techniques that required students to draw on recall, memory, and comprehension using strategies such as drill, worksheets, and competitive games. Rita particularly liked students who were neat, organized, and respectful, and completed work on time.

Mastery of subject-matter content — what teachers know — was the barometer of educational excellence and teaching effectiveness in the reform movement of the 1980s. Teachers with dunce caps and students unable to compete with their foreign counterparts were the icons of the decade. The Bridenthal program and its eventual evolution into Central College's "Humanitas Curriculum" reflects the centrality of knowledge articulated by its education faculty. In comparing the interns' preparation as teachers with that of other Central education students, Don Wright stated: "I don't think the interns would be any different. They might have had an extra practicum or two. Again, the quality depends on what they know."

The Discipline Orientation: Teacher as Inquirer

As noted earlier, some educational researchers and teacher educators, particularly during the past decade, have focused on subject-matter pedagogy. Rejecting Wright's and other reform-minded persons' beliefs that teaching methods have little place in the university curriculum, leading educators such as Lee Shulman, Sharon Feiman-Nemser, and Jere Brophy have underscored the importance of subject-matter pedagogy. Liberal arts graduates knowledgeable in particular subjects are not equivalent to professional educators "teaching the 'structures of the disciplines,' fostering 'meaningful' understanding of content" (Feiman-Nemser, 1990, p. 221). From this vantage point, problems in classroom learning are less the result of the absence of subject-matter knowledge and more the consequence of teachers

> unable to manage classrooms when the academic tasks are more unpredictable, as conceptual and problem-solving tasks are; teachers don't perceive some or

all subjects as conceptual subjects; or teachers don't understand conceptual aspects of the subjects themselves, and therefore are able to teach only the more trivial aspects of these subjects. (Kennedy, 1990, p. 6)

Like Gene and Rita, Lucy is intellectual and knowledge-oriented: her preferred teaching techniques emphasize critical thinking and her content focus is on conceptual objectives rather than measurable results. Preferring students who are excited by ideas and who can work well independently, Lucy prefers to encourage collaborative work among students who, it is hoped, will be more interested in ideas and theories than in the minutiae of facts. Like Rita, Lucy places much more emphasis than Gene on the "sensing/thinking" aspect of teaching, with an emphasis on a classroom well defined by rules and procedures and a curriculum whose content is approached in an orderly manner.

The Progressive Orientation: Teacher as Child-Focused

The educational philosophies of Harold Taylor and John Dewey were as evident at Central College as its number of minority students and faculty. For both reasons, Roberto found himself outside of Central's institutional ethos.

Roberto, like the other interns, did not expect the Bridenthal program or the Central curriculum to enable students to respond positively to the ethnic diversity of pupils or to expand their tolerance for different people and ideas. Recalling nothing memorable as a Central student and confessing he knew few of the 2,500 mostly Anglo undergraduate students, Roberto remarked candidly: "I came here thinking that Central would be the best place for me to get my education. I came here for an education, and I really wasn't going to worry about prejudice and all that goes with it. But it's out there and it's hard to deal with sometimes. It just gets to you." Nevertheless, asked if he had to start over again whether he would choose Central, Roberto unhesitantly answered yes. While Roberto continued to rate Central's liberal arts curriculum low on developing an awareness of different cultures and ways of life, the value he places on a Central-type collegiate education differs from that of other Chicano educators:

How many of you people in the liberal arts know about "barrio economics?" When you teach Chicano people, you teach us the [greatest economic principles]: marginal utility; the law of diminishing returns, and so forth, but such principles taught as they are presently taught do not help my people to buy a chuck steak. They do not help my people to cope with situations where they buy pure grease when they are supposed to buy hamburger. . . . The college of liberal arts is teaching our people the wrong subjects in the wrong way. (Burruel, 1971, pp. 121–122)

Roberto viewed himself, and struggled for others to view him, first and foremost as an individual. This individualistic focus was partially shaped by conflicting messages Roberto had received from his family, peers, and schoolteachers. Given these experiences, it is not surprising that Roberto differed from the other four interns in the great emphasis he placed on students' feelings of self-worth and the comparatively lesser importance he placed on developing students' intellectual development:

> I believe in universal public education. People don't stress that concept much anymore. We have tracks: academic, vocational, general. The kids are going into your middle schools already thinking I've got to be this. They aren't even given a chance to experience what an honors class is like because they already have that label that says "vocational." I can't possibly do something like that.

While most interns stressed school-related and acquired components to teaching like mastery of school knowledge, acquisition of pedagogical and interpersonal skills, and ability to make sound instructional decisions, Roberto underscored personal-related and acquired components of teaching such as the importance of caring, the establishment of a teaching presence and a classroom ethos, and the ability to relate to students from personal experience.

Roberto's preferred classroom atmosphere was warm, friendly, and supportive. He especially liked students who were honest with their feelings and sensitive to others' rights and enjoyed working collaboratively with others. However, in the area of classroom management, Roberto was more technical and outcome-oriented. Here he emphasized the importance of establishing well-defined classroom rules and clear expectations for student behavior.

The Technical Orientation: Teacher as Worker

"Being prepared" was important for Jan, who found a lack of correspondence between the knowledge she acquired as a Central student and what she was expected to transmit as a public school teacher. As she later wrote: "In college we would spend the whole semester on the French Revolution; in the classroom it was one or two days. Then, there was a lot of stuff that I didn't know anything about. When I first started teaching world history (almost all of my credits are in U.S. History), I was teaching ancient Egypt and that was really hard for me."

Jan's primary teaching orientation was "outcome-oriented." While other interns like Rita and Roberto shared this orientation—particularly in areas of classroom management—Jan was the only intern to embrace this orientation in the majority of teaching preference areas. Jan preferred a teacher-driven classroom in contrast to Roberto's and Lucy's "warm and friendly" atmosphere and Gene's and Rita's intellectually oriented environment. Like Rita, Jan felt most comfortable when her lesson plans followed a prescribed curriculum or mirrored chapters in a text. Again, this was in variance with Gene, Roberto, and Lucy, who wanted to follow a broad outline that encompassed a variety of perspectives. Finally, Jan viewed teaching as "pragmatic" and "efficiency-oriented," which distinguishes her from all the others who viewed themselves as fundamentally "knowledge-oriented . . . encouraging independent thought."

Jan, one of the interns who had always planned to become a teacher, reflects the image of a conventional teacher education graduate that has been fostered by efficiency minded, scientifically oriented educators beginning with Franklin Bobbitt and W. W. Charters, extending to George Beauchamp, and culminating in Madeline Hunter and Frances Hunkins and criticized by an array of contemporary educators such as Elliot Eisner, Peter McLaren, and Maxine Greene.

CONTENT KNOWLEDGE—the currency of the academic marketplace—provided a focal point for the Bridenthal curriculum and an apex for some of the interns' images of a competent teacher, their conceptions of the quality of their education, and their views regarding the transmission of knowledge. Nowhere during their liberal arts studies were these interns encouraged to "engage in the prior examination of what is considered valuable knowledge both overtly and covertly in school settings, why this is considered valuable knowledge, and how this conception of valuable knowledge is linked to institutions in the larger society" (Apple, 1974, p. 13). Had such questions been posed, the interns might have realized that what knowledge is of most worth is a question of ideology, not epistemology.

Central's traditionally oriented liberal arts curriculum honed their intellectual abilities and shaped their understanding of the nature of knowledge. For some interns, like Gene and Rita, Central's perspective coincided with their deepest epistemological understandings. However, for others, such as Roberto and Lucy, the belief in the universalization of knowledge was more problematic. While they found an occasional oasis in a professor or a specialization, the institutional ethos was incompatible with their often unarticulated beliefs about teaching, learning, learners, and subject matter.

CHAPTER 6

Specialization and Teaching

Beginning in the latter half of their sophomore year and continuing through their senior year, the Bridenthal Interns disappear into Central College's "regular" programs for students seeking elementary, secondary, and special education certification. Gene is optimistic that "we are being prepared in a good program. You can look at Central's placement ratings and how well students do on standardized tests like the Pre-Professional Skills Test (PPST). Preparation is no problem. The fact that students are coming to Central means that they are going to get a good preparation program." As a graduating senior, Gene easily checks off several professional program outcomes: "I learned methodology—the different teaching techniques, I learned methods of discipline, I learned how to deal with parents, and I learned the history of the educational system."

As we will see, the Bridenthal program included all the components recommended for the preparation of professional teachers, and its effectiveness as far as student teaching goes is the focus of Chapter 7. Here we portray not only the specialization decisions made by the interns but how their accumulating professional knowledge and experiences affected the ways in which they understood their future roles as teacher and reformer.

BECOMING A PROFESSIONAL

Chapter 1 reminded us that every profession claims to have a codified, systematic body of knowledge. The uniqueness of these bodies of knowledge separates one profession from another, while the mere possession of such elite knowledge separates professionals from laypeople. To attain this knowledge, professionals must go through lengthy, specialized periods of training (Ornstein, 1981; Weil & Weil, 1971). Although the length and nature of this period of education and training are specific to each profession, the preparation must be extensive and rigorous enough to allow society to recognize professionals as experts and to "view the profession as possessing the kind of *mystery* that is not given to the ordinary" person (Goode, 1969, p. 278).

Debate continues about the existence of a codified body or bodies of knowledge for teaching professionals. Most will agree, however, that teaching is a complex, multidimensional act that requires various sorts of actions, behaviors, and decision-making abilities (see, for example, Barnes, 1989; Spring, 1985), and that teaching requires not only knowledge of content and pedagogy but knowledge of the intricate relationships between them (see, for example, Grossman, Wilson & Shulman, 1989; Macklin, 1981; Tamir, 1988). Representing reform-minded efforts to professionalize teaching in the 1980s and beyond, Gideonese (1989) talks about the kinds of knowledge that should inform the design, development, and delivery of programs that prepare teaching professionals, including (1) liberal arts or general knowledge, (2) intellectual foundations knowledge, (3) subject-matter knowledge, and (4) professional knowledge.

As noted in Chapter 5, most professional preparation, by virtue of the fact that it takes place within institutions of higher education, is built on a foundation in the liberal arts and sciences—typically encountered within students' first two years in college. The "intellectual foundations knowledge" of which Gideonese speaks can be found in most teacher preparation programs beginning at various points in a student's progress through college or university and taking the form of courses with titles such as Introduction to Teaching, Philosophy of Education, and History of Education.

Specific subject-matter knowledge represents the established disciplines (mathematics, science, English, social sciences, etc.). Within the structure of schools as we know them, secondary school teachers require a thorough understanding of the subject matter in at least a single discipline area and take a substantial number of courses in that discipline as part of their professional preparation. These discipline-based teachers should also learn pedagogical knowledge specific to their subject or discipline. This "subject matter pedagogical knowledge" (Carter, 1990) combines knowledge of subject matter with knowledge of learners and instruction to produce a "weaving together [of] ideas about how people learn and knowledge about particular pupils with a thorough understanding of the subject in ways that respect the integrity of each" (McDiarmid, Ball, & Anderson, 1989, p. 194).

Elementary school teachers, in contrast, are expected to have a much more general understanding of the knowledge contained in specific disciplines. Their subject-matter pedagogical knowledge, therefore, will focus less on discipline-specific knowledge and more on a way of teaching that includes the ability to see and make connections across the various disciplines. In both cases, the extent to which teachers are familiar with the content and inherent structures of the disciplines has much to do with their professional decision-making ability (Grossman et al., 1989)—an ability that enables teachers to understand "how a subject matter can be useful to students in discovering personal levels of meaning, and how students can translate this meaning into humane daily action" (Howsam et al., 1976, p. 85).

What Gideonese (1989) terms "professional knowledge" is often discussed within the educational literature as "general pedagogical knowledge" (see, for example, Carter, 1990; Shulman, 1987; Tamir, 1988). Unlike the subject-matter pedagogical knowledge discussed above, general pedagogical knowledge is comprised of the knowledge, techniques, skills, and behaviors useful in various contexts, regardless of the specific subject taught. Sockett (1989) offers examples of what he terms "a common-sense classification of teaching knowledge" that, in part, makes up the general pedagogical knowledge of teachers: management of pupil learning, individually and in groups; pedagogic skills, such as demonstrating a method or telling a story; and an understanding of the context in which the teacher works (p. 102).

Within general pedagogical knowledge we find a more complex way of knowing called "practical knowledge" (Elbaz, 1983; Feiman-Nemser & Floden, 1986; Lieberman & Miller, 1984). Practical knowledge is a form of personal knowledge that incorporates knowledge of the social structure of the classroom, the roles that various participants play within the classroom, and the impact that these aspects of schooling have on the learning process.

Finally, the component of professional knowledge common to most programs preparing professionals of any sort is "clinical knowledge." Most teacher preparation programs require students to spend numerous hours in actual school classrooms seeing and eventually performing the work of teachers. This program component allows future teachers the opportunity to learn, from seasoned professionals, how to put professional theory into practice (Wise, 1989).

Fitting Everything In

In his initial funding appeal developed for the Bridenthal Foundation, Don Wright not only stressed the need for bright young people in the teaching profession but underscored their need in typical shortage areas. As a result, Wright encouraged all of his recruits to consider mathematics, science, or special education as eventual certification areas. Lucy and Rita proved to be remarkable "finds" for the program in this regard: two young women who decided to become certified to teach *both* mathematics and science.

Lucy stays busy enough during her first year at Central, balancing a full course load of between 16 and 19 credits each semester and managing her complicated life as a mother. During her second semester she meets with her academic advisor and generates "a long list of required classes" needed to complete majors in mathematics and science. She spends her first summer as a college student taking 12 credits, and plans to spend the next two summers (and possibly a third) accumulating these requisite courses. Under the circumstances, Lucy leads a highly organized life, balancing schoolwork, time with her young son, and home life. Sunday is the day she sets aside to complete all of her homework for the coming week of classes at Central: "When I do my homework in advance, my attitude is much better because I chose to do it, I didn't have to do it. Plus, it's out of the way and I have more flexibility with my time during the week."

Lucy's decision to complete a double major follows her decision to become certified at the secondary level. Like her content-area decisions, this one is tied to her sense of personal and professional pride. Despite her initial interest in elementary teaching,

> I picked secondary because I wanted people in college to respect me. I love kids, and I love to work with kids, but elementary education majors in college just seem "Mickey Mouse." I have this urge for people to say, "Wow, you do that?" That's one of the reasons I picked science — because a lot of people can't do that. I'm not terrific at it but I'm better than some people.

Lucy believes that "a different type of person goes into elementary teaching . . . more all around, general. They're into everything and not just one specific thing." Lucy has no plans to be a generalist.

Yet by the end of her second year Lucy is forced to make several decisions she is not too happy about. That fall she learns that she will need to complete at least 24 education credits (including student teaching) to graduate. While this is not new information (all secondary students at Central take at least 21 credits; the interns accrue an additional 3 credits for their special seminars), many interns have not given it much thought. Lucy writes in fall semester of year two:

> For the first time, I am having negative feelings toward the Bridenthal program. Rumors are circulating (among the Interns) that Dr. Wright expects us to take 24 hours of Education classes. The three hours we have already taken do not count for anything. There is no way I can earn a math and a composite science certification in four years if I have to take 24 hours of Education. . . . Not only do we have to meet the requirements from our major, plus Central's general education,

plus state requirements for teacher certification, but we also have to take classes mandated by Central's Education Department. . . . There better be some kind of mistake.

But there is no mistake.

None of the interns discuss this "news" with Professor Wright in any of their seminar gatherings. Lucy's life becomes problematic now: Chuck, her son's father, hopes to increase the number of hours he is taking at college, which means that both Lucy and he will have fewer hours to spend caring for their son, Daniel. Yet Lucy knows that "I can't afford to send him to daycare every day."

By the time her second college summer arrives, Lucy has "decided not to take any more math classes, but just to get my composite science major." Caught once uninformed, she has learned that the state will certify her to teach mathematics with only 12 credits, whereas Central's mathematics major requires 24 credits. "I don't have enough time in my schedule for that," Lucy notes; "I plan on taking summer school already."

A science major, Lucy finds herself among one of Central's "little groups . . . the science teachers that know each other and the social studies teachers—that's a bigger group—and the English teachers know each other." Like most of her new cohorts in Central's secondary education track, Lucy takes one "education" course each semester, beginning with a foundations course called Schooling in America (sophomore spring term), then on to Secondary School Curriculum (junior fall term), and finally Secondary School Teaching (junior spring term). Each course contains a practicum requirement as well—clinical experiences that, when added to those of the three Bridenthal seminars, have the interns in public school classrooms every semester of their first three college years. Lucy's time spent in public school classrooms is no different in quality from the time spent by all of the interns: some good, some not so good. She even spends one semester visiting an inner-city classroom, writing in her journal that "the facilities are comparable to suburban schools I've been in—maybe a little nicer. The difference is the students (98 percent minority) and the attitudes."

As for her education courses, the first two are taught by Wright—a situation most "regular" secondary education students relish, though for the interns, "it's all material that we've had before." Lucy recalls, however, that in Schooling in America she met "some very important people," including several school superintendents and a school board member. For the most part, though, she describes her courses with Wright as focused on "theory" and requiring more "papers." Indeed, she looks forward to the Secondary School Teaching course since it "looks like it's going to be totally different because the teacher is not a professor—she's from the public schools. . . .

It's going to be more practical, hands-on things, not theoretical philosophy which is what we're ready for." Recalling the course a year later, Lucy characterized it as "more practical and helpful. We talked about discipline and behavior modification and different techniques of presenting materials." She believes that "that course should have been a year long. . . . I thought the course was okay, but some [students] didn't like it."

Lucy concludes her third year at Central anticipating needing no more education courses except student teaching—which she will do in the spring term of her senior year because the remaining content courses required for her science certification are offered only fall term. She will spend her last summer as a college student taking two courses needed for her teaching certificate.

With Whom and How

For many students of pedagogy, deciding what to teach has much to do with the question of whom to teach—younger children or older adolescents. As a second-semester junior, Gene mulls over differences between those who choose elementary and those who choose secondary (his choice) education. "It seems to me that the people who go into elementary education are more child-focused. The people who go into secondary education are more field-focused—they are more interested in what they want to teach." Secondary education allows him to work with junior high school students, too, but after numerous field placements, including student teaching, Gene is even more sure that "I would rather be a high school teacher than a junior high school teacher."

The Bridenthal Interns remained special among their preservice peers because they had been hand-picked from a small group of top-ranked high school seniors. Rita basks in this specialness and believes that, while these years at Central will give her a strong grounding in physics and mathematics, her membership in the program will provide her with professional respect and land her a good teaching job when she graduates.

Rita knows she is good in mathematics and science—she has had a knack for them as long as she can remember. By the time she reaches her junior year at Central she knows that as a teacher, she is "interested in the higher math and physics courses that require more cognitive development. I have a hard time," she admits, "bringing myself down to a lower level." Unlike her preservice peers, however, Rita does not matter-of-factly correlate a deep interest in subject matter with teaching at the secondary level, for she has a friend in the mathematics program who is interested in both teaching calculus and working with special education students. For Rita, the selection of elementary or secondary teaching preferences has more to do with how one feels around young children — and she feels "nervous." Her dilemma, when eventually choosing secondary education, lies in her ongoing concerns about her diminutive size and ways in which her stature may inhibit her ability to develop and maintain classroom control. She goes as far as asking to be placed with a teacher of similar size for her fourth semester practicum (so that she can see how a woman as tiny as she handles classroom management). Even into her final year at Central, Rita harbors this fear.

As a junior Rita acts on a felt need related to what we earlier identified as subject-matter pedagogical knowledge. Although all secondary education students take a general pedagogy course (Secondary School Teaching), Rita and Lucy (who thinks she might still obtain two teaching certificates) feel the need for a course directed specifically toward the teaching of mathematics. Together, they approach the chairperson of Central's mathematics department and begin a series of discussions about the possibility of instituting such a "math methods" course. Eventually, Rita becomes one of the first Central students to take the newly developed course for teachers of high school mathematics. To her dismay, she takes it along with student teaching; to her delight, she feels it helps to ready her for the job ahead.

Through it all, however, Rita remains solid in her belief that the Bridenthal program is the key to her eventual teaching success. She believes as a junior that the intern group has more general knowledge about education because of their special seminars, and that interns feel more self-confident going into their practicum placements because they have had so many by their junior year. In short, the interns benefit from "a wonderful introduction that others did not have."

The Benefits of Special Education

Several interns select a teaching area that allows them to work with all age levels (e.g., music or special education), and a few even prefer middle-level or junior high school students. Roberto formed early plans to teach elementary students, later deciding to get certified to teach special education students at all levels as well. Still clinging to his pre-college dream of child psychology, he hoped to complete an academic major in psychology on top of everything else. By the end of his sophomore year, Roberto identified himself primarily as a teacher of special students.

Throughout his years at Central, Roberto pays a high price for wanting to accomplish so much. He carries no fewer than 16 credits each term and attends school (while working) for three summers. In the second year, when the interns begin to complain about the amount of work they have in their single-credit seminars, Roberto encourages them to see beyond this surface level to

all the things that we're learning that most people going through the
regular education program are not learning or getting the chance to experience. . . . To me, this amount of work was something that was expected. You just don't go around with the label of being a Bridenthal
Intern and then sit in class and do nothing, experience nothing.

Much of what makes Roberto able to cope with his own labor-
intensive dreams is his tendency to want to understand himself and his
world. Roberto works hard at trying to make sense of each experience, each
class, and each relationship, often doing so in conversation with others. For
example, following one of his classroom visits as a sophomore, Roberto
goes to see Don Wright, confessing a desire to tell the classroom teacher
some of what Roberto thought she was doing wrong. He recognizes a
tension in having begun to feel that he has better ideas, yet no right or
authority to share them.

Roberto realizes during the latter part of his sophomore year that he
has come to prefer discussions focused on practicum experiences rather
than those (such as the early seminars) focused on books, because he is most
interested in trying to make sense of what he sees happening in classrooms.
Unfortunately, such discussions have become rare and Roberto finds himself looking for students and faculty with whom to explore some of his
ideas and "looking for Dr. Wright a lot more, just to talk to him on that
basis." His reflective nature and willingness to work through problems and
ideas with others allows Roberto to establish rapport with many other
faculty at Central whom "we knew we could go to and talk with about
what's going on."

Of the more than 20 students working toward special education certification at Central, Roberto is the sole male in the group. By the time they
complete their junior year, members of the group have become quite close,
working and studying together through their program coursework. Roberto
feels unique as a special educator "in the sense that you know you're going
to get into something that's really going to be difficult for you, not only in
terms of more hours, with all the work, but the responsibility of knowing
how these kids are and the challenges you're going to have."

One of the strongest beliefs Roberto develops during his special education program is that teachers preparing as special educators are "gaining so
much more" than their regular education peers, in that "you're given better
ways to remediate, better ways to handle the school environment, classroom management, lesson plans." Though Roberto is committed to working in a special education classroom, several of his friends among this
group—including a few Bridenthal interns—plan to first teach in regular
classrooms. Roberto agrees with them that their preparation as special

educators provides them with "the best of both worlds" and will actually make them better teachers in a regular classroom environment.

While student teaching, Roberto suggests that his efforts to make concepts concrete come from his special education preparation: "I'm not like the regular ed teacher who doesn't understand what a learning disability is or why a child can't read." He holds firm to the belief that it is specifically his special education program that gives him the biggest boost toward his teaching goals: "I learned a lot. I learned how to be a teacher, I guess, and how I wanted to be as a teacher, and what I was going to try to do with my kids, and how much was going to be realistic, and how much was going to be idealism."

CANONICAL CONCERNS: TECHNICAL, RATIONAL, INSTRUMENTAL KNOWLEDGE

A Nation Prepared: Teachers for the 21st Century (Carnegie Task Force, 1986) says little about "professional knowledge," recommending, instead, that the National Board for Professional Teaching Standards judge "the quality of candidates' general education, their mastery of the subjects they will teach, their knowledge of good teaching practices in general and their mastery of techniques required to teach specific subjects" (p. 66). Programs designed to prepare teaching candidates for these assessments would all exist at the graduate level within colleges and universities, according to Carnegie recommendations, so that "candidates [could] take maximum advantage of the research on teaching and the accumulated knowledge of exceptional teachers. [These programs] would develop their instructional and management skills, cultivate their habit of reflecting on their own practice of teaching, and lay a strong base for continuing professional development" (p. 76).

Like its Carnegie contemporary, the Holmes Group (1986) situates teacher preparation at the graduate level of study, arguing that to do so eliminates the pressures felt by undergraduate programs, which must constantly struggle with issues of program duration and content. Because of its membership, however, the Holmes Group believes that these graduate-level preparation programs should look and operate differently and that the universities in which they are housed (as opposed to a national board) should exert primary responsibility for determining their efficacy. The issue of teachers' knowledge is paramount to the Holmes Group's efforts, as represented in their number one goal: "*To make the education of teachers intellectually more solid.* Teachers must have a greater command of academic subjects, and of the skills to teach them. Teachers also need to become more thoughtful students of teaching, and its improvement" (p. 4).

Members of the Holmes Group argue for a set of interrelated and coherent courses that would reflect at least five components of a teacher's professional studies:

> The . . . study of teaching and schooling as an academic field with its own integrity . . . knowledge of the pedagogy of subject matter . . . the skills and understandings implicit in classroom teaching . . . [and] the dispositions, values, and ethical responsibilities that distinguish teaching from the other professions. Finally, all these aspects of professional studies must be integrated into the clinical experiences where formal knowledge must be used as a guide to practical action. (p. 51)

As Gardner notes, "teacher education has for too long been a normative enterprise," its knowledge perceived as "pedestrian" in character. The new knowledge base for teaching has been "generated in research . . . and in the tested practices of leading professionals, moral propositions, legal precedents, and more. A new and higher norm is now possible . . . one which reflects the best that research and experience can offer" (1989, p. ix). Unfortunately, like the classic liberal arts canon with its Platonic emphasis "on mind not hand, thought not action, production not reproduction, and reason not emotion" (Zeichner & Liston, 1990, p. 5), this new pedagogical canon for teaching contains problems of its own.

Reformers' fixation with what Schön (1989) describes as a "crisis of confidence in professional knowledge" results from the positivistic epistemology "that dominates most thinking and writing about the professions, and is built into the very structure of professional schools and research institutions." This particular way of understanding knowledge, he argues, treats "rigorous professional practice as an application of research-based knowledge to the solution of problems of instrumental choice" (p. 190). We see this evidenced not only in specific reform recommendations that address content and coursework, but in the way reformers literally structure their programs: "first, the relevant basic science, then the relevant applied science, and finally, a practicum in which students learn to apply classroom knowledge to the problems of practice" (p. 192).

Rationalizing Teaching

Contemporary reformers believe that teaching can become more professionalized because pedagogical knowledge has finally become specialized (i.e., no longer dependent on the disciplines), authoritative (i.e., scientifically generated), and inaccessible to the layperson (i.e., counterintuitive). Most reform agendas argue for more pedagogical knowledge because of this—hard, positivistic, or scientific knowledge born of careful research and disciplined inquiry. Our efforts to professionalize teaching become, as a result, efforts to rationalize teaching—what Popkewitz (1991) calls the rationalization of classroom instruction. This more rational approach to instruction requires a "common, technical language" that, while allowing educators to relate to teaching as a science, "homogenizes social distinctions and conflict by casting them as procedural categories" (p. 194). While providing a feeling of "commonality, community, and objectivity," this language of objectives and performance criteria also creates

> a poverty of expression about teachers' knowledge. As one examines the common language, its unidimensionality becomes apparent. Priorities [transform] teachers' work into actions that can be defined in explicit, hierarchical, linear, and sequential ways. The importance of aesthetics, the playfulness of experience, and the use of intuition [are] lost. The "common" language of the reforms [refocuses] teachers' understanding on a narrow range of communicative competencies. (p. 208)

Gene seems to have fallen prey to the rationalization of classroom instruction. For him, learning to teach becomes equivalent to learning how to prepare appropriate materials for lectures. He recalls a typical example of a practicum experience during his junior year:

> I taught every time I went in. I observed the first two times and didn't say a word. But the teacher didn't even want me to grade papers, just teach. I remember doing very extensive research for some of my lessons. For instance, we discussed World War II and the interaction between the United States and Great Britain, and I talked about the devastation in London as the result of the bombing of London. I used actual newspapers from the time and took out quotes and gave them handouts on that, asked them questions, and asked them to develop hypotheses about how they felt it would affect U.S. and British relations.

Everything important about teaching for Gene revolves around content. Recalling his visit to an inner-city high school, he claims that:

> I was depressed at Far South because the teacher did things like give the students a six weeks test of 50 capital cities, and these students were 10th graders! I decided that I would use only the actual historical documents and . . . things other than the textbooks, which is all this teacher used. I would also use very practical experiences with the stu-

dents. . . . I would definitely not interview at Far South. . . . I just can't see myself teaching there. It would be very admirable and very virtuous of me to want to go there and contribute my teaching skills to those who are less advantaged, but maybe I'm an elitist—I just cannot do that. I cannot teach students who have absolutely no respect for learning.

While at Central, Gene continuously makes statements about the value of early and frequent field experiences. Interestingly, he is among the few interns who seem to have routine opportunities to develop practitioner skills in the classroom. Concurrently, he never loses sight of his belief that "we would rather try to improve the teaching profession by bringing qualified, talented, and enthusiastic individuals into it, and after we have brought them into it, we should prepare them well and work on the conditions of teaching to keep them in the profession." But Gene ponders how to change the conditions of teaching.

Gene learns during the summer prior to student teaching that he has been placed at the high school he listed as his first choice. He recalls spending "a lot of time writing out lecture notes. I didn't spend a lot of time planning activities because I find that they're better if they're spur of the moment." He also learns that his mentor, Dr. Wright, is off on a trip to the Far East and will not be there during Gene's student teaching.

A lot of us are going to be doing our student teaching then. And we won't—I don't feel as comfortable with the other professors as I do with Dr. Wright. And I won't feel as comfortable when I have my student teaching experience, and say something wrong, and come back and tell someone else about it. I would feel a lot more comfortable getting moral support from Dr. Wright.

In order to maintain his Bridenthal scholarship, Gene carries two additional courses while student teaching. "I don't think I was able to be as creative as I wanted to be during my student teaching," he later sees, "because so much time was spent trying to do well in my other two courses. I got A's in them, but there were some things that, had I had more time during student teaching, I could've been more innovative and creative in."

Nor, it turns out, is he as prepared as he should be: "I knew my weakness in world history, and I knew my weakness in economics. I know, now, that I have an additional weakness—evidently of dealing with discipline." Gene presumes that he can employ discipline as necessary, never imagining that both teachers and administrators have a say in the matter.

The basic view in the administration is that they don't want to cause waves. . . . Ms. Rouse said that if she hadn't written up anybody in two years, she didn't see any reason why I'd have to, despite the fact that I had a student threaten me. . . . I've done everything in the book for classroom management. . . . And Mr. Ribald told me today that in his entire eight years of teaching he's never written up anybody . . . I watch him, and he's very ineffective . . . as far as classroom management goes. . . . I didn't anticipate the total lack of respect by the students, so I didn't anticipate that trauma . . . or the additional trauma of not having any support from the administration.

The influence of and complex relationships between school policy and teachers staggers Gene, who acknowledges during student teaching that he hasn't taken into account

that the school district had a strict policy on the minimum number of grades that each student can have. Aside from that, the teachers' policy is a higher minimum than that . . . you have to have a certain number of grades for each student or the parent calls and says, "Why did my child flunk? You only gave him ten grades." So I'm spending five or six hours a night grading. . . . The off-periods you spend filling out progress reports, because every time a student slips under the F-level, you have to fill out a progress report. Progress reports have to go out every three weeks. Of course, three weeks later you have a report card. Then in three weeks, another progress report. . . . I don't know if anybody else is in that situation. I don't know whether that's state policy or a district policy, but if they're in that situation I would be willing to bet that, like me, they're not feeling very professional.

Teachers' Knowledge

One problem with "intellectualizing" teaching within a technical/rational model is raised by Giroux (1988), who suggests that the reform emphases on instrumental and pragmatic factors and functions of teaching threaten teachers' ability to become what he calls transformative intellectuals. These are teachers who can recognize and resist "the tendency to reduce teachers to the status of specialized technicians within the school bureaucracy, whose function then becomes one of managing and implementing curricular programs rather than developing or critically appropriating curricula to fit specific pedagogical concerns" (p. 122).

The relationship between a common technical language for teaching and its resulting poverty of expression and intellectual dulling is also apparent to Berlak and Berlak (1981), who, among others, make apparent an inherent knowledge that many teachers have lived with for years—that teaching is an act of struggling with dilemmas and inherent tensions that McDonald (1992) describes as pertaining to rational versus intuitive action, technical versus moral problems, and "pedagogical knowledge that is contextual rather than instrumental. This is knowledge about the limits of technique, about the place of uncertainty in practice, about all the webs— moral and otherwise—that catch teachers and their students" (pp. 49–50). Yet there was nothing obviously transformative or problematic about the knowledge learned by the Bridenthal Interns. Jan and Lucy provide clear examples of the technical, rational, and instrumental professional knowledge that guided their professional thinking.

We see Jan's ideas about teachers' knowledge through some of the work she did in her Secondary School Curriculum course during fall term of her junior year. Jan understands curriculum development as hierarchical in nature, with power, authority, and responsibility for curriculum decisions flowing from top to bottom. Teachers, near the bottom of this curricular edifice, have little influence: "After a teacher is handed his/her copy of the curriculum and materials," writes Jan, "there is not much left for the teacher besides regurgitating the material."

In a second paper Jan constructs an ideal high school curriculum, which consists of three tracks (general, academic, and vocational), plus a provision for an honors component within the academic track. She gives considerable attention to the scope and sequence—which courses would appear where within each track. Building on this ideal, Jan uses a third paper to work through her ideas about current high school social science curriculum and instruction. In it she addresses censorship; what should be taught (here, Jan develops social science coursework for each of the three tracks of her ideal high school curriculum); recognition of the need for "relevancy of courses"; a discussion of inquiry versus expository teaching (here, Jan calls the inquiry approach, popular in the 1960s, "brainwashing" by teachers "ill-prepared and incapable of discussing the issues with students"); and the need for "high-ability" teachers. After suggesting changes to current social science teaching, Jan paradoxically concludes this paper by noting that "of course, there is always the possibility that the system . . . will not change and that our students will have to forever suffer through long, boring, fact-filled lectures that only develop and overuse their listening skills and never let the students state how they feel or what they think. Let's pray for a better way!"

Jan's final paper depicts a unit plan designed to accompany a textbook chapter. She notes the relationship between all of the choices of content for her supplemental unit and several sources (e.g., state curriculum guidelines) listing content requirements. Her teaching methods focus on lecture, reading, and handouts. The course instructor, Professor Wright, assigns the paper a grade of A and adds, "An excellent unit, particularly its content."

In the same course, Lucy writes about curriculum influences, noting examples of national, state, and local influences and recognizing that "because administrators are in a leadership position, they, too, influence curriculum." The paper concludes with the argument that teachers are the most important mix in this situation because they have the "ultimate power" when it comes to applying this much-influenced curriculum in their classrooms.

Applying curriculum knowledge is something Lucy looks forward to, having reached the point during her third year when visiting schools and watching others teach has become, in her words, "*boring*. I'm sure things will be different when I am in charge of my own classroom (not because I'll be a more exciting teacher, but because I'll be in charge)."

Lucy enjoys taking science courses and seeing how they all relate to one another, and how basic ideas from science can be recognized everywhere. Nonetheless, she admits in her junior year to finding little enthusiasm for this choice of majors: "I have these hours in science," she explains, "and science is really needed, so I might as well. . . . Plus, I'm plowing my path. I can't turn around and get in another furrow because the first one would be all wasted." Gnawing at her is the worry "that I won't know the subject matter because I've taken such a sprinkling" of various science courses. Based on conversations she has with friends who do their student teaching before her, as well as her six semesters of being in classrooms, Lucy predicts minimal transfer of value between her coursework at Central and success in student teaching.

Lucy is good at "making things simple. That's my strong point." While student teaching she plans lessons that correspond closely to the school's science curriculum guidelines and tries to give only the kinds of tests she likes to grade. According to her, she's also good at keeping big ideas and goals separate from the "little details." She'd rather teach biology because she feels better prepared in that area than, for example, in physics. She'd also like to teach "an easy class, like physical science," because of the freedom it would give her to experiment and discover.

Concluding her teacher preparation, Lucy has developed the belief that teaching success depends more on one's personality than on "the program you've been through." Her advantage as a Bridenthal Intern has come to rest on her sense that the interns have a more positive self-image as future teachers, which "might allow us to be more creative or innovative, or take more risks."

Knowledge Transfer

Lucy's prediction about minimum transfer value is a good bet. Paramount to the creation of programs for professional preparation is the assumption that what students "learn" will stay with them or transfer to their work in classrooms with young people. However,

> There is much evidence that the knowledge, skills, and dispositions introduced to students in these [professional] courses have little influence on their subsequent actions, even during initial training. . . . Many researchers have concluded that teacher education has a weak impact on at least some of the values, beliefs, and attitudes that students bring with them into their teacher education programs. (Zeichner & Gore, 1990, pp. 336–337)

And when students of teaching do take specific ideas or skills with them into classrooms they are often the ones that "work" in purely utilitarian ways.

Jan hopes to transfer three important lessons learned during student teaching. First, she learns that high school teachers must "move fast" in order to cover all of the content in the curriculum. In both of her student teaching placements, Jan finds teachers who "lecture a lot" in order to get through the content (typically two chapters of the textbook each week).

In addition to learning about the demands of covering content, Jan finds that perhaps she's been right all along—that she is not as bright as the rest of the interns, because she sometimes feels "shaky" with the content: "The history we did in college was so different. It's like we spent a whole semester on the French Revolution rather than having two days to spend on it in the middle school setting. In these situations you have to look back on the teachers you've had, not your professors."

At the same time, Jan uncovers her greatest strength: an ability to "warm up" to and get along well with students. Student teaching convinces her that high school students understand her better than middle-school students do. She enters teaching with the belief that a good teacher cares about her students and has the ability "to get information across" to them. She is most proud of three students who pass in her class after failing with other teachers: "That was kind of a neat feeling, knowing that I'd helped them understand maybe better than they could have otherwise." The only students she fails during student teaching are a couple who Jan believes lack interest.

Reflecting on her entire teacher preparation program Jan feels she's been "fairly well" prepared, learning how "to get in front of a classroom" and deal with discipline problems. She's benefited the most from time she spent with teachers in classrooms, though she wonders whether she couldn't have learned more from those opportunities. Jan feels no better prepared as a Bridenthal Intern than those who did not go through the program, and believes that the primary difference between her and practicing teachers is "experience." Her commitment to teaching is strong her senior year, though "it's not bursting out of its shirt or anything."

Little that students learn in teacher education programs seems to transfer well to their own classrooms, and when it does, the meaning is immediate and utilitarian. We can understand this happening in large part because preservice students, including Jan, bring with them strong and deeply embedded role identities of teachers. Unless programs work to make these role identities problematic, any learning preservice students do will relate to preexisting ideas about the roles of a teacher (Zeichner & Gore, 1990).

The structure of teacher preparation programs further segments preservice teachers' knowledge into various categories (psychological, foundational, pedagogical, and clinical), working against the likelihood that these classroom rookies will ever imagine how and why these categories are interrelated. Without exploring these various understandings even the most conscientious teacher educators remain at a disadvantage (Zeichner & Gore, 1990).

Simply put, a professional preparation program must recognize the complicating factor of the presence of the student candidates it aims to serve. Expecting everyone to accumulate some professional body of knowledge without recognizing the human nuances at work in complicating that expectation is naive at best; expecting this to occur within the complex structures of teacher preparation programs asks too much of the canon while simultaneously uncovering its weaknesses.

ALTERNATIVE EPISTEMOLOGIES

None of these critiques is meant to suggest that teaching ought not to seek enhanced professional status or develop stronger knowledge bases of practice. Concern lies not only with epistemological decisions about valued knowledge but with questions about who should undertake such efforts toward which ends and at what costs to whom. And alternative visions abound.

Schön (1989), for example, has suggested his now famous concept of "reflective teaching." Alan Tom (1987) understands teaching to be a fundamentally moral craft. Teaching is moral because of the inherently unequal power distribution in the relationship between teacher and students, and because it is carried out with the presupposition that something worthwhile is taught through the curriculum. And teaching is a craft, ac-

cording to Tom, because it contains ends that are pursued with strategies
that sometimes work and sometimes don't, thus requiring teachers to analyze complex situations, decide to pursue a particular strategy for each, and
monitor the results of these provisional attempts. Like Schön, Tom rejects
a technical/rational model for preparing teachers in favor of a more constructivist one that highlights the interpretive value of experiential knowing,
adding to his acceptance of this uncertain craft the call to infuse a deeper
appreciation for the morality of teaching.

Cornbleth (1989) also sees current efforts to reform the knowledge
base(s) of teaching (found in the Holmes and Carnegie reports, in particular) as problematic in their technocratic conceptions of knowledge and its
instrumental value—an epistemological perspective that assumes that experts can discover knowledge and make it available to teachers, and that
these facts and guidelines "eventually add up to productive teaching and
learning" (p. 21). She joins both Schön and Tom in pointing out the power
and value of an interpretive use of knowledge. Yet Cornbleth goes further,
noting (like Popkewitz, Giroux, and many others) that the technocratic
rationality promoted by popular reform agendas "fosters expert control and
demeans teachers. . . . Reform requires coherent conceptions of knowledge
and its use in teaching and teacher education that are consistent with the
reflective practitioner ideal and sensitive to the conditions of teaching" (p.
21). Combining these concerns, Cornbleth argues for a constructivist conception of teaching knowledge that would be informed by critical rationality—that is, knowledge constructed rather than given or revealed, tentative
rather than fixed, personal as well as public or formalized, and integrated
rather than fragmented.

Epitomizing a self-developed constructivist perspective, Roberto leaves
his two student teaching experiences working through his own feelings and
ideas about the differences between teaching in regular and special education environments. As in encounters with everyone, it seems, Roberto
learns much from his two cooperating teachers, who readily share their
experiences and ideas and help him to build files of information and materials for future use. No less important, according to Roberto, is that both
give him lots of positive reinforcement and allow him to make mistakes. He
is entirely comfortable in his fourth-grade special education placement but
"iffy" with the regular classroom of fifth-graders: "I didn't know if I wanted
to do regular education," he recalls wondering at the time.

Roberto's uncertainty in the fifth-grade classroom grows from his assignment to teach reading to the children Roberto describes as

> low readers. . . . Mine were the kids that were low, but it was a mat-
> ter of being low-low, to medium-low, to high-low. I got stuck with

them. I don't know that I did all that I could for them because I really don't know how to attack that kind of a problem. There were many times when the lesson just fell apart because they don't have the skills.

Student teaching convinces Roberto to seek work with emotionally disturbed (ED) students in a school that has strong parental support. As a special educator, his ideal teaching environment is a residential hospital (like the one he worked in the summer prior to his senior year) where the teachers work with the staff: "It's a perfect opportunity to teach kids and plan good lessons. If students don't perform in the classroom, there are consequences in the classroom and in their residence."

He also leaves student teaching confident in his belief that every child can learn, his ability to communicate with children and make them feel safe, his ability to motivate, and his ability to teach every child something. He recognizes, too, the likelihood that he will "probably overdo it and try to be the person that's going to change students around and fix their lives."

But as much as anything else in his last year as a preservice student, Roberto senses that perhaps members of the Bridenthal group have placed too much emphasis on the correlation between student teaching and future success in the classroom. He watches as interns he characterizes as good teachers grow despondent during student teaching, yet his characterization of them as "good teachers" rests almost exclusively on their academic success: "You see them in classes and you know they have the knowledge." He has arrived at the belief that many variables must be in place to make student teaching (and any teaching, for that matter) successful, including what Roberto calls the "fit" between student teacher and the district, the school, the cooperating teacher, and the college supervisor. "You have good and bad days," Roberto recalls. "For some, it was 12 weeks of bad days. That's unfortunate, and it's not necessarily their fault."

As a graduating senior, Roberto recognizes that, despite the efforts of the Bridenthal Internship in Teaching program and Central's department of education, the public schools, which provide clinical sites, exert significant influence on readying new teachers. This fact proves to be the great leveler for the interns—that which makes them no different from their nonintern peers. Though perhaps the interns "were maybe taken care of" in their first few semesters, subsequent placements seem to be hit-and-miss. He also recognizes that placing students has to do with "an interest in a particular area or grade level, things like that, but pretty much it's where teachers are willing to take you, and we don't have any control over who we work with."

Much of the success of Roberto's four years of teacher preparation, even as a Central student and Bridenthal Intern, comes down, in his view, to "chance." He sees no relationship between successful student teaching and prior study or experiences, nor ties to the values, attitudes, or awareness of the players involved. "I was lucky," he says. "I've been lucky most of the time in my placements. . . . There are others who haven't. . . . I've just been lucky."

REFORMING THE PRACTICE OF REFORM

Beyer (1987), too, critiques our current "focus on technical rationality, linear thinking, and psychometric analysis" (p. 19). In its place he offers that "since educational discourse and a great many teaching practices are political, moral, and ideological, the knowledge most appropriate for teacher education must be based in such social and moral traditions" (p. 19). "The aim of teacher education, accordingly, ought not to be achievement of prespecified outcomes that are rationalized, sequenced, and individualized, but the encouragement of practical reason that can help reconstruct a world dominated by inequality and alienation" (p. 29).

Beyer's (1987) most important point, however, is that which concerns the *act* of reform. Beyond rethinking the epistemological bases of appropriate teaching knowledge, we "must resist the temptation to prescribe in detail the routes toward improved teaching and programs designed to foster this. . . . To change these knowledge forms without also shifting our strategies for reform of education is to be caught in the very dualisms . . . generated out of the very hierarchical and patriarchal system of domination we seek to replace" (pp. 19–20). We cannot, he argues, work for more democratic, contextual forms of change in teacher education without first committing ourselves to promoting those values and practices within our own reform contexts. Genuine reform "can only happen in specific locations and in collaboration with those people—teachers, parents, students, administrators, etc.—involved in the day-to-day operation of schools and programs of teacher preparation"; it "is not possible within the more typical context for reform that is hierarchical, divisive, and impositional" (p. 30).

The practice of becoming a teacher at Central College, despite the early programmatic influences of the Bridenthal program, showed scant evidence of teacher education reform as Beyer understands it. Indeed, by the time she's ready to leave Central, Rita has begun to doubt the program in general, and teacher education reform in particular:

Student teaching is when it hit me; I was thinking, the other Central students are just the same as I am. . . . I don't know how truly differ-

ent . . . how really different the Bridenthal Intern program was as opposed to being in the regular program. Because, the people I know in
the regular program didn't do any worse or any better than I did in student teaching. . . . I had the same problems they did, which were all
uncontrollable by the Bridenthal program.

Rita's problems, it turns out, have to do with discipline and motivation. The students she has the greatest trouble working with are those in
the lower mathematics track. Reflecting on her preparation, Rita offers
that:

fewer classes on theory would be okay. We need more observations in
the classroom, especially at the lower track levels. . . . Experience
with the lower classes is best because usually that's what the beginning
teacher will get. It would be better if schools could allow the beginning teachers to teach the (upper) level students because they don't
have to worry too much about the discipline problems and just concentrate on the materials. But the veteran teachers do an awful lot of complaining, thinking that the lower level classes should be for the rookie,
they shouldn't have to be punished by teaching basic classes.

With hindsight, she now criticizes her general pedagogy course, Secondary
School Teaching:

The teacher . . . came from an elementary school background, and so
all the examples she used related to elementary school, like discipline
and management. Also, they were more directed toward English and
history and those types of courses. It's hard to compare what goes on
in that type of classroom and what goes on in a science lab classroom
and a math classroom. . . . We learned about classroom management
and teaching strategies . . . they've changed it now to more of a secondary focus . . . but I found that useless.

Rita concludes her stay at Central doubting her specialness as a Bridenthal Intern and wondering whether educational reform can ever truly occur.
In late spring of her senior year she acknowledges that while the interns
initially felt they were going to make important changes in education, they
now realize how hard it will be to change much of anything: "I don't think
change will ever happen, because we don't have enough grass roots support.
Mediocrity, or below mediocrity, it seems, is the aim; get these kids to pass

and get them out." Through four special years, the "problem" has never changed in Rita's eyes: "We don't have enough good . . . quality math teachers available at the elementary level. That's why it's creating so many problems at the secondary level. We are having to re-teach all the stuff at the secondary level." With her nationwide reform beliefs now set aside, she expresses hope that she'll at least make a difference within her own classroom.

THE NEED TO DECLARE a teaching specialization pushed the interns to consider their continuing clinical experiences in light of this and related decisions (e.g., to teach elementary or secondary students) as they shaped and reshaped their teaching identities. Eventually, all but Roberto see themselves as best suited for teaching specific subject matters to high school students, though these decisions help little to soften the thrilling trepidation of these graduating seniors and job-seeking novice teachers. Meanwhile, the mantle of reform has begun to slip almost unnoticed from their shoulders.

CHAPTER 7

Ready or Not: Testing the Mettle and the Model

One test of the Bridenthal program came during the interns' student teaching. As they stood on the verge of transition into the profession, the interns found in the context of student teaching a time to rethink old decisions and to ponder new ones. In this chapter we focus on student teaching and look primarily at how cooperating teachers, college supervisors, and an independent evaluator viewed the interns as would-be teachers. These observations are cast within our ongoing discussion about career decision making.

The career-development process is characterized by an ongoing decision-making cycle; in Super's (1990) words, "a series of mini-decisions of varying degrees of importance" (p. 220) wherein previous decisions inform future decisions and guide individuals through the various career-development tasks. As we pointed out in Chapter 3, career decisions are further influenced by a number of determinants internal and external to the individual and are both present or historical in nature. Thus, while professional courses and clinical experiences develop and inform a developing teachers' knowledge base, interactions between experiences of the past and present form the basis for decisions that shape future career directions.

PAST DECISIONS

Becoming a teacher involves a series of decisions, all of which undergo a "reality test" during student teaching, when individuals confirm or contradict all or some earlier career decisions. Like other teacher education students, the Bridenthal Interns made many major career decisions prior to student teaching, though unlike most others, they made their initial commitment to teach prior to entering college.

Preservice students make different sorts of career-shaping decisions, including those regarding age/grade level (e.g., early childhood or secondary), secondary-level content area (e.g., English or mathematics), and general or special education. Entering Central, nine interns could clearly articulate their decisions in each of these areas, while the remaining eight indicated some age/grade level preferences but held no firm ideas about content areas or special education. By the end of their sophomore year, eight interns maintained their interest in secondary education and two others joined them. Special education won six interns (five at the elementary and one at the secondary level), and one intern, who entered the program with her sights set on working with young children, chose certification in early childhood/kindergarten. These decisions formed the foundation for their specialization phase.

Through a variety of experiences not limited to the formal teacher education process, students add to their knowledge base about teachers and teaching, prompting some to rethink their earlier career decisions. Many students reconsider their initial decision to teach during the student teaching experience, sometimes abandoning teaching for another career alternative (Chapman, 1983). In 1985, for example, only about 60 percent of teacher education graduates entered the teaching work force immediately (Darling-Hammond, 1990). Cohen, Klink, and Grana (1990) found a similar proportion not entering the teaching work force after graduation: Offering various reasons for not teaching, the majority of graduates "learned as a result of student teaching that the field was not for them" (p.12). The interns, of course, did not have the luxury of acting on such decisions without incurring considerable financial debt. Nolan was the single exception.

As an intern, Nolan was unique in that he joined the Bridenthal group by special arrangement without accepting the program's scholarship support. During their junior year Nolan announced to the group that he was leaving the program to pursue a law degree (a career he had always favored). While most interns knew about Nolan's arrangement, some were surprised by his decision. Others defensively argued that Nolan's commitment to teaching was never strong to begin with.

Lucy had always doubted Nolan's priorities:

He used to talk about teaching and it wasn't the same kind of teaching that the rest of us talked about. He talked about giving the kids busy work and using the book a lot. Those weren't the things the rest of us wanted to do. [It seemed] kind of like he was going to teach partly because it was easy. . . . Then, all of a sudden he becomes a workaholic and works all the time at a law firm and starts getting real good grades and wants to become a lawyer. . . . That surprised me.

Rita, feeling herself tied to the program, knew of Nolan's ultimate career plans and suspects that he "didn't take the money because he didn't want to be trapped." Gene simply insists that Nolan differed from the other interns all along and that his departure should not be viewed as a blow to the program. Wondering aloud about retention, he offers: "We've lost one and he never, of course, received any money. The question comes down to how many people stayed in as a result of coercion and the possibility of paying all that money back and how many people stayed in because they really want to do it."

Nolan's departure served as a visibly personal reminder of each intern's financial obligations. Jan suspected at the time that some of the interns would probably take a different path if they did not have the loan to pay back. As they rounded the corner into their senior year, all but Gene indicated that the scholarship influenced their decision to remain an intern— sentiment that would not change throughout the coming year.

STUDENT TEACHING: SAVING "REALITY" FOR LAST

Student teaching is the most universally implemented curriculum component in teacher preparation programs (Guyton & McIntyre, 1990). Typically a final step in the teacher education process, it is referred to as the "capstone" experience for students and viewed as the first opportunity to try out one's decision to teach—to get a feeling for the role and work environment of teaching. "Theoretical knowledge must be translated into practice. Ideal images are confronted with demands of reality" (Hoy & Woolfolk, 1990, p. 280).

Zeichner (1987) concluded, after a review of the research, that while the basic *structure* of student teaching is the same everywhere, no agreed upon set of goals exists nor is there consensus on how these school experiences should be conceptualized, organized, and actually implemented. Furthermore, research has failed to provide the kind of information necessary to establish its effectiveness in teacher preparation (Guyton & McIntyre, 1990). In the end it seems that "perceptions" and "tradition" account for maintaining student teaching on the basis of history rather than merit (Watts, 1987).

This traditional regard for the value of student teaching is apparent in contemporary educational reform agendas. Both the Holmes and Carnegie groups discourage the emphasis given a single and final experience, preferring multiple sites that include youngsters with diverse ability, motivation, and cultural background. However, reformists also seek to control the contexts in which field experiences, including student teaching, occur in order to manage many of the problems that plague these experiences. The solution, according to the Holmes Group (1986), lies in Professional Development Schools, where practicing teachers and university faculty could together "improve teaching and learning on the part of their respective students" (p. 56) and for the research and development of the teaching profession. The Carnegie Task Force's (1986) recommendation is to develop "clinical" schools, analogous to teaching hospitals, that would "exemplify the collegial performance-oriented environment that newly certified teachers should be prepared to established" (p. 76).

A second theme of these and other reform reports is "reflection": "The typical student-teaching experience is not a genuine laboratory experience. . . . The emphasis is upon imitation of and subservice to the supervising teacher, *not upon investigation, reflection, and solving novel problems*" (Holmes Group, 1986, p. 55; emphasis added). Reformers suggest redesigning curricula to better tie methods and content courses more directly to student teaching in order to "develop an ethic of inquiry and professional judgment" (Holmes Group, 1990, p. 35), and provide "a strong element of field-based preparation, emphasizing opportunities for careful reflection on teaching integrated with a demanding program of academic coursework" (Carnegie Task Force, 1986, p. 76).

While reform tries to create new frameworks for "in-school" experiences, the fundamental ideas are reminiscent of tradition: model and practice. Such tradition emphasizes the technical orientation that has long been associated with student teaching and relies on a "transfer" model: transferring techniques from teacher to student teacher, transferring theory into practice, and transferring academic coursework into teaching. Reflection, then, becomes merely reflecting a model whose roots are in old mind-sets instead of new frameworks.

Yet student teaching as a transition point from "student" to "teacher" is viewed by some as the most significant experience in the entire teacher preparation process (Applegate, 1986). Within the context of career development it signals the transition from the growth to the exploration stage. Career exploration is associated with crystallizing (clarifying) and acting on one's vocational self-concept (Harren, 1979). The exploration process is defined by Blustein as "those activities in which individuals seek to assess themselves and acquire information from the environment to assist in career decision-making" (1989, p. 111).

Exploration during student teaching can not only clarify preservice teachers' perceptions of their own strengths and preferences but can allow them to explore traditional orientations and mind sets they bring to the teaching and learning context. Margaret Yonemura (1987) views student teaching as part of a developmental process in which student teachers assimilate information and make accommodations in ways that "shift" their prior understandings of important relationships between teachers, students, schools, and society. Because "human beings of all ages struggle all their lives to shift perspectives in order to gain wider worlds" (p. 475), student teachers must be supported in their exploration of new orientations instead of being coerced or left to adopt old ones.

EXPLORATION: A MATTER OF CONTEXT

Perspectives on the value of the student-teaching experience range from claims of positive changes to those who find change negligible or even negative. Zeichner and Tabachnick (1984) blame this variability on the failure of research to address issues of context, contending that the interaction of variables within the context of student teaching has the greatest impact on student teachers. In this "ecological" perspective the interactions of program features, settings, and people become most important.

Having become part of the larger group of teacher education students at Central, the interns appear to receive "equal treatment" during student teaching. The context of this experience is revealed through aspects of the student-teaching setting and the teaching education program. All Central students completed two student-teaching experiences over 12 weeks for which the student teaching office at Central, in cooperation with school principals, coordinated the assignment of schools, cooperating teachers, and specific courses/classes to be taught. While students could indicate a preference, final placements were made by personnel officers within each school district. Basic criteria for the selection of cooperating teachers, on the other hand, were set by the individual building principals. As the interns learned, neither years of teaching experience nor experience with student teachers seemed critical to their student-teaching assignments; neither did their status as Bridenthal Interns.

Lucy asks to be placed at the middle-school level for her two student-teaching experiences, though she is "not sure if I want to teach in middle school. I'm not closing that door, but I don't really prefer it except for student teaching." She chooses this level based on doubts she has about her youthful appearance and how that might cause her problems in high school, and "because I've been told by several sources that middle school is a fun place for science because there is more leeway: you can be more creative; it's not strictly lecture, tests, and a few labs." She predicts that her greatest strength will be organization and her greatest weakness, discipline.

Lucy eventually completes student teaching near her home (a nonnegotiable prerequisite for her), in the same district where she attended school. In fact, Lucy requests (and receives) permission to remain for both placements in the same school, where she works with two earth science teachers—one in the morning and the other in the afternoon. She describes her first cooperating teacher, who has experience with student teachers, as

> very, very structured, very ordered, very in control. . . . I do consider this a strength. At first I thought it was too excessive, but after having control myself, I realized that you had to be in control completely. . . . She tended to do everything the same way. It was easy for me to fit in and do those things, yet I considered this a weakness. She didn't try to teach the kids too much. She wasn't a really hard teacher as far as subject matter.

Lucy's second cooperating teacher is the opposite in every respect, perhaps because

> they had to scrape up somebody else. And the person they found was an experienced teacher; she was a good teacher, but she had never had a student teacher before. She had a lot of anxiety about the whole thing. She was worried that students' grades were too low [as a result of my teaching], that I was making mistakes on the computer, and that I was letting them tear up the room. She was just real worried.

As things turn out, Lucy struggles with discipline problems: "The teachers kept telling me 'You're too nice. You let them get away with too much.'" Worried that she has made a poor impression at Jack Simper Middle School, Lucy becomes even more convinced that she should teach high school students.

Jan, too, remains in one school for her two placements, both with American history teachers, her first a male teacher and her second a female. She characterizes both of their teaching styles as "primarily lecture," determining that since there is so much information to be covered this seems to be the most efficient method. Jan feels the least comfortable in her first placement during times when her own insecurities about content knowledge are enhanced by a specific group of students she sees each day: "They were a really sharp class and it was harder, so I didn't really get along with them. But not just because of that. Out of all my classes they were the more predominantly wealthy class and they let you know it quite frequently." Her second placement is with "older kids." Jan feels more comfortable here, noting that these students seem to understand her sense of humor.

Gene also requests and receives placements near where he resides—in this case, Professor Wright's home, where Roberto and he are "house-sitting" while the Wrights travel abroad. Both of Gene's assigned teachers—his first a female social science teacher in a middle school, his second a male high school teacher—teach advanced classes, and both have experience with student teachers. Yet Gene encounters difficulties during his first placement and appreciates the chance to move:

> There were times when I thought, "I don't want to do this." They were all in the first six weeks. Due to the teacher that I had, it was definitely a personality conflict. The second six weeks, when I had another teacher, I was given the responsibilities that I should have been given the whole time, and I was communicating better with the teacher like I should have been the whole time.

Because he's done most of his practicum work with middle-level students, Roberto asks that both his placements be in middle schools. As things turn out, neither of his cooperating teachers has ever had a student teacher before Roberto, who later recalls them as "scared" in this new role, yet outgoing, friendly, and willing to bend over backward for him. At the end of his student teaching, Roberto calls each of his cooperating teachers "real good friends."

Rita teaches in a local high school with teachers she had visited in earlier field experiences. Her first placement is with a "high-level" physics class, followed by a second six weeks teaching "low-level math." Rita had requested previous placements in similar math classrooms because she knew that beginning teachers typically receive such assignments.

Along with student teaching, the interns shoulder other commitments, like the student teaching seminar they attend along with other Central student teachers. While the purposes of the seminar are not explicit, the interns see it as an opportunity to share stories or, in Roberto's words, "complain." In addition, all graduating Central seniors take a "senior seminar" course that requires them to conduct an "independent research" project. Students enrolled in the seminar meet with their faculty instructor as a group twice: once to receive instruction on how to conduct and prepare their projects and later to present their papers. In the interim, students must individually consult with their seminar instructor as their inquiry progressed. According to one of these seminar instructors:

> The paper is something that should be a significant study conducted by a person who is exiting the formal education process and entering into the professional world. [Students should have] some sense about how to conduct research and some self-motivation, self-directed learning in the ideal sense that I would like to see from a student leaving a school like Central.

Many of the interns, however, admit putting off this rather formidable task until the last minute, not only because of their student-teaching commitments but also because of additional coursework they are taking to complete certification and graduation requirements. Rita takes her final physics course and the new math methods course during student teaching; Gene enrolls in two history courses; and Roberto starts but eventually drops a psychopathology course.

The interns emerged from a program that placed traditional emphasis on scholarship and reflected commonplace technical and rational orientations toward teaching and learning. Though their student-teaching contexts provided restricted career-decision opportunities, none offered alternative, innovative, or reform-oriented models of teachers' work.

ON-THE-JOB DECISION MAKING

As the "specialness" associated with the Bridenthal program faded, the interns moved into the uncharted waters of student teaching. No different from others, they responded to the requirements of the context as they engaged in traditional student-teaching tasks and assumed gradual responsibility for teaching. They also confronted numerous decisions. At one level, the interns reexamined their initial decision to teach and their earlier decisions concerning age/grade level, subject matter, and the kinds of schools in which they hoped to teach. At another level, they worked on more subtle decisions that influenced their orientation to classroom teaching. Ultimately, these more subtle decisions would define the kinds of teachers they became.

The model of career decision making developed by Harren (1979) serves as a lens through which to view the interns' experience during student teaching and includes three stages: (1) Awareness (reality testing); (2) Planning (seeking identity); and (3) and Commitment (career action). The interns made a number of career decisions at the outset and during the first two years in the program, yet student teaching forced them to consider the degree to which they recognized and reconciled differences in their "awareness," how they personally and occupationally "identified" with the role of teacher, and what their future career directions might be. Each step in the process either brought them closer to or pushed them away from a long-term commitment to teaching as a career.

While various data helped us evaluate the interns' student teaching experience, videotaped samples of classroom instruction provided documentation of aspects of interns' teaching. Each intern was videotaped at least once during student teaching and at least once during each of the first two years of teaching. Each of these "teaching episodes" was subsequently evaluated using the Teacher Performance Appraisal System (TPAS), a formative instrument used in North Carolina and typical of others used to evaluate teacher performance. When using the TPAS, a trained observer (in our case, a veteran North Carolina school principal) creates a running record of the lesson, then uses this to identify the presence or absence of specific teaching behaviors in five areas: (1) Management of Instructional Time, (2) Management of Students/Student Behavior, (3) Instructional Presentation, (4) Instructional Monitoring, and (5) Instructional Feedback. Our primary purpose in introducing these data is to provide an account of these teaching episodes from the perspective of someone completely removed from the lives of the interns and the conduct of this study, not to suggest inherent value in this sort of detached, technical, and obviously behavior-oriented judgment of effective teaching.

Awareness: Confronting the Myths

Harren (1979) describes awareness as "appraisal of self-in-situation." The context of awareness for student teachers is the reality they bring to student teaching in contrast to the reality they meet and come to know through their student-teaching experience. Discrepancies between these two realities and an individual's goals, values, and needs are evaluated, and alternative courses of action are considered. Eventually, the student teacher must consciously recognize and reconcile these discrepancies in preparation for the next stage of decision making: planning.

One reality most salient to student teachers is their own school experience. Lortie's (1975) research in *Schoolteacher* identified the role of "biography" as important in the development of a teacher because internalized teaching perspectives can actually restrict one's potential for change. Tabachnick and Zeichner (1984) find even more frustrating the fact that aspects of teacher preparation serve to support the internalized perspectives that individuals bring to teaching. Britzman (1987) views this as a process of "reproduction," where student teaching actually perpetuates myths about teaching, like "Everything Depends Upon the Teacher," "The Teacher Is the Expert," and "Teachers Are Self-Made." Confronted with such cultural myths, the interns made important decisions that reinforced and shaped their own teaching orientation. For example, since everything depends on the teacher, the teacher must establish and maintain control in the classroom.

Despite prior examination of the demographic characteristics of students, dropout rates, social ills, and the decline in student performance in schools, many members of the Bridenthal group were literally astonished by the everyday behavior of their students. In their student-teaching classrooms interns seldom found students with the same seriousness and discipline they recall having when they were in school themselves. Years of classroom experience provide students with very specific expectations of how teachers should act. In particular, students expect that teachers will maintain classroom control and enforce rules while delivering subject matter. The interns, like other student teachers, struggled to meet these expectations. Lucy claims that if she had it to do over again,

> I probably wouldn't have student taught in middle school . . . it was too much. When you're teaching middle school, you're not a teacher so much as you are a policeman. Even if they like you and they think you're cool and everything, they still are just out to get you, constantly seeing what they can get away with. And that was a real struggle.

Her only practicum in a middle school was with a teacher who had good control, so "I didn't know how bad it could be."

Confidence in her ability to control students' behavior wanes during Lucy's student teaching. Having agreed with statements such as "I know specific behavior management systems to adapt and use in the classroom," and "I feel confident in dealing with many types of behavior problems" on a written survey completed prior to student teaching, she disagrees with these and other, related statements afterward.

Lucy's difficulty in identifying strategies for controlling behavior is evident in a lesson conducted three weeks into student teaching. During a science lesson on barometers, her attention and responses to "inappropriate" and "off-task" behaviors become entangled with her instructional goals. Below, Lucy's lesson is logged, with occasional observer statements:

First 12 minutes: Students are told to begin warm-up exercises while Lucy takes roll. She discusses procedures for handing in late work. The observer writes: "Materials were not ready prior to beginning of class. . . . Lesson did not start quickly and efficiently because teacher did not have a system in place to make sure materials were organized from the previous class's activity."

Next 2 minutes: Lucy demonstrates the lab experiment for students.

Next 5 minutes: Students begin working at their lab tables. Lucy notices that students are too loud and establishes consequences: "Quiet. If you get too loud. . . . *Listen!* . . . If you get too loud, I'll bring my pen over and take 5 points off your grade. Please remember, 5 points off of a 50 point lab is one letter grade. If you're goofing off or talking, you just jeopardized yourself one letter grade." The observer writes: "I noted a *very inappropriate* measure taken to control behavior. . . . Teacher told students that she would take 5 points off their grade if they became too loud during lab—a different consequence for unacceptable behavior should have been stipulated."

Next 25 minutes: Students work independently at their tables. Lucy asks students to raise their hands if they have questions or need materials. She soon becomes overwhelmed in her attempts to attend to students' many requests and simultaneously attend to inappropriate behaviors. Lucy continually asks students to quiet down: "You're getting loud. *Shhh!* Keep it down." One student who stands up and hits another on the arm is told to sit down. Lucy tells another student who is off task to turn around. Several students are often out of their seats and others talk continuously.

Final 6 minutes: Lucy closes the instructional period by talking generally about the lab and what happened during their experiment.

At the end of student teaching Lucy diagnoses her primary weakness as management of students and readily admits that she is inconsistent: "Like, if I'm in a good mood some days, I let them go get a drink or go to the bathroom. Other days I say, 'No passes.' And I just treat them differently discipline-wise, too." Inconsistency is out of character for Lucy, who has managed to survive and excel by organizing almost every aspect of her life. She feels that entering a classroom in the middle of the year does not help, because she has to learn the rules herself before she can enforce them with students. Her "solution" is to try to become more consistent. She predicts that behavior management will be easier in a high school setting—a belief confirmed by her college supervisor, Hilda Williams, who sees Lucy as "a very caring teacher . . . a very enthusiastic teacher." However, Dr. Williams holds "some concerns" about Lucy's classroom control and, along with both of Lucy's cooperating teachers, encourages her to take charge, set the rules, and hold firm.

Jan, too, encounters difficulties with students' behavior but develops a different approach to gain control. Jan's management problems become apparent in her first placement. Her supervisor, Dr. Williams, who taught these interns methods in secondary education as an adjunct Central faculty member, comments that Jan seems shy and speaks with a timid voice. Further, "the kids [student teachers] spend the first six weeks concerned about whether they make this report on the pink sheet, the yellow sheet, or the blue sheet. How do you report attendance? What period do you put the attendance outside? What period do they come in to get it? Jan had to work into it!" During Jan's second placement with older students (seniors), Williams watches her transform:

I wasn't impressed with her at the beginning. She's kind of sleepy.
. . . And then, I saw her conduct a mock senate. She put together all
of the materials. She conducted it herself as President of the Senate. It
was a remarkable thing to watch. . . . It was incredible . . . her voice
and her "in-charge" attitude. It was a revelation because I thought she
was going to be very timid.

Although mock senates did not happen every day, Jan's vocabulary
lesson described below reflects a similar strategy for control:

First 6 minutes: Jan organizes students in the classroom, gives directions,
and demonstrates a vocabulary game modeled after "Pictionary."
Next 5 minutes: First student selects a word (from the glossary of their
social studies textbook) and goes to the board to draw a picture clue.
Other students attempt to guess the word.
Next 30 minutes: Jan changes the rules and re-explains the game. She
restricts the amount of time allowed for clues, coaches students, and
tells them when they are taking too long and need to pass their turn on
to someone else. She awards points for a successful guess.

In 41 minutes, students cover nine vocabulary words and guess three cor-
rectly as Jan manages the words, the clues, the points, and the time. The
observer writes:

Social studies game did not appear to be well-planned. Ultimately, the
directions to the game were understood by the students, but the
teacher took an inordinate amount of time to explain the game and
also failed to explain certain rules. . . . Teacher did not give a pur-
pose/objective for the social studies vocabulary game. . . . The social
studies game related to the material being taught, but it had little value
other than a mental exercise.

While Jan's social studies game does not appear to accomplish much
instructionally, it does put her in charge. She has successfully developed a
strategy for control that is routinized, easy to deliver, and gives the appearance of student learning. Jan's second cooperating teacher, in whose room
the game occurs, describes her as "terrific" — and why not: Jan has changed
the regular teacher's lecture approach to one that is activity-based. Professor Williams is equally impressed with the changes she has seen in Jan
during her two student teaching placements: "Jan is a teacher through-and-
through and feels comfortable with that role," Williams exclaims. "I ob-

served her walking around here [Central]; it was a metamorphosis. She appeared to be someone who was more sure of herself. She was incredible."

Evident in both Lucy's and Jan's cases are student-teaching contexts that supported and even modeled Britzman's (1987) myth regarding control: that when students' behavior is under control, learning is taking place. Other myths were equally apparent.

The "Teacher Is the Expert" myth reinforces the notion that teachers should be all-knowing. This is especially problematic during student teaching because student teachers are "educating at the same time they are being educated" (Britzman, 1987, p. 459). Because this myth perpetuates containing and controlling knowledge in order to maintain the position of expert, "to the student teacher, any condition of uncertainty is viewed as a threat to becoming an expert" (p. 451).

Built on a perennialist liberal arts foundation, the Bridenthal program placed great emphasis on knowledge. One result of this was that many interns felt unprepared to *teach* their content, often staying only "one chapter ahead" of their students. Some struggled unexpectedly with "what" to teach as well. Although Gene spent the summer prior to his fall student-teaching assignments preparing content, his primary teaching difficulty came in his struggle to teach the content he'd mastered in the ways he wanted. He most epitomized the struggle to emulate "the expert."

Troubling, for Gene, is the fact that in his first placement he is treated as a "student teacher" and not the full-fledged teacher he feels like. In addition to the discomfort he feels with his cooperating teacher, he appears uninspired working in a junior high school environment. During one lesson, for example, he spends a considerable amount of time checking vocabulary worksheets, walking students through a discussion of individual vocabulary words, and playing "Trivial Pursuit." He receives low marks on the TPAS for, among other things, getting off to a slow start and not responding to inappropriate behaviors.

Another lesson—this one during his second student teaching placement, in a high school philosophy class—demonstrates Gene's preferred teaching contexts. The topic is the "Death of Socrates." Throughout this 45-minute lesson (with the exception of the first 3 minutes of class during which students write their conceptions of Socrates' philosophy), Gene employs a shared-discussion format, entertaining topics ranging from Socrates' basic philosophy to concepts such as the perfect state and the good life. During this lesson Gene experiences no student behavior problems.

Asked about Gene's teaching, his college supervisor opens with, "Oh, my God!" and continues: "Gene has a totally in-charge personality. . . . It wouldn't occur to him that he wasn't the principal. When he would talk and ask the students questions, he wouldn't have the faintest idea what he might get for an answer. Whatever off-the-wall ideas students gave, he could answer. He had a dialogue with his class."

Gene's second cooperating teacher also emphasizes how impressed he is with Gene's command of the subject matter:

> Gene seems to be a bit more sure of where he's going and how to get there [than other student teachers]. I didn't have to take nearly the time in terms of having him research and structure a particular lesson. Perhaps that's a result of training he's had in the education curriculum at Central. But I suspect a lot of it is his own personal pride in what he's about. He came to me with a desire to do his best and he's done it.

In her final evaluation of Gene's teaching, his supervisor writes: "Gene knows his subject matter very well and has a lot of leadership characteristics." Gene had finally succeeded in impressing these students, this cooperating teacher, his college supervisor, and other teachers in the building that he was an expert.

A third myth that Britzman (1987) claims student teachers play out is that "Teachers Are Self-Made." Student teachers have difficulty seeing the connection between their college coursework, liberal arts and professional coursework, and the work of teaching. The expectation that one can or should rely on coursework in child development, sociology, pedagogical theory, or educational history is replaced with intuitive, trial-and-error learning during student teaching.

As a group, the interns shared the general impression that their teacher preparation was "too theoretical." And while they believed they had a realistic view of teaching stemming from opportunities to try it out in clinical experiences, they still viewed student teaching as a "test" of their ability to teach. During his senior year Roberto frequently expresses concern about the ways in which some interns complain or seem to have a lower level of commitment than they ought to, simultaneously noting genuine anguish that some "good people" become so negative about themselves during student teaching:

> It was tough. You really had to talk to them, try to get them back and give as much positive feedback as we possibly could. I felt it was important that I kind of help them if they came to talk to me—let them know that they really are good teachers and can change things around if they just stop thinking the way they were thinking. But sometimes they kind of went through those weeks hoping to see the end of it and survive.

Rita finds interacting with students in ways other than through formal instruction difficult. Teaching and learning are serious business for her, especially in upper-level classes. According to Professor Williams, Rita "was scared absolutely witless when she started" in her physics placement:

> I remember her saying . . . "They don't talk to me." And I asked, "Rita, do you talk to them? Honey, you know, the problem is that they're seeing you as this university person. You are in this position and they don't know what to say to you. They would love to have you acknowledge them. They're kind of waiting for the invitation to speak to this neat lady from the university." Well, she came back later and said, "I tried that and now they're all over me." And they were. She made such friends. Well, not really friends. She's one of those people that keeps an appropriate distance.

A second opportunity to warm up to students greets Rita in the "very low level" math class she enters next. Dr. Williams admits wondering "if Rita could come down" to successfully teach these students, though with lowered content expectations Rita actually feels more free to interact with them. In Hilda Williams's words: "When they would act up, Rita's sense of humor was wonderful. She would just say something to them in a firm but humorous way. And no one resented her reprimands. They didn't feel like she was cutting them down."

While teacher/student relationships are sometimes puzzling to Rita, delivering instruction is not. Because Rita herself is task-oriented, she has no problem figuring out ways to keep her students busy during class. Instinctively, she runs her classroom like a drill team. She is well prepared, maintains a high level of on-task behavior, cuts off inappropriate behavior, and moves both herself and students quickly through instructional activities. The following is an episode from one of Rita's physics classes:

First 5 minutes: Rita provides instructions for the labs and calls out pairs of students to work together. (Note: Materials for a series of six labs and two activities called "circuits" are set up around the room prior to the lesson's start.)

Next 5 minutes: Student pairs begin working on labs. Rita circulates around the room to make sure they understand the directions and have adequate materials. Students work in groups of four.

Next 35 minutes: Students continue to work on labs and circuits. Rita circulates, providing feedback, answering questions, and giving directions. The observer writes: "Teacher exhorted students to pick up the pace as she noted their progress throughout the class; she also reminded several students of the deadlines they faced. . . . Students got on-task quickly and remained on-task throughout. This appeared to be more a function of the type of student population, however, than of what the teacher did. Students in this class appeared to be bright, intrinsically motivated students."

In this case, Rita is teaching students who appear similar to her. While concerned with students' learning of math and science concepts, she focuses her instructional goals on getting the work done and done right. Instinctively, Rita follows her own efficiency model of learning.

Roberto is pleasantly surprised by his two student-teaching experiences, and episodes from his classroom performance support his positive self-assessment. He conducts the following lesson in early October, one month into student teaching. In a 42-minute lesson, approximately 35 minutes are classified as "teaching time" while the rest represent "work time":

First 5 minutes: Roberto introduces the lesson with a drawing of the earth on the board, the core and mantle labeled. He reminds students that in social studies they learned about the outside of the earth and today they will learn about the inside. Also, as in social studies, they will use a "model."

Next 15 minutes: Roberto reads a story about drilling to the center of the earth as students follow along in their books. During the oral reading Roberto asks students to "pretend that you are in a machine (like the one in the story). . . . Close your eyes for just a little bit. . . . Can you imagine drilling to the center of the earth? . . . What will you find there?" Roberto focuses student attention on the lesson's objectives by asking, "What do you think are the three layers? How are the layers of the earth like the layers of an apple?" Teacher/student discussion runs throughout the lesson, and Roberto shares pertinent information as the story moves from layer to layer (distance, temperature, etc.).

STUDENT: How do you find out about the mantle and the core?

ROBERTO: Remember when *you* told *me* about volcanoes and what comes out? Lava. Well, that lava from deep in the earth comes up from hotter layers like the mantle and the core. . . . Scientists, geologists, study lava when a volcano erupts. . . . They can't go down, but they can measure temperature . . . with a special thermometer. It may not be exact, but remember, scientists have to make guesses.

This conversation serves as Roberto's transition into his demonstration. The observer writes: "Teacher got students on task during oral reading about the earth; students stayed on task. . . . Numerous student comments and responses to teacher questions were made; teacher gave his students feedback on these."

Next 15 minutes: Roberto and the students move to a desk, where he demonstrates how the layers of the earth are like an apple. He sets the demonstration up as a problem-solving situation and walks students through the problem-solving process. During the demonstration Roberto and the students discuss volcanoes in Hawaii, earthquakes in California, and ways in which geologists study the inside of the earth. The observer writes: "Teacher did exhibit adequate knowledge of the subject matter in answering student questions and during lecture/discussion. He spoke fluently and precisely throughout all phases of the lesson . . . explained all concepts pertaining to the earth clearly."

Final minutes: Roberto asks students to write their conclusions to their demonstration/experiment. "Your conclusions are going to be how the inside of an apple is like the earth. . . . See if you can answer that."

According to the observer, Roberto's use of instructional time is optimal and his transitions are quick. Further, Roberto maintains student attention and presents concepts clearly using examples and demonstrations. Roberto's college supervisor, Barney Friend, is also impressed, referring to Roberto as "boy wonder": "Roberto, who seemed somewhat reserved and cautious in his ways is just tremendous; he is just outstanding . . . my surprise, because sometimes he appears not to have too much energy." Friend expected a few more problems for Roberto: "Because of his timid personality I thought that he might have difficulty relating to the students." In his final evaluation, Professor Friend writes of Roberto: "He was not the best, but certainly not the worst."

Student teaching presented surprises to many of the interns. The ways in which they dealt with these had a significant impact on their teaching styles. In some cases they attempted to change or modify their orientations (e.g., Rita moving from her intellectualist orientation to be more student-oriented). However, for most interns, the contexts of student teaching reinforced existing orientations and myths, setting the stage for their plans to become teachers.

Planning: Matching Identities Toward Change

Planning, the next stage in career decision making, is the active consideration of alternatives (exploration)—a process that guides individuals into a gradually more specific direction and prepares them for making a commitment (crystallization). The planning context of becoming a teacher includes the development of a student teacher's image of self in the role of teacher. Within this context, student teachers begin to see job preferences that more clearly match their own sense of identity. Eventually, they consider alternatives and move closer to specific job commitments. Key to this process is the search for "identity": determining "who I am," "what my need-value priorities are," "what I am good at," "where I am heading," and "what general life goals are important to me" (Harren, 1979, p. 130). Many of these questions are answered during "occupational socialization" (Hoy & Woolfolk, 1990).

Bureaucratic or institutional structures are often blamed for perpetuating environments of conformity rather than change in teaching and schools. Hoy and Rees (1977) refer to this phenomenon as "bureaucratic socialization," which they define as the organization's attempt to induce consensus between the newcomer and the rest of the organization: "Student teachers appear quite vulnerable to the pressures of bureaucratic socialization as they try to succeed and earn good grades" (p. 24). They argue that such a posture encourages status quo practices as "correct" and "natural" while discouraging any critical analysis or interpretation. Field experiences and student teaching, thus, "revolve around adjustment, containment, and control" (p. 38). Though recruited as ambassadors of educational reform, the interns found maintaining the hope of change to be a difficult task. As they departed the student-teaching context, some found conflict at a personal level while others had problems with bureaucracy.

Lucy finds it hard to be "revolutionary" as a student teacher, but her desire to be dynamic and change the profession remains strong: "I want to be interesting. . . . They've constantly been telling us, 'You're special. You're special. You're going to be great. Everybody's going to want you. You're going to succeed.'" She goes on to note: "I think we should stand out; be recognized; maybe get like a new teacher award or something. . . . I don't just want to be just any teacher."

Student teaching prompts Rita to bridle in her enthusiasm, otherwise it will "just get pounded out by other teachers, which is really sad." She trades her plans for systemic change for hopes that she can make a difference in her own classroom: "If not a major difference, I just hope to do my best in the classroom and make a difference with the students, especially the lower-level students whom teachers just pound down."

Through it all, Gene holds tightly to the Bridenthal vision: "We were trained not only to be teachers but to be leaders among the teachers . . . I see there's a 20 percent chance that I'll get fired in my first two years for being too radical or outspoken." He tells of how, while student teaching:

> I was working with a world geography curriculum that was terribly outdated. And I went to the library and started revising it with very current things . . . none of the other teachers in the other 14 sections of world geography had any of this material, nor had they planned to introduce this material at any time during the year. . . . I see myself as a changer in that school. I introduced material they didn't have; I introduced a new way of doing assignments that they weren't using. And the students loved it.

Nonetheless, his vision for reform is now bounded by his own teaching contexts: "I don't think that I'm going to be able to change the system. I'll try to work the best I can within the boundaries that are set."

Jan never did give much credence to the interns' being change agents. As far as the Bridenthal program, "I don't know that it has necessarily prepared us any more than, you know, any other student that was in the program. But I don't know that it was really meant to prepare us more."

Roberto's dreams of becoming a reformer find new life when he is encouraged by Professor Wright to continue his "innovative" career path by becoming involved in Wright's latest reform endeavor—the Alliance Schools: "It is sort of the same thing that happened to us when we were graduating seniors in high school and not really sure where we were to go in the future. Here comes Dr. Wright and talks about exciting things."

The interns were set apart from practicing teachers and other teacher education students in the beginning of their program, though by the time they left Central most had erased the artificial boundaries and viewed themselves as a part of the larger group of teacher education graduates. During student teaching the interns negotiated similar relationships with their future colleagues—classroom teachers they had scoffed at throughout teacher preparation. For some interns, becoming "one of them" produced great internal turmoil.

For Gene, the Bridenthal promises and its potential for impact are fading. While he finds community with his fraternity brothers, a few interns, and some other Central students, he can find no community among teachers with whom he works during student teaching:

> I got tired of the lunchroom Mafia. . . . If I had another Bridenthal Intern there, at least I'd have someone that wasn't soured by all their experiences in school . . . and someone my age, because that's the biggest thing I've noticed. Young people aren't going into teaching any more, and so I'd sit in this room and all these people were talking about denture fixatives.

Roberto seems to be a born teacher. He recalls how his fifth-grade cooperating teacher praised him, saying that "she had never seen anybody so quickly take to teaching. She thought I was just another teacher—part of the team there, already. She was kind of awed about it."

Rita socializes primarily with other Central student teachers (not the interns), though she views her cooperating teachers as "life preservers" who often rescue her from trouble. Focused on the student-teaching task, she negotiates few inroads to the school community. Most of her support during student teaching comes from fellow student teachers in her building with whom she commutes: "I depend a lot on them just to talk, support each other and help each other."

Bergsma and Chu (1981) explain how beginning preservice students tend to be motivated by their liking for children, whereas graduating seniors tend more to be motivated by criticisms of schools and a desire to change and influence schools through teaching. Those interns who approached student teaching holding on to serious hopes to affect change, like Rita, began to see those hopes tarnished in the harsh light of school practice. Others, like Jan, who never assumed an identity as reformer, worked more comfortably into the school community. And still others, like Gene, adjusted their ideas of change. Only Roberto emerges with hopes of influencing others and aware of his budding teaching abilities. With first-year survival looming, their Bridenthal-imposed images had become tentative; the interns' images of themselves, teaching, and reform—shaped on the anvil of student teaching—became more visible.

Commitment: Establishing Career Direction

When making career decisions, individuals arrive at the commitment stage when they feel ready to plan ways to implement their personal and occupational self-concepts. Commitment, in other words, implies action. Throughout the exploration process, individuals collect and analyze data regarding environmental contexts (awareness) and the internal context (identity). Ideally, they use the information gleaned from these explorations to direct or influence their next steps toward implementing career decisions. It is at this point that one's career is put into a broader context, which includes shaping one's immediate and long-term future and personal life space.

At the commitment stage, preservice teachers take steps to become practicing teachers. If, after progressing through both awareness and planning stages, one sees his or her choice of becoming a teacher as the best alternative, then specific actions to implement and integrate this role into the life space follow. Commitment can be expressed as short-term and long-term career goals, the first of which is securing a teaching position. If, on the other hand, teaching does not appear to be the best alternative, one begins a search for more suitable alternatives.

The interns' ability to use the information they gleaned from the awareness and planning stages of student teaching was limited. Their contract with the Bridenthal Program left them little choice regarding teaching as a career for the next two years. Their student-teaching experiences, however, did have the potential to influence their selection of a teaching job.

Throughout their program the Bridenthal Interns knew they would one day have teaching jobs. Indeed, from the earliest months they had been showered with interest and "promises" of work by school administrators and central-office personnel. Yet in their senior year some interns began to worry about finding work, and whether they would have to repay their Bridenthal scholarship if they didn't. Several accepted jobs during their student teaching in spring term, or early that summer, to remove these worries.

Practically all of the 16 graduating interns sought and eventually found work in suburban districts, many in the districts they attended as K–12 students. Despite a tight hiring market, few even applied to the major metropolitan school district serving the inner city. Members of the group readily admitted not wanting to work with students in lower socioeconomic districts.

By the time they left Central, the Bridenthal Interns' label seemed to have lost its allure as far as the job market went. A few experienced summer worries of finding a suitable job. In some ways, the Bridenthal requirement to teach in one of the city's districts seemed to limit the number of opportunities available to the interns. But in fact, only a handful of interns applied to more than 3 of the 15 school districts; many applied to only one; and some (like Roberto) had no need to look for jobs in any district.

However, several interns found themselves faced with job options. One school district, for example, seriously courted Lucy before her senior year to come and teach science in one of its high schools, yet she decided, instead, to sign an "open contract" with the district where she completed her student teaching. By signing such an agreement, Lucy understood that she could be placed wherever the district decided, to teach whatever the district needed. She made this decision knowing that most openings would probably be at the middle-school level. Lucy's decision was tipped in favor of this opportunity because of the support and encouragement she received from those who worked with her—in particular, the building principal.

As it turned out, nearly half the interns signed similar open contracts, giving up almost any hope of choosing where, what, or with whom they would eventually work. With the exception of the single intern certified in early childhood education, these open contracts eventually turned many an intern's specialized knowledge of and accumulated experiences in special education, or physics, or middle school, for example, into a moot point. Interestingly, this situation is common to teachers in their search for initial employment. DeLong (1984), for example, found that the most significant motivation for selecting a job was geographic location. Further, statistics support the fact that a good proportion of new teachers accept jobs in their home towns and even in the same school districts and schools in which they grew up (Zimpher, 1989). This was the case for most of the Bridenthal Interns.

Individuals leave student teaching with the intention of teaching forever (continuously or intermittently), teaching on a trial basis, or never teaching — and again, the interns look similar. Although they were forced to attend to short-term career decisions first, this did not stop them from speculating on decisions regarding the more distant future beyond the two years they had committed to the Bridenthal program. Many reconsidered their initial decision and began plotting beyond the next two years. While some long-term plans revealed upon graduating from Central included teaching, others did not.

Rita, for example, leaves student teaching exhausted and worried about "going it alone." She now bemoans the fact that she will have to put off her real desire — to live and work in Japan — rationalizing that "I think the two years that I gain here might help me later anyway." Gene still plans to enter graduate school after spending two or three years in the classroom, and Roberto struggles with the decision to teach more than two years because of his unmet goal to pursue psychology. Despite talk among some interns about becoming school administrators, Roberto shows no interest in this career direction. Lucy and Jan see themselves continuing to teach indefinitely. Lucy plans to begin work towards a master's degree in the next five years, and Jan's long-term plans include marriage and family.

THE DECONTEXTUALIZATION OF TEACHING

Career decision making results from the interactions between individual and environmental contexts. Career-decision-making theory proposes that long- and short-term decisions are responses to developing impressions from direct and indirect experience and create one's commitment to future action. This theoretical perspective, when applied to the process of becoming a teacher, implies that individuals' impressions of teaching shape projections of themselves in their future role as teacher in an attempt to play out their own occupational self-concepts. In order to do this, however, individuals must understand their relationship with the breadth and depth of increasingly diverse contexts of teaching in the 1990s.

While many aspects of schooling have remained constant even during this most recent era of reform, the broader contexts of teaching and schooling have changed, especially through altered social and demographic conditions, shifts in perspectives on the focus of teaching and learning, and expanding knowledge regarding teacher development (Lieberman, 1992). When the old meets the new, however, a tension emerges between allegiance to a perennialist tradition (which seeks to preserve contexts of the past) and commitment to change reflected in a progressive orientation (which presses for new contexts for the future).

The changed contexts of teaching and learning now encourage a focus on students. Rather than have teachers seek to efficiently develop skills in students through "passive, impersonal, and generally print-bound" methods, changed contexts require that we recognize what students bring to the learning process and emphasize more student-centered approaches in our teaching processes (Lieberman, 1992, p. 4)—in other words, encourage a view of students as experts in their own right.

The contexts of the developing teacher also have changed, especially with respect to job skills, knowledge, behaviors, attitudes, and concerns (Burden, 1982; Fuller & Brown, 1975; Sprinthall & Thies-Sprinthall, 1983). Thus, the myth that good teachers are born and thrive, regardless of the context, must also be changed. We can accomplish this by making preservice students privy to their own developmental processes during preparation. Increasing the amount of information they have on teachers and the teaching career, providing a more explicit view of beginning career development, and teaching students ways to determine their teaching strengths and areas in need of further development will address this need (Burden, 1990).

Change in education, however, meets strong resistance embedded within the institutional bureaucracy—the same bureaucracy student teachers learn to see as valid and unchangeable (Beyer, 1984). Student teaching often results in the development of a stronger sense of personal teaching efficacy and a weaker sense of general teaching efficacy; that is, student teachers develop a greater confidence in their own ability to teach, but at the same time lose confidence in their ability to influence children's learning because of factors they feel are out of their immediate control (Hoy & Woolfolk, 1990). Essentially, the power to change structures and situations beyond oneself is diminished during student teaching and the tendency for conformity is reinforced long before one lands a teaching job. Ultimately, while the contexts of teaching become broader and more dynamic, those over which a beginning teacher feels control grow more narrow and static.

In the process of making career decisions, individuals view and interpret contexts. Teacher preparation and field experiences, in particular, are responsible for revealing the contexts of teaching and providing preservice teachers with opportunities to explore teaching in ways that help pose critical questions, engage individuals in self-assessment (beyond merely examining "skills"), and support the developmental process of becoming a teacher. Most important, individuals must have the freedom to test and act on their decisions in search of alternatives.

CHANGE OR REFORM is not as prescriptive as reformists would have us believe. If change is to occur in a system as entrenched in tradition as schooling, change agents must enter the profession with an awareness of the dynamic nature of the contexts of education, an understanding of their own identity within the profession, and a commitment to a direction that challenges current practice at all levels of the system. Revealing the contexts of teaching is not sufficient; preservice teachers must be able to view them from a critical perspective. As we discuss in Part III, Jan, Gene, Rita, Roberto, and Lucy enter public school teaching groomed as "pace-setters" for reform as a "new breed" of teacher, though tainted by their first descent into the trenches of everyday school practice.

Part III

PROFESSIONALIZATION

CHAPTER 8

Inducing Reform: The College Comes to the Classroom

If it is possible to recruit high-ability students and give them a first-rate teacher education program, can they be retained in the schools? In the final analysis this is the most important question. —Don Wright

On the basis of educational research, we know that the "brighter" a teacher education graduate is, the less likely it is that that person will enter into the profession or will continue in the profession for more than a couple of years. We also know that the quality of a person's first-year teaching experience is more strongly related to teacher attrition (within five years) than either their academic performance or the perceived adequacy of their training program.

Traditionally, beginning teachers have received little support from either teacher education institutions or school districts. Moreover, there has been little genuine collaboration between school-based practitioners and education professors as new teachers enter the profession. Not surprisingly, then, reform advocates in the 1980s underscored the importance of long-term induction of novice teachers and the necessity of university/school collaboration in this induction process.

Of course, the problems confronting beginning teachers were well documented long before this generation of reforms and leaders of earlier educational reforms had made proposals regarding professional induction and school/university collaboration (Association for Student Teaching, 1968; Cuban, 1990; Flowers, 1948; McDonald & Elias, 1980; Shaplin & Powell, 1964). The first section of this chapter explores the parallels between the reform movement of the 1980s with its generational predecessor. Following this historical overview, we examine how effectively Central implemented its collaborative internship model and the effectiveness of the school districts' formal and informal induction process against the backdrop of the interns' journeys as beginning teachers.

SURVIVING THE FIRST YEARS: REFORM AND RESEARCH EFFORTS

Thirty years ago, in the *Education of American Teachers*, Harvard educator James B. Conant (1963) proposed that local school boards adopt an initial probationary period for new teachers, asserting that not even an adequate teacher preparation program can ready "first year teachers to operate effectively in the 'sink or swim' situation in which they too often find themselves" and admonishing local school boards for being "scandalously remiss in failing to give adequate assistance to new teachers" (p. 70). Conant made several recommendations for the employment of new teachers.

First, he advised that new teachers have limited teaching responsibilities and that students likely to be the most difficult to instruct because of discipline or learning problems not be assigned to novice teachers. Second, he proposed that the school provide assistance to new teachers in the selection of instructional materials. Third, he recommended that experienced teachers receive a reduced teaching load in order to consult with new teachers in their classrooms. Finally, he suggested that new teachers have an understanding of the community from which their students come.

These recommendations, consistent with beginning-teacher research studies of the 1960s and early 1970s, were evidenced in the research and reform efforts of that era, which focused on the developmental needs of beginning teachers.

In 1964, with the financial support of the Carnegie Corporation, the National Association of Secondary School Principals (NASSP) initiated the Project on the Induction of Beginning Teachers, incorporating Conant's recommendations (Hunt, 1968; Jerry, 1968; Swanson, 1968). First implemented in Detroit, Richmond, and St. Louis public school systems, this first-year induction program eventually reached into more than a hundred schools nationwide. A related reform effort, stemming from a $40 million initiative by the Ford Foundation, was a five-year teacher education program culminating in a Masters of Arts in Teaching (MAT). Key to these programs was a university/school collaborative effort to develop a well-supervised fifth-year internship (Dunbar, 1981). MAT students participated in workshops addressing their teaching needs and personal concerns as they taught with mentors who were adjunct faculty. Another multimillion dollar reform was Indiana University's Bureau of Educational Personnel Development–funded Options in Teacher Education Program. By the mid-1970s there were more than 20 program options for elementary, secondary, and special education students as well as several program for students pursuing a master's degree (Sears, 1990a).

By the late 1970s, however, facing dwindling enrollments, financial cutbacks, fundamental conflicts between the university and school cultures, and a conservative political environment, only remnants remained of these reform efforts to ease the entry of young professionals into teaching and to connect universities with schools (Brookhart & Loadman, 1992; Sears, 1990b). There were only remnants of independent research efforts assessing and evaluating the effectiveness of such programs.

Veenman's (1984) thorough review of empirical studies on problems confronting beginning teachers conducted in the 1960s and 1970s revealed substantial overlap with the NASSP and Indiana University findings and evidence significant consistency over time: The most common problem was classroom discipline followed by student motivation, learner differences, student assessment, parental relations, class work organization, materials, student personal problems, and heaving teaching loads.

Many of the reform programs developed at Indiana University as well as the NASSP Project encouraged experienced teachers to develop induction activities arising "from the needs of the individuals" (Swanson, 1968, p. 77). Though the specific phases articulated by these researchers differ, all share three fundamental assumptions:

> First, they acknowledge the reality of individual differences among preservice and inservice teachers and the necessity for more individualized training opportunities. Second, they focus on changes in teachers over time, which calls for interventions and support spread over time. Third, they take into account teachers' present needs and interests in developing appropriate interventions. (Burden, 1990, p. 318)

In the late 1970s and early 1980s the emphasis on teacher preparation and induction programs shifted from meeting the concerns of beginning teachers to satisfying systemic needs. Teacher performance and teaching competencies replaced issues of emotional support and personal development. "Induction"—a word long associated with military training and industrial research—became vogue.

While the political center shifted from the Kennedy-Johnson years to the Reagan-Bush era, educational reform was no less affected by economic and ideological forces (Popkewitz, 1991). With their neo-Taylorian emphasis on efficiency, standardization, and measurement, educational reformers of the 1980s sought to reverse the nation's economic, intellectual, and moral decline. Though the problems of the beginning teacher persisted, the emphasis shifted from meeting the developmental needs of the novice teacher to fulfilling state mandates for higher student performance and teacher competence.

During the first wave of educational reform, many state legislatures mandated proficiency examinations for would-be teachers and assessment of their classroom teaching. The use of proficiency examinations and other assessment techniques focused on the measurable: subject-matter knowledge, discrete teaching behaviors, pupil test scores. Unaddressed were beginning-teacher pedagogical concerns, such as classroom management, student motivation, individual learning differences, and planning/preparation, as well as school survival concerns, such as inadequate supplies, student personal problems, supervisors' and co-workers' expectations, and parental communication.

Mid-way through the 1980s the second wave of reform reports, while echoing many of the criticisms and proposals of earlier reports (e.g., necessity for a liberal education, strenuous education courses), asserted that teacher education reforms would be effective only if concomitant reforms were made in the structure of the school, in the work place, and in the governance within the professions. Their proposals, following numerous calls for in-service teacher education reform (e.g., Grant & Zeichner, 1981; Vaughn, 1979), included renewed calls for induction systems and collaboration among university faculty, classroom teachers, and school administrators.

In *Tomorrow's Teachers*, the Holmes Group (1986) advocated professional development schools in which preservice and classroom teachers, school administrators, and university faculty members would collaboratively develop a professional teaching culture. The group further recommended a three-tier system of licensing beginning with new teachers, possessing nonrenewable certificates (instructors), leading to a mass of proven competent educators (professional teachers), and at the apex a cadre of outstanding teachers exerting leadership in teacher education and school change (career professionals). Instructors would begin their career through a year-long, well-supervised induction program.

A Nation Prepared (Carnegie Task Force, 1986), recommended the restructuring of the teaching work force by designating lead teachers who would uphold standards and exercise key leadership in the redesign of schools. The report advocated providing students in graduate teacher education programs with internships and residencies in schools as key "support staff" for professional teachers. During the second year of the graduate program, prospective teachers would serve as interns at schools with "diverse student populations" while taking additional graduate coursework. During the internship, these graduate students would assume "substantial teaching responsibilities" with supervision from a lead teacher holding a joint appointment in the graduate school. Acknowledging that this approach would have many variations, the report emphasized that "what is essential is a strong element of field-based preparation, emphasizing opportunities for careful reflection on teaching integrated with a demanding program of academic coursework" (p. 76).

Calling for a new generation of teachers, *A Call for Change in Teacher Education* (National Commission for Excellence in Teacher Education, 1985) advocated one-year induction or internship programs beyond the provisional teacher certificate. "During this period, the school, the profession, and higher education should work together to help the new teacher become successfully immersed in the teaching profession" (p. 24). The document further recommended that interns receive reduced teaching loads to ease their participation in professional development activities such as seminars.

The Bridenthal program appropriated the language of collaboration and incorporated an induction model. In this chapter and in the following two chapters we chronicle the stories of Roberto, Gene, Rita, Jan, and Lucy as they moved from college student to classroom teacher and become inducted into the teaching profession.

REFORMING THE SCHOOLS

As 16 reform-minded, high-ability interns prepared to enter the public schools, Don Wright knew that their transition from college to classroom would not be easy. Many would enter public school districts that had integrated only the most basic recommendations from the second-wave reform reports on teacher induction; some would enter schools whose administrators and teachers remained largely unaware of these very reports. The interns, he knew, could be overwhelmed by the bureaucratic minutiae of everyday school life and the acceptance of educational mediocrity reinforced within the teacher lounge and at faculty meetings.

Providing the interns with a $2,000 extra annual stipend, Wright envisioned their return to Central and a seminar format reminiscent of their first year: an open exchange of ideas, the development of an esprit de corps and group support, and the infusion of new ideas through guest speakers and occassional readings. Wright also recognized that in order for his brightest and best to truly serve as "catalysts for change," educational reform required university collaboration with public schools.

In 1987, Wright formed partnerships between the college and several city public schools in order to create what became known as "Alliance Schools." Alliance Schools emerged as a collaborative effort between Central College, two school districts, the Bridenthal Foundation, and a psychological organization. Like other professional development schools that sought to bring about simultaneous renewal, the Alliance Schools aimed to improve the professional preparation of teachers while developing, in

Wright's words, "effective partnerships" among related educational institutions. Two elementary and two secondary schools "will be experimental and demonstrational in nature and will serve as magnet schools for faculty who want to work in an environment dedicated to the development and dissemination of best practices in teaching, learning, and schooling."

The emergence of the Alliance Schools coincided with the completion of the interns' four-year teacher preparation program. Wright described the project in the spring of 1988:

> King-Jackson elementary school is one of the four professional development schools. It is as close to an ideal situation as you can get. I was on the selection committee to pick the principal. She has two degrees from Central! I was involved in talking with faculty throughout the district about what we were going to do and why they might be interested in seeking transfer. We are going to have about 20 faculty; they will be the best teachers in the school district. The district will save two or three spots for the "wet behind the ears" Bridenthal Interns.

Roberto: Working in a Glass House

Roberto was one of these three interns "targeted" by Wright. Initially, Roberto had other career plans. Roberto's ideal job was working with special education kids "in a supportive, fairly wealthy" district on the city's northside which has "great parent support." He recalls wanting "to teach a self-contained, emotionally disturbed unit at an elementary level. Well, as I interviewed at a northside district school, I found that they wanted to move me into a middle school if I wanted to teach educationally disabled students. But I really wanted to work with elementary level kids." About that time, the Central-initiated Alliance Schools reopened King-Jackson elementary school:

> That kind of piqued my interest. I went to the meeting to see what they were talking about. Dr. Wright didn't push; he just mentioned that this would be a good thing to do. He set up an interview with the principal, Ms. Lillian—I had met her when she was the vice-principal during one of my field experiences. After talking to her I felt this was it. It was falling into my lap. I decided that I wanted to be part of this alliance and work to improve the education program and teaching.

Joan Lillian recalls the Christmas interview she had with Roberto: "I didn't expect Roberto to come here. I really didn't. I don't know what he went through to decide to come here. But I wasn't even going to interview him. I had put out a couple of feelers and hadn't gotten anything back."

The teaching position at King-Jackson was different from Roberto's vision of his first year teaching assignment. But, as Ms. Lillian noted: "I didn't have special ed to offer him, all I had was fifth grade. I think it was the best decision he could have made. I taught self-contained three years and was a resource teacher for five. But you need to start in a regular classroom. How can you be a special ed teacher if you don't know what a regular teacher must go through?"

During his senior year, Roberto also had a more personal issue to resolve. Professor Friend, who supervised Roberto's student teaching, recalls several conversations he had with Roberto: "Frankly, I was surprised that Roberto chose King-Jackson. I had thought he would have wanted to work in an inner-city school. Sometimes you have this image of a minority, particularly one who is a male, elementary teacher—itself a rarity—going back to help others who are oppressed and to serve as a role model." Though Roberto had long felt a personal and social responsibility to teach in the city's inner city or southside, he deferred this sense of social obligation until "I have a few years under my belt"—a decision, again, that Joan Lillian thought wise:

I started on the southside. The children are the same; the facilities are different. It's the materials you have and all the support that you have. Roberto has a lot of things here that people in this district take for granted; he probably doesn't even realize it. If he needs paper clips, we have them. If he needs the laminating film, we have it. If he needs to photocopy material, we have those resources. All these can make your life easier as a beginning teacher. We also have a newly renovated building with all new audio-visual equipment—every teacher has an overhead projector! We have all new books. If they need something, I get it for them. If they want to go to a conference, I pay for it. So, we're very fortunate and he's very lucky to work here as a beginning teacher.

Despite the modern facilities and strong faculty, King-Jackson's student population does not reflect the northside's wealthy Anglo image. As a magnet-type school drawing students from four low-income schools, King-Jackson attracts a different "type of student." Lillian continues:

Sixty-six percent of our kids are on free lunch. We have a high turn-over rate. I had a parent of two children today for whom this is their sixth school this year. That's unusual, but three schools in a year is not unusual. Parents don't have a phone and they don't have a car. They're hostile toward the school. They didn't do well in school and they expect the school to fail them and their children.

These are the children to whom Roberto, writing in an early journal entry, is committed:

My concern begins as a teacher with the "type of student" we have: a child from a divorced, low SES family, usually Hispanic, with a negative attitude toward school. I worry how, as a teacher, I am going to instill in this type of student the idea that school is an okay place to be. That, as my parents instilled in me, it is a way out—a stepping stone for future success. Most importantly, they must forget the type of student they are and become motivated to succeed in school.

Hired to teach in an Alliance School, Roberto began his in-service in early August—"a lot sooner than most teachers." In addition to the responsibilities of teaching fifth grade, he felt the stress of "working in a glass house" of an Alliance School:

We had to be willing to read research and to be part of different kinds of in-house research. We have an Exxon grant in mathematics, and we have committees that are meeting to develop new approaches for the teaching of elementary math which involves Central College and some of the King-Jackson staff. We're also getting a lot of practicum students and student teachers from Central.

OF THE 16 INTERNS who completed the preparation phase of the Bridenthal program, five worked in professional development schools. The remaining found themselves in a variety of school districts—generally on the more affluent northside of the city or in districts where they had attended as students—and with diverse teaching responsibilities. This diversity is well illustrated in the teaching assignments received by Gene, Rita, and Jan, all first-year teachers in another northside school, Justin High School—a traditional non-Alliance School of 4,000 students situated on two nearby campuses.

Gene: Teaching the Best

As a new social studies teacher, Gene expressed less than overwhelming enthusiasm about returning to his alma mater:

Justin has a serious discipline problem. The administrators do not back up the teachers like they should. I knew this going into Justin. However it was the only school that offered me a job and I accepted it despite the fact that my father, who just retired from the social studies department, had pretty well informed me of the chronic discipline problems.

His teaching assignment, however, was far from a typical first-year teacher's: an advanced placement European history class, a course for the International Baccalaureate (IB) curriculum (Justin is one of only three schools in the state to offer this program), and three basic economics classes. The district provided Gene with a two-day IB teacher workshop in Kansas City preparing him to teach history using a thematic approach. In his second year of teaching, Gene was given two teaching periods to work with gifted and talented students in the New Jersey–based Odyssey of the Mind Program and one Advanced Placement European history class, and allowed to develop an Asian studies course based on his summer trip to China with Don Wright.

Recalling Gene's long history with Justin, Mrs. Weller, his supervisor, offers insight into Gene and the nature of his teaching assignment:

Gene's dad taught in the social studies department for 20 years. His dad transferred Gene to the Justin schools even though they did not live in the district when he was in elementary school. He used to sit out in the office over there. This little boy with his books waiting for elementary school to begin across the street. In high school, he was a gifted and talented student, but he was a high mid-range IQ person. He was not a genius; he recognized that and he worked hard.

So, Gene has had a different kind of relationship at the school because of that. It has helped because I don't think there has been a lot of jealousy about Gene getting upper-level classes. He is like our child, our son.

Gene was essentially hired to work in the IB program. The teacher who had taught the course was leaving and it was a critical course. We had to select carefully because a high level of scholarship is demanded of the students. We felt that Gene would be able to do it. Part of that has to do with trust. Gene was not an unknown commodity to us. He was my student, and I helped to sponsor some of his speech events.

We have given Gene a lot of responsibility. We have to be careful that we don't create a monster. This little egghead running around with no perception of reality. That's why we thought it would be good for him to teach a regular economics class.

Mrs. Weller was Gene's "gatekeeper" long before she became his supervisor, alerting him to the Bridenthal Program and assisting him in his Central admission.

Gene and I specifically discussed his decision to apply for the Bridenthal program. My first question was, "How does your dad feel about it?" His dad was not very happy with teaching. I said, "Gene, do you think that you really want to be a teacher?" At that point not only was it an economic advantage but he could feel very proud that his parents weren't going to have to spend a lot of money to send him to college. It was a lifeline thrown to Gene.

Mrs. Weller, a curriculum specialist, paused for a moment before continuing:

What is the purpose of a college education? Is it to acquire more learning, more knowledge, more education? Or, is it to prepare for a profession? I think Gene was realistic enough to know that he needed to have something by which he could support himself and also something by which he could pursue his intellectual bent. He made an appropriate choice.

Rita: Breaking in at the Bottom

Like Gene, Rita had attended Justin. When she graduated second in her class, the teachers and administrators had "expectations because they knew me as a student and they had heard of the Bridenthal program." Along with the high expectations came strong support: "A lot of the teachers that I had are still there and I seek advice from them. That's why I sort of feel a part of the school, I don't feel isolated. They're always asking me how I'm doing, 'Oh, we knew you'd be a successful teacher.'" Unlike Gene, being an intern was still important for Rita : "Knowing that I am a Bridenthal Intern, it keeps you going. I'm glad to be a part of it. It makes me feel special."

Just as Gene had hoped against all odds that he would be able to teach in an IB program, Rita had relished the prospect of working in a school with other interns. Her wish, too, materialized. Rita, working with Gene and Jan (though their paths seldom crossed during their two-year assignment), taught in the mathematics department at Justin with two course preparations: three classes of Algebra I and two Informal Geometry courses for remedial students. One section of geometry "folded" after three weeks and was replaced with a fourth, newly created section of Algebra I.

Rita's transition from college to classroom was somewhat more typical for the first-year teacher than was Gene's: "For the beginning teacher, I think it should be the administrators' goal to make it as easy as possible as far as the paper work, the convenience, and the classes. I know that they dump on you all the remedial classes for the beginning teacher and that's not the way to go." Nevertheless, she offers, "It was a lot better than some people's experiences. I consider myself very fortunate . . . not really getting stuck with Fundamentals of Math or Consumer Math."

Rita did face such an assignment as she neared the end of her first year. She became furious when she learned of her pending assignment at the other campus to teach one remedial algebra class for eleventh- and twelfth-graders. Her department head told Rita "to get used to the real world of teaching." When she began her second year of teaching, however, her assignments were to teach two ninth-grade Algebra I classes and three tenth-grade classes of Informal Geometry—all on the same campus. Nevertheless, Rita still credits her new teaching load with being a beginning teacher: "I know last year my department head said, 'You need to teach a few more lower-level classes to break you in, to really see, to learn how to teach those kind of kids.' So I think that's why I got three informal geometry classes."

Jan: Fitting into the Mainstream

Although Wright had been telling the interns all along not to worry about a teaching position, only about one in four had one at the time of graduation. Many of the interns applied to only one or two of the 15 city school districts and others, like Jan and Gene, were in teaching areas with less demand. Jan was one of the last interns to receive a teaching contract. When August arrived, even the obvious fact that her Bridenthal membership *required* a two-year teaching commitment and the likelihood that Don Wright was scouring the city's high schools for vacancies did little to make her optimistic. Finally, Jan got lucky: She received a contract to teach at Justin High School.

Another intern commented, "I think Dr. Wright made a few phone calls and got her a job." As this intern noted, personal connections were critical: "In almost every case somebody knew somebody. I got my job because I student taught with that teacher and she recommended me. Gene got his job because he knew the people at Justin, and Rita knew the people at Justin."

Justin is a huge, comprehensive high school with shuttle buses taking students to and from classes on two nearby campuses. Serving mostly middle- and upper-middle-class students is a faculty of 250 teachers. Jan's assignment was teaching classes in American and world history. She did not feel well prepared in either subject, perhaps because she had a composite social science major. She had no additional or extracurricular assignments. The beginning of her first year found Jan optimistic: "I feel like I'm really going to have a positive first year experience—which they say really makes a difference in your attitude about teaching the rest of your life."

As we detail in Chapters 9 and 10, Jan is happier at Justin than are the others—especially Gene, who works in the same department: "I can't remember one minute when I've seen Gene actually happy about his job at Justin," Jan observes. She also fits well into the history department, in part because of her "laid back" personality and other characteristics that are similar to those of her co-workers. By her second year, she was teaching only American history: three regular classes and two "fundamentals" classes (students who have tested at or below a third-grade reading level). In addition, Jan was assigned bus duty for part of the year, given a different schedule (first period conference, an early lunch—"One thing I really hated"), and provided with a new textbook.

Lucy: Accepting a Sought-After Position

In her senior year, Lucy had described her ideal job as a place with "hungry kids. Kids that are just thirsting for knowledge and they want to soak it all up. . . . And to have an administration that's really liberal, that lets you do what you want, that doesn't put a lot of strings on you. And to have peers . . . that don't look at me funny when I have a new idea." Lucy also expressed a desire to work in a school near home ("I like that part of town and my family lives there") and within a district that's respected ("I probably shouldn't have that attitude, but that's the way I am") and "that really wants me and appreciates me and values me and needs me." Lucy's wish, too, became reality.

When Lucy completed her student teaching at Jack Simper Middle School, Jean Hawkins, the head of the science department, thought Lucy would be a good hire for the northside district. Although this sought-after school district only had five openings for teachers holding a composite science certificate, Lucy filled one of those slots, becoming one of only three beginning teachers in all content areas hired by the district.

As a graduate from this district Lucy confessed "I guess I always wanted to teach there," and quickly accepted an open contract in the early spring of her senior year. Like Gene, she also had a gatekeeper, Peggy Carnahan, the district's science coordinator. Long before she was offered her teaching contract, Lucy had interviewed Ms. Carnahan for a paper she wrote in Dr. Wright's secondary school curriculum class during the first semester of her junior year. The following semester Lucy accepted Ms. Carnahan's invitation to "give her a call and we'd go out to lunch." The lunch extended into a large part of the school day, during which Lucy was chauffeured around to three different middle schools as well as the district's high school. During those conversations, Ms. Carnahan advised Lucy to "student teach in the district in which I hope to be hired." Eventually Lucy elected to student teach at Jack Simper partly because of the "good things I heard about teaching science in that environment." Following that experience, "Peggy told me if I'd come and teach for her, she'd put me anywhere I wanted."

Although Lucy had no control over which school she would work in (she would have preferred to teach at the high school level and to work with another intern in the school), she accepted her first-year teaching assignment at Jack Simper Middle School. The school is a large, modern complex that already has outgrown its building. Lucy teaches five classes of regular and one class of basic sixth-grade science in one of the school's dozen "portable" classroom trailers. Her "basic students" are poor achievers because of low reading levels or behavioral/motivational problems. Three are repeating sixth grade and many of these students would be classified as "at risk." The other classes include a wide range of achievement levels but most students are hard-working, responsible, and eager. Most of Lucy's discipline problems resulted from this overenthusiasm: "Kids are so anxious to get in on the discussion they don't raise their hands."

LUCY, GENE, RITA, JAN, AND ROBERTO all received different job placements. As we highlight the induction experiences of these five beginning teachers, we discuss two fundamentally different induction models evidenced in their experiences.

SUPPORTING THE BEGINNING TEACHER: INDUCTING AND COLLABORATING

During the late 1980s, as reformers sought to connect universities with schools and to ease the entry of young professionals into teaching, *collaboration* and *induction* became educational buzzwords. Most states were implementing or planning to implement induction programs (Defino & Hoffman, 1984; Huling-Austin, 1990). The thrust of many of these programs was enhanced teaching performance through modification of teacher education programs and greater collaboration with school districts. At the end of the decade, Schlechty (1990) stressed the importance of such reform efforts:

If reform in teacher education is to be anything more than curriculum time-keeping and standard setting, it is essential that teachers learn to teach on the job. Any effort to restructure teacher education that does not involve a fundamental realignment of the relationship between public schools and schools of education is . . . misguided. (p. 24)

Many teacher induction programs, however, "seldom arose above the procedural compliance level" (Hoffman, Edwards, O'Neal, Barnes, & Paulissen, 1986), lacked any credible research or substantive evaluation component (Griffin, 1985; Kester & Marockie, 1987), and operated under a "deficit model" of induction, stressing management and instructional skills and emphasizing accountability (Fox & Singletary, 1986; Runyan, 1990). Not surprisingly, many such programs, particularly those developed as the result of legislative mandates, evidenced a narrow and utilitarian focus (Little, 1990), failed to address individual needs of women and minority first-year teachers (Lawson, 1992), and were often associated with the neo-Taylorian emphasis associated with industrial psychology in which teachers are seen in a technical rather than a professional role (Hall, 1982; Hargreaves & Dawe, 1986).

Consistent with the goals of most induction programs, many school districts and several states have mandated mentors: seasoned teachers who meet various career and psychosocial functions ranging from exposing novices to new opportunities and coaching them in the craft of teaching to serving as role model and counselor (Hawk & Robards, 1987; Kester & Marockie, 1987). While one would expect that to function effectively as role model, promoter of thinking skills, and demonstrator, the mentor would receive preparation in areas such as clinical supervision, subject-matter pedagogy, stages of teacher development, and teacher reflection (Feiman-Nemser & Parker, 1990; Livingston & Borko, 1989; Odell, 1990), these and other related areas are often absent in induction programs (Huling-Austin, 1992).

In a survey of 1,100 local school systems in 17 states, the ATE Commission on Teacher Induction (Kester & Marockie, 1987) found that 112 of these had some type of induction systems. Though induction programs ranged from a systematic three-year process to half-day orientation sessions at the beginning of the school year, few programs extended beyond the first year and most centered on a series of special in-service sessions and included frequent teacher performance evaluations; about one-half of the programs had a mentor component. Only a handful of school systems reduced the inductees' teaching load, gave more planning time, eliminated extracurricular activities, or collaborated with a college or consultant. Again, the primary focus of most induction programs was socialization, with emphasis on teaching assessment. A similar pattern appears in statewide teacher induction programs (Hawk & Robards, 1987).

As a proponent of the reform recommendations of the late 1980s, Don Wright saw support for first-year teachers as the core of the Bridenthal program. He comments: "During the next two years we will have a support system, one way or another, for them in each of the districts. There will likely be different models depending how the school district wants to work with us. What we do at King-Jackson, obviously, will be different than what we do at Justin High School."

For Wright, induction and collaboration were the cornerstones for this phase of the Bridenthal program. As the interns graduated in the late spring of 1988, however, Wright had yet to determine the exact nature of their two-year, school-based internship—the purpose of which had changed in Wright's mind:

> When we decided six years ago that we would keep in touch for two years, the principal reason was to see what unique problems first year teachers experience and what that had to do with retention. As it turns out, I am not sure that is the right question. . . . It's really tied into a longer term project of how we support first-year teachers and how do we make teaching more rewarding, how do we professionalize teaching, and how do we make it a career that people are willing to pursue.

As Gene, Rita, Lucy, Roberto, and Jan entered into the profession, Wright's assessment of the interns and Central's preparatory program, however, had not changed: "The interns are all unique characters. Some of them in their first year are like five-year veteran teachers because they are so mature and self-confident. Others will resemble first-year teachers. But, *all* will be better prepared—I hope they are; they should be; I think they will be."

Being an intern once again distinguished these high-ability first-year teachers. Not only would they participate in some, as yet to be defined, support program, but for some interns their status provided job opportunities or placements not usually garnered by a "wet behind the ears" first-year teacher. Their status also created a higher level of expectation. Roberto states:

> I would never have gotten this offer at this type of school had I not been in the Bridenthal program. There are five of us in Alliance Schools and then there's Gene who is teaching in the International Baccalaureate program at Justin. What first-year teachers would get those kinds of positions? Of course, people are expecting me and the other

interns to almost be like veteran teachers with a dedication, a drive, and a willingness to accept that kind of challenge.

When the interns began their first year of teaching, all entered differently supportive environments, although all were expected to participate in Central-sponsored seminars. The school-based induction programs experienced by Gene, Lucy, Jan, and Rita generally reflected the diversity of induction programs and their narrowness of goals discussed above. Roberto, working in a professional development school, was the exception. The most prevalent model experienced by these interns (like many other beginning teachers) was the industrial model.

Industrial Model of Induction

Similar to the industrial leadership model emphasized in the Bridenthal program that we discuss in Chapter 9 and detail elsewhere (Marshall, Otis-Wilborn, & Sears, 1991), this approach to induction is reminiscent of the early twentieth century managerial concepts embodied in Taylorism (Taylor, 1911). The central goal of Taylorism is efficiency, with emphasis on measurement and product output and an underlying assumption of the interchangeability of workers. Within this context, the purpose of induction is to effectively socialize novice workers into their production roles while assessing their performance vis-à-vis predetermined production goals. Examples of this model of induction can be found in the assignment and role of the interns' mentors, the role of the interns' supervisors, and the hidden curriculum socializing the interns into the school culture.

With the exception of Roberto, the interns found that their two-year school induction process stressed assessment and socialization. Activities to promote personal and professional well-being or to enhance the likelihood of retaining these novice teachers were largely absent. Induction activities encouraging pedagogical reflexivity, questioning authority, or challenging tradition were absent.

Gene, Rita, and Jan attended Justin's new teacher orientation at the beginning of the school year. Gene described this opening in-service session as "mostly useless. The administration had people get up and describe the forms, what a hall pass looks like and what a discipline notice looks like, to make sure that we all signed them in all the right places . . . that was kind of an insult to my intelligence."

All of the interns had specific suggestions for revising this in-service orientation. Rita thought that the beginning teachers should have been introduced to all the supervisors and administrators and told their duties, as well as receive a thorough briefing on discipline. Gene, in a characteristically lengthy lecture, observed:

> I would cut the induction program for new teachers to one half day.
> The current program used by Justin is a full day with a lunch break. I
> *do* think the lunch break is valuable. I *don't* think that a beginning
> teacher coming out of an induction program should feel six inches
> shorter from all the burden and weight they they're carrying on their
> shoulders . . . after the administration wastes time trying to induct
> them into a particular form of administrative minutia.

Justin's induction program was not limited to the opening in-service session. Each beginning teacher at Justin had an assigned "buddy" teacher to ease the transition to school life. As in many schools, the intention fell short of the reality. The teacher assigned to Gene was transferred at the last moment, leaving Gene "mentorless." Rita didn't talk much to her buddy teacher, preferring the company of a second-year Central graduate teaching across the hallway and a couple of second- or third-year teachers in classrooms nearby. "We've got a cluster of young teachers. We talked a lot yesterday about the stress and about controlling your classes or getting them to work and getting them to be quiet." Reflecting on the value of her district-assigned buddy teacher, Rita, echoing the recommendations of many induction experts, commented, "It would be better to have one person who has enough time and who has the same courses that you have. An experienced teacher is so far removed from the first-year experience that they forget."

Ironically, by their second year some of the interns, notably Gene and Rita, found themselves as assigned "mentors" for other beginning teachers. Gene, for example, became the buddy teacher for a woman teaching economics—a course that Gene's administration had hoped might keep him "out of the clouds." Being a mentor, perhaps, was more of an educational experience for Gene than for the first-year teacher:

> One thing I have noticed is that the beginning teachers get trial by fire
> when they're hired. For two of the classes she does not even have
> enough desks in her classroom. This first-year teacher is also involved
> in some extracurricular activities with the band. They pile these duties
> onto new teachers, and new teachers will stupidly agree to do them be
> cause they want to be hired. Then when they wisen up and they say
> that they don't want to do it anymore after two or three years, they
> give it to some other dumb, poor schlock who comes along. A first-

year teacher should not get that kind of treatment; not if the district wants the teacher to return.

While mentor programs are developed with the goals of "emotional support" and "instructional assistance," for Gene and Rita the school-based support system was less than helpful in these areas. Gene complains, "I don't feel like I get any professional support. I have needed emotional support and I have gotten it, but not from the school. I'm not getting support from the administration who asks me to be innovative and creative and then are unwilling to help me out. I'm not being supported from the rest of my colleagues." Rita's concern was instructional immediacy: "When I was student teaching if I had a problem, I could talk to my teacher right away about the problem and solve the problem for the next class period. But you don't have anybody to talk to that split second after it happens, and by the time you talk to them you've probably forgotten about the problem anyway." Some of the interns, like Rita, found support elsewhere. However, after two years of teaching Gene felt close to only one member of Justin's faculty—a geography teacher who taught across the hallway: "He and I are kind of birds of a feather. He's given me useful tips and when my backbone felt like it was going to turn to water he refortified my confidence. He's kind of a rabble rouser, I guess. The administration, I think, is really afraid of him, but he's a good teacher and they don't dare get rid of him."

Building collegial relationships within their schools proved difficult for some interns. Because the Bridenthal model did not highlight the importance of group cohesion, the interns left Central College with friendship groups identifiable largely by proximity (program colleagues, roommates, and frequent classmates), which may or may not have included their intern peers. Central did not encourage them to see the value of developing or nurturing new adult relationships among teacher colleagues. One result was that some interns, as new teachers, did not easily network among faculty—a major task for any educator seeking to be a "catalyst for change."

While Rita spent considerable time speaking with others on matters of concern to her ("I've talked to English people about discipline; I've talked to Science people. I'll talk to anybody who is willing to listen and give me advice"), when it came to participating in or establishing genuine support networks among her colleagues, she resisted: "I go to school, I stay in my room."

Gene's contemptuous feelings for his fellow teachers created barriers in developing networks of colleagues:

I've consulted people who were supposed to be master teachers in my department. They were some of the biggest jokes I've ever seen. They haven't done anything new in six or seven years. . . . I don't have colleagues that are great thinkers. There's nobody to bounce ideas off. Some of the other teachers are now using my material, but I have received nothing from them. They are deadbeats!

Mrs. Weller, though aware of Gene's concerns, sees much of the problem as stemming from his intellectualist orientation:

Gene's not the "party boy" kind of teacher. He doesn't go down to the lounge and chum around. He's very intense; he's very organized. He usually has his day scheduled at least a week in advance. He does talk with other teachers and other teachers talk with him, but Gene's rapport with teachers is based on his perception of how intellectual that teacher is. His rapport with this geography teacher is very good because he perceives him to be an intellectual that is on his plane. Gene doesn't have a lot of time for people that are not on his plane.

Along with their teacher buddies, Gene and Rita also worked with a supervising administrator. This person conducted several formal classroom assessments and served as a liaison between the beginning teacher and the school administration. Gene's immediate supervisor was Mrs. Weller. When asked who had provided him with support during his first year, he replied: "Well, theoretically it was supposed to be the vice-principal for curriculum, Ms. Weller, but she hasn't been all that much help. I find her most often justifying the position of the counselors or the administration rather than trying to give me a hand in doing what I'm trying to do." Gene had few good things to say about his administration throughout his tenure at Justin: "I think there is something that administrators inherit. It's a disease that deprives them of their spine. They just turn into a jellyfish right there in front of the parent."

Prior to first-year teaching, Rita also wondered about administrative support: "I don't know how the administration is going to support me, the beginning teacher. Sometimes they are more supportive of beginning teachers, sometimes they are not. I don't want to become an isolated teacher—that's one of my greatest fears." Later, after noting how comfortable she felt knowing that she could approach any of her administrators with a teaching concern, she conceded: "But really I don't. I just concentrate on teaching and what I have to teach." Although Rita received support from her department head, "At times I didn't particularly care for her advice."

In addition to providing informal advice, a major responsibility of educational supervisors such as Mrs. Weller and Joan Lillian was to formally assess the beginning teachers' teaching performance on the basis of several scheduled and unscheduled classroom visits. All the interns were subject to the statewide assessment procedures mandated legislatively. This highly structured observational protocol, discussed in Chapter 10, appraises teaching performance in five domains: instructional strategies, classroom management, presentation of subject matter, learning environment, and professional growth. Within each of these domains, supervisors score teachers according to evidence of specific behaviors ranging from soliciting student participation and reinforcing correct responses to providing clear administrative directions and beginning the lesson with an appropriate introduction. Teachers who evidence mastery in any subdomain receive "exceptional quality" (EQ) points.

While the specific evaluations from supervisors and our own independent evaluator will be discussed in Chapter 10, it is important to note how this system of assessment inducted these interns into the realities of classroom teaching. Gene remarked: "I don't really like the EQ game. It is an absurd way to measure something that's very difficult to measure: *my* teaching style. They have virtually no meaning. The supervisor comes in, I get the evaluations two weeks later after I've all but forgotten what the lesson was. If they write anything it's usually nothing positive." Rita cynically declares, "It's all a staged game when it comes down to the evaluation, to me. You learned what they're looking for." Again, Roberto is the exception. While he understands how some teachers get so defensive and believes that the integrity of the system relies largely on the evaluator, he was especially comfortable when Ms. Lillian evaluated him, given his respect for her.

In addition to the assessment component, the socialization process pervaded the life of these beginning teachers. Suggestions and recommendations for classroom practice often moved beyond pedagogical issues. In a large school such as Justin, the emphasis was on system maintenance—keep the machine running as smoothly as possible. Various rigid structural components were integral facts of organizational life: grading standards; criteria for entering and exiting academic tracks; standard operating procedures defining student-teacher-administrator relationships, expectations, and behaviors. These structural components—not the persons who ostensibly benefit from the structure—delineated the parameters of everyday school life. During their first year of teaching, each intern felt this enculturation process.

Rita discovered the importance of unambiguous grading when she gave a student 69 percent on his report card:

My department head asked, "How good of a teacher are you? What qualified you to give him a 69 percent? Couldn't that have been one question on a single test that he might have messed up on?" Well, I didn't think that was true. One test question could not raise or lower a kid's overall grade. She just said, "Nobody will give a 69 percent! If he is gonna fail, lower it. Kids can handle 68 percent; parents can handle that." Well, I had a real problem with that and so I wrote my decision on a piece of paper justifying how I came up with 68.9 percent. Maybe I should have given him a 68 percent.

Jan found out about the hidden rule of student discipline, soon becoming frustrated with the need to explain her reasoning each time she "wrote up" a student and the reluctance of the administration to back her up. She finally got "to the point where I don't even want to write a kid up. I haven't. I have only written up kids if its for something unrelated to me like if the kid has skipped out. This is fine with the administration. They certainly don't want them down there."

Gene resents being "strictly controlled in my subject matter by the administration." In one case, his supervisor told him to remove Renaissance reproductions from his bulletin board because of the nudity. On this issue, he resisted, noting its relationship to the college-level course he was teaching and declaring, "I'm not going to be neutered by this administration!"

Formal and informal induction programs do "neuter teachers" (Frymier, 1987) by socializing them into the bureaucratic mentality of a school system, blunting enthusiasm, stifling creativity, and constraining change. They seldom meet the developmental needs of young adults nor do they seek to transform schools by encouraging any professional action that challenges the culture of authority and conformity.

Human Relations Model of Induction

Another, often advocated but seldom implemented, model of induction is rooted in human relations. Like induction programs of past generations, this model, most recently espoused by a variety of educators (e.g., Fox & Singletary, 1986; Lawson, 1992; Runyan, 1990), articulates a developmental base; teaching authority in this orientation is person-oriented and needs-centered. In a client-practitioner relationship, concerns of management, control, and discipline are means to a larger end: the maximizing of opportunities for personal freedom within an interdependent schooling community. A human relations–oriented induction model places much less emphasis on performance assessment and greater emphasis on collaborative teaching and learning models to develop the interns as teaching professionals. The only intern to experience a version of this model, however, was Roberto.

Although Roberto laments in his first teaching journal about "all the days of in-services for every reason imaginable giving me a taste of bureaucracy," unlike the other interns, Roberto ended his initial in-service induction program "motivated." Describing the school's principal and counselor as wonderful and the teachers as "top guns" sharing a similar sense of mission and commitment, Roberto felt that these sessions clearly affected his success as a new teacher. "We're talking about teachers who were sharing from the very start the same mission, the same goal. I mean, we met . . . before school started and built together. . . . We knew what we wanted; we were all working for the same kinds of things."

Although Roberto felt overwhelmed with "district things" to the point where he occasionally lost control of his lesson planning, within the school he valued the sense of community and the sharing of authority evidenced at King-Jackson: "Ms. Lillian is a tough, respectful person who expects a lot and gets it because all the teachers there were hand-picked." Even in the midst of his second year, Roberto expresses amazement as he watches this group of hand-picked professionals with strong ideas and personalities working together. "She doesn't always get what she wants. . . . "

Unlike Rita and Gene, Roberto felt great support from his colleagues, especially his assigned mentor and his fifth-grade chairperson, Judy Haley. At the start of his first year, the fifth grade had only two teachers, Roberto and Judy—a "very nurturing, very calm, caring person" who, according to Joan Lillian, worked closely with Roberto all year.

In Gene's second year of teaching, Judy assumed other teaching responsibilities at King-Jackson. His new colleague and informal mentor in fifth grade was a woman with 28 years of experience, Peggy Justice: "a real dynamic lady. She's real neat and that's going to introduce me to a whole different perspective on things." Mrs. Justice was quite different from Judy Haley. Peggy's philosophy, according to Lillian, was "TNKB—Take Names and Kick Butt. Roberto needed that. He needed somebody to help with classroom management. This year his class is very much on task and academically oriented all the time. They don't waste time on classroom management."

During both years, Roberto—the only male teacher at an elementary professional development school—received extraordinary support on a personal as well as professional level. The faculty, Lillian confesses, "refers to Roberto as 'our baby.' When he sneezes, 20 women say 'Have you gone to a doctor?' We just tease him to death."

Unlike the Justin interns, Roberto and the other King-Jackson interns received greater support from the Central faculty. At this Alliance School, Wright's presence was keenly felt by these interns. Roberto relates:

> I know that some way or another Dr. Wright is going to hear about it or someone's going to mention something about how I'm doing in teaching. The professors are always around King-Jackson, and people will talk and I would definitely want them to say good things about me. It's like parents . . . the way you behave as a child kind of reflects back on your parents.

Returning to Central

As noted earlier, one element of the Bridenthal program was a $2,000 stipend for each of the interns' first two years of teaching. Although some of the interns viewed these stipends simply as salary supplements, for Wright they were compensation for additional, though as yet mostly unarticulated, induction-type activities—particularly seminars similar to those the interns attended in their first year at Central. These seminars reflected Wright's preference for an emergent design relying on the interest of the interns to guide his sessions. Given his close personal relationship with the interns and his human relations skills, these seminars had great potential as a human relations induction program—in sharp contrast to the industrial model experienced by most of the interns.

Within this orientation, induction activities are facilitative. Mentors collaborate with the interns in carrying out many of the day-to-day teaching responsibilities, and university faculty assist the interns as they pass through predictable developmental stages. In this model, the role of mentor would not be to simply comply with state- or district-mandated induction, but to provide personal as well as professional support. The role of university faculty would be to serve as a liaison between the school and the college, bridging the conceptual with the practical. Here, the developmental concerns expressed by Jan, Gene, Rita, and Lucy, detailed in Chapter 9, would be center stage.

For the interns, professional concerns included the time-honored issues of beginning teachers: classroom management, administrative paperwork, parental communication, grading, and appropriate instructional materials. Personal concerns generally centered on the need for encouragement and support, reflecting doubts about self-confidence and fears of isolation.

Rita's personal concerns centered on not having "enough self-confidence" and the technical aspects of teaching. She conceded, "I need a lot of guidance on controlling my classes. Getting them to work, not necessarily having total control over them, to make it more enjoyable so it doesn't create an atmosphere for discontent and discipline problems." Paperwork also created stress for Rita. "I don't have enough time to do my preparations and do all the paperwork that's involved in teaching." There was also the lack of "materials to pull from to teach for the next day so you're preparing the night before along with grading papers." Finally, the ability to meet individualized needs: "How are they going to react? What problems are they going to run into on a certain topic?"

Gene yearned for intellectual stimulation. Reflecting on the ineffectiveness of the internship seminars, he suggested that the goal of retention could have been enhanced "through maintaining that sense of community where we could hash out some of our problems or get the intellectual stimulation that we're lacking from our colleagues at schools." The intellectual wasteland that Gene found himself in was never far from the surface of his concerns:

> I've seen a lot of my intellectual skills deteriorate in the setting that I'm in. I don't have colleagues that are great thinkers and there's nobody to bounce ideas off. Now, I have lots of people telling me I'm wrong in paperwork. But they don't broaden my own education which is still very important to me. So, I have a harder time now challenging my students to be the best in their scholarly endeavors when I don't feel that I am doing that myself.

Unlike the others, Roberto does not feel like a cog in the organizational bureaucracy, although he questions whether the school district is concerned with his or his students' needs. He only agrees mildly that his work allows him to be creative and finds the technical aspect of paperwork bothersome: "The daily kind of stuff. If you want to get a kid into tutoring it's four copies, and they have to be signed by four different people."

Jan's concerns often revolved around the personal: the need for sleep, time for herself and with her fiancé. Much of this stemmed from her spending six days a week on school work, particularly grading papers and preparing for class. Jan is most concerned about the mismatch between the content that she received in her liberal arts education, with particular emphasis on twentieth century U.S. history, and her teaching areas.

Aside from a general unease about classroom management, Lucy was most concerned about being a positive force within her school, not necessarily because she went through the Bridenthal program but because she wants her ideas to affect others. Veteran teachers, she notes, "need some idealism to rub off on them; some fresh ways to do things. Maybe it's because of the person I am. Maybe it has nothing to do with the fact that

I'm young. Maybe I'll always be this way—a pioneer or someone that wants to make a difference."

All of these interns, however, understood their job as primarily one of getting students to learn material and understand it well enough to pass. These former "good students," however, saw much of what teaching entails, from classroom management to parental involvement, as being inevitably tied to their students' academic success. They anguished over their responsibilities from differing personal vantage points: Gene worrying about the numbing of his intellect, Rita concerned with her physical stature, Lucy from the perspective of single mother, Jan planning her wedding and facing the impending transfer of her husband-to-be to another city, Roberto deeply conscious of *la raza*.

The induction procedures of schools employing interns, with the exception of Roberto's school-based assistance, did little to address these developmental needs. As a beginning teacher, Roberto experienced problems relating to classroom management and parental communication. By the winter of his second year, however, he had received the support necessary to resolve them. Excited about "a lot of good parent involvement" he garnered during the fall term with parents coming in to see him and his writing and calling them, Roberto attributes it to the "homey" feeling that his school represents, the school parental involvement committees, funded in part by the Bridenthal Foundation through its alliance with Central, and the ideas he received from his principal following her formal teaching evaluation.

While the interns' induction programs varied, Wright's fundamental induction goal did not: to "provide an umbrella of support services for every intern in order to ensure that teaching would be a career that people are willing to pursue." Rita described the initial seminars as opportunities for the interns to talk about the issues they face and the problems or joys that they experience. These sessions resembled a "rap session. It's a stress relief . . . that gives each other support. Most of the time Dr. Wright will just sit back and let us talk. . . . I feel a closeness to him and it's just . . . well, his support means a lot—or at least his listening ear means a lot. Even though he might not have much to say, he's a very important figure in my life."

While the interns welcomed these sessions at the beginning, there were few occasions where these sessions went beyond sharing one another's woes or pressing the comfortable ear of Dr. Wright. As Rita observed, "A lot of times it's encouraging because other students have the same problem or problems that are much more difficult than yourself. And that's kind of sad to say but misery loves company." Lucy asserted, "They could have been better, but some of the interns acted like the meetings were a hassle or an intrusion or just one other responsibility that they didn't want to deal with."

Jan was one such intern. Quickly, she grew weary of these "gripe" sessions. "I can't agree with these interns who are doing all the speaking. But I never say anything. That's always been a problem for me, how negative some people are."

The interns seldom communicated with one another beyond the occasionally scheduled seminar, and there were no structured activities designed to provide professional assistance to the interns about their concerns. By the end of the first year, interest in the seminars waned; at the final meeting, fewer than one-third of the interns attended. "I could only assume that we needed it less then or maybe we'd already gone our separate ways," notes Gene.

Wright's second-year seminar agenda was more ambitious. In their September meeting, Wright talked about "keeping us together every single month with some kind of get-together, formal or informal." Roberto also pointed out that the second-year meetings were more focused, although they still tended to resemble a "social gathering" more than any type of systematic support service. As the seminars were interspersed with social festivities such as a pre-Christmas function and occasional visits with prospective Central teachers or educational groups, the dominant format continued to be the informal rap session. By the end of the second year, even the most ardent supporter of Wright could find little of value in the Central-sponsored seminars as interest again waned and attendance lapsed.

Beyond the seminars, Central faculty occasionally visited the interns. However, with the exception of the Alliance Schools, these visits were brief and generally uneventful. Gene declares, "I really haven't got much help from anyone. Dr. Carol dropped by one time, but she wasn't very helpful; she told me that I had a nice decoration in my room. And, to this day Dr. Wright has still not seen me teach." Rita recalls receiving suggestions from Dr. Carol about a discipline problem, which consisted of "(1) separate them, (2) call their parents, (3) just try different ways, (4) just say, 'You're going to have a quiz at the beginning of every class period unless you are quiet and listen to what I have to say.'"

At the college level, Wright's reform-based induction model was more emergent than predetermined in form. Certainly, the interns never knew from one month to the next what to expect. The technical force evidenced in many of the school-based induction models, emphasizing a predetermined structure and the development of competencies directly related to day-to-day classroom performance, was absent. In the end, the program simply consisted of a series of disconnected seminars often unrelated to the interns' teaching concerns with a sprinkling of high-visibility events. The piecemeal nature of the program did not provide interns the opportunities to build and develop understandings about schools, teaching, or leadership based on their accumulated school-based experiences and cumulative knowledge.

THOUGH THE INDUCTION PROGRAMS varied from school to school, with the exception of Roberto's Alliance School placement, the emphasis was on socialization and assessment. This industrial model of induction is clearly evident in the type of mentors assigned to each intern, the roles assumed by the interns' supervisors, and the hidden curriculum that socialized them into the culture of the school. Although Roberto's induction experience was more akin to a human relations model, he too faced the structural constraints of state-mandated student testing and teacher performance evaluation. As we detail in the next chapter, the teaching environments at Justin, Jack Simper, and King-Jackson coupled with legislative and district-mandated reforms profoundly affected how each intern experienced, interpreted, and responded to day-to-day classroom struggles between the work they were prepared to do as Central graduates and Bridenthal Interns and the job they were expected to do as beginning teachers and fledgling professionals.

CHAPTER 9

Renewing the Vows: Autonomy, Stratification, and Cultural Change

Much of the wisdom found in recent educational reform proposals stems from their recognition that those who would change teachers must reshape the culture(s) of teaching, and that to accomplish this, the culture(s) of schools must be altered as well. Yet so much of the analysis underlying these reports, while necessarily tying the professionalization of teaching to professionalizing, as well, the places where teachers work, tends to dwell on behavioral and structural manipulations to bring about such cultural change. In this chapter we follow the interns through their first two years of teaching while exploring the ideas of autonomy and career stratification. We suggest in this chapter that such behavioral and structural changes will more often than not fall far short of enhancing teachers' professional culture.

GOING TO WORK, DOING THE JOB

In their exhaustive review of the cultures of teaching, Feiman-Nemser and Floden (1986) state: "Teaching cultures are embodied in the work-related beliefs and knowledge teachers share—beliefs about appropriate ways of acting on the job and rewarding aspects of teaching, and knowledge that enables teachers to do their work" (p. 508). These various cultures receive their shape and meaning from (and help to shape the meanings of) the interactions of three contexts: classrooms, schools (institutions), and larger social contexts (neighborhoods, cities, states, etc.). These contexts of teaching become important as we look at the emphasis each has in affecting *teaching* cultures. For example, we consider the classroom context when we think about teachers' practical knowledge and their relationships with

182

students; issues related to teachers' extrinsic rewards and interactions with others are typically raised in the context of the institution; and questions of image, status, and the gendered nature of teaching seem best framed within the larger social contexts (Feiman-Nemser & Floden, 1986). Understanding these multiple contexts and their various arenas of focus helps us to better understand and effect cultural change in teaching and schooling. New teachers develop their understandings of teaching cultures over long periods of time, beginning with their first contact with "a teacher." However, their most intense enculturation process occurs during the early years of teaching.

Much of the conflict new teachers confront lies between the work they're prepared to do and the job they're expected to do:

> The *work* of teaching includes all those aspects directly related to the realization of educational goals: motivating students, getting to know them as individuals, assessing their understanding. The *job* of teaching is concerned with the realization of organizational or bureaucratic goals: maintaining order in classrooms and corridors, keeping students busy, categorizing students so that they can be processed by the administrative machinery. (Feiman-Nemser & Floden, 1986, p. 517; emphasis added)

Though cultures both shape and are shaped by their contexts, teaching culture is disproportionately shaped by the culture of its institution (schools) in this exchange. Depersonalized institutional and bureaucratic goals and standards tend in time to change teachers' work to better fit their jobs. It takes an awfully strong internal vision to successfully resist the myriad forces at work to reshape one's ideas of the work of teaching. Roberto seems to have had such strength during his baptismal teaching year.

To describe Roberto as child-focused is an understatement. He recognizes himself as primarily a sensitive, thinking person whose greatest fear as a teacher is that he might "harm a child's life or teach them something in the wrong manner." For Roberto, success will be judged by students who might someday return and tell him, "Hey, I remember you when you were my fifth-grade teacher." He continues, "I want to be able to see that kind of success and really know that I've positively influenced a child's life and my own life and that I've improved my own teaching and my profession and what I believe in. . . . I hold myself accountable for what my kids learn and do not learn."

Even his talk of classroom management and discipline reflects this emphasis on human interaction and responsibility. Though King-Jackson has a schoolwide discipline program, Roberto gives it little thought. He establishes a good rapport with parents and describes them as "real supportive." At various points throughout his first teaching year he reports no discipline problems and can't recall ever sending students to the principal's office. Though Roberto describes himself as demanding and holding high expectations for students, he quickly adds, "I'm not abusive. The kids know when I'm angry, and I don't yell." Yet Roberto does not attribute his enviably "trouble-free" environment to his deeply held human values or to his never-ending efforts to establish a collectively generated and maintained family atmosphere in his classroom. Instead, he learns that as long as he has his "lessons done in such a manner that we can move smoothly from one thing to another" he'll never "lose them" to discipline problems.

Roberto fully recognizes that he is becoming the sort of teacher he had always imagined he would (a "dream come true") and believes that this development has a good deal to do with his colleagues and with working in an Alliance School, where everyone shares the same mission and commitment. At King-Jackson, teachers work in teams, and team leaders work closely with their principal, Ms. Lillian, "a tough, respectful person who expects a lot and gets it because all the teachers there were hand-picked." He elaborates at year's end: "But she was always very careful about checking in on us and seeing that we were having a good year, also."

"Having a good year," Roberto quickly learns, has more to do with his job than with his work. In his classroom Roberto appears anything but new to the ranks. He spends most of the day in motion, visiting various small groups of students scattered throughout the room. He is always experimenting with seating arrangements and dreaming up new ideas for presenting material. He and his charges laugh together often. Roberto is a confident teacher, his greatest worries resulting from other responsibilities.

By October he finds himself swamped with administrative paperwork and grading. King-Jackson teachers attend "a lot of meetings," and Roberto feels constantly overwhelmed with "district things." Though he sees all of these additional tasks as "stuff that really has to be done," he finds them quite "time consuming, and it doesn't always free you up to want to do other things. . . . You're always kind of in a rush trying to put things together, hoping that you'll find the time and get yourself ahead." What he's constantly trying to get ahead of is lesson planning, and he eventually admits: "That's what I've been trying to work out; how much time am I willing to spend. How much time should I spend?"

As a fifth-grade teacher, Roberto must administer the state achievement exams. He recalls being "blind-sided" when, shortly after the December/January holiday break, the teachers begin talking about the tests, which students at several grade levels (including fifth) take each spring. The talk continues over the following months as colleagues strategize and eventually practice for the tests with their students.

This "testing atmosphere" begins to destroy even the environment within Roberto's classroom. He knows his students and knows, too, that the state test scores are "used to evaluate their and my success or failure in the teaching-learning process." He becomes physically affected as he adjusts his teaching efforts to prepare students for a test he knows they will not do well on. His teaching hardens, and he even puts his desks in rows as the test date nears. "I lost confidence in myself," he confesses.

But the testing date passes and Roberto concludes the year in a more upbeat mood, though tired "physically and emotionally. It was the most challenging, demanding and fun time I ever had in my life." Acknowledged at a superintendent's breakfast for one of his innovative teaching ideas (he later wrote about and published this idea in a regional teaching magazine), Roberto responds to a question about his teaching skills by noting his "natural need for empathy, to make learning important and safe, and somehow a part of real life. Are these teaching skills? I'm not sure. All I know is that my feeling of success stems from these aspects." Given the tears and hugs in his room on the last day of school, he believes that the students saw it as a successful year, too.

CULTURAL ASPECTS OF TEACHER REFORM

Each of the major reform reports makes clear that changing the professional nature of teaching will require changes within the bureaucracies of schools. What they may underplay is the embedded nature of the cultures of teaching and schools. As Susan Florio-Ruane (1989) notes: "Cultural knowledge includes propositions, procedures, beliefs, values, and history. While rarely taught directly, this knowledge is largely acquired by its members' participation in the activities comprising everyday life within a social group. . . . [This] knowledge regulates our communication and underlies our social practices" (p. 163). While changes in practice and structure may be important beginning steps toward deep and lasting cultural change, they stand little chance of survival within cultural contexts whose histories, existing beliefs, and values are not addressed with equal and simultaneous attention.

Two areas of emphasis in recent reform proposals are outlined below and analyzed within the context of the cultures of teaching and schools: teaching autonomy and professional stratification. Reformers see both of these as requisite in their efforts to professionalize teaching.

Autonomy: The Behavior of Reform

We can understand professional autonomy as the distance from bureaucracy—that is, teachers' freedom and ability to implement the knowledge and skills they've learned from training and experience (Macklin, 1981). Autonomy is critical to teacher professionalism, and good teachers have always taught professionally when allowed to do so (Wise, 1989).

Teacher autonomy encompasses most aspects of teaching and is manifested through both group (or national) autonomy and individual (or local) autonomy. We will follow the agenda of the reform reports and look, here, only at teachers' individual or local autonomy.

Focused primarily on the freedom of teachers to make decisions on matters that directly affect them, local autonomy is typically evidenced in the desire for shared decision making regarding choice of curriculum, choice of teaching methods, and the right of teachers to judge their own achievement as well as that of their students (Cattell, 1932; Ornstein, 1981; Wise, 1989, 1990). When restricted to discussions of teaching cultures, individual teacher autonomy is often thought to be a strong and appealing aspect of teachers' work (the much-touted "behind-closed-doors freedom"). When expanded to include the institutional and larger social contexts, however, the question of autonomy as a cultural aspect of teaching receives a different hearing.

Work-Related Autonomy. The fifth goal of the Holmes Group (1986) reads as follows: "*To make schools better places for teachers to work, and to learn.* This will require less bureaucracy, more professional autonomy, and more leadership for teachers" (p. 4). Noting several institutional aspects (structures, working conditions, and division of authority) that "are all seriously out of step with the requirements of the new professional," the authors acknowledge that "if the construction of a genuine profession of teaching is to succeed, schools will have to change" (p. 67).

Within their vision, new, more professional teachers would enjoy various "degrees of autonomy" relative to the various categories the Holmes Group (1986) would establish, though all teachers, regardless of their status or label, would be competent.

> Central to [our] vision are competent teachers empowered to make principled judgments and decisions on their students' behalf. They possess broad and deep understanding of children, the subjects they teach, the nature of learning and schooling, and the world around them. They exemplify the critical thinking they strive to develop in students, combining tough-minded instruction with a penchant for inquiry. (pp. 28–29)

Clearly, professional autonomy for the Holmes Group rests squarely within the classroom as it pertains exclusively to the work of teaching. The report continues:

For competent professionals, students' learning is the *sine qua non* of teaching and schooling. . . . Such professionals are deeply concerned by mounting evidence that *many of this country's teachers act as educational functionaries, faithfully but mindlessly following prescriptions about what and how to teach.* . . . Truly competent teachers find it as important to discover ways of helping those who find learning difficult and frustrating as they do helping those students more like themselves, who find school learning easy and rewarding. (pp. 29–30; emphasis added)

Graduated from Central as one of the hand-picked Bridenthal Interns, Jan was anxious to begin work as a teacher—work she'd anticipated since childhood. After two months, Jan identifies students as the most enjoyable aspect of her work. "They're all so different," she notes, meaning different from her when she was in high school. Jan had an easy time in high school, never studying much to do well. Her Justin students do have to work hard and study, and they don't "grasp information right away." So Jan takes their feedback to heart when they tell her, "We don't really learn, we don't really grasp it as well when you do *that*. But when you've done *this*, it's really helped us a lot."

Certainly, her strong desire to help students learn illustrates Jan's fit with the Holmes Group's image of a competent, autonomous teacher. She quickly learns that requiring students to take notes as she explains content (Jan's own preferred learning pattern) results in information that goes "right through them." Eventually, she develops a routine whereby everyone writes a series of definitions first, followed by Jan's lecture—during which she highlights definitions at appropriate points. This way, "they get all their notes done at first and then we spend time talking about it." Additionally, she settles into using a good many worksheets and giving frequent quizzes as a way to keep students on task. Consequently, she finds herself "grading papers" almost every night and constantly trying to keep up with this chore. Free to do as she pleases, Jan wishes she knew "20 different ways to get a point across."

On the other hand, the benefits of support and collegiality delight Jan. She speaks glowingly of her "buddy teacher" (assigned by the department) and her department head, noting their invaluable aid during the opening weeks of school: "I felt a little lost at the beginning but I figured out pretty quick that if I wanted to know what was going on I had to ask. . . . The other teachers don't know if you need help unless you tell them you do." She notices early that the American history faculty seems "more communicative" than those who teach world history—a problem for Jan, who feels woefully underprepared and entirely uncomfortable teaching the latter. After one semester, world history is removed from Jan's teaching schedule (to her relief) and replaced with an additional American history class.

Jan believes that experience is what makes a good teacher, and as the year wears on her experience begins to shape her understanding of the work and the job of teaching. Calling the year "a tremendous learning experience," she notes how difficult it is making history relevant for students. She learns much about the system at Justin (in terms of grading policies and failure rates, for example) and the importance of deciding "what to teach." Autonomy notwithstanding, Jan's colleagues encourage her to focus on teaching basic facts (because students might remember these while forgetting the rest of the information) and even help her select the "right" facts to teach. Instruction is driven by end-of-year "exit exams," and admonitions such as "they'll *definitely* be asked this" direct Jan's decisions. Rather than wishing for greater autonomy, she ends the year wanting more "tricks of the trade" to help her get this basic, test-specific information across to her students.

Jan's most apparent shift in understanding teaching is evident in ways she now talks about students. When asked to elaborate on the importance of knowing "about the students that you would be teaching," Jan offers the following explanation: "Some of the things that I think would help me would be to know . . . if they're going to be highly motivated . . . or completely unmotivated. Another thing that is very important to know or to have some sort of background with is some discipline program that really works."

Memories of students as motivational challenges allow Jan to admit that sometimes students drive her crazy and make her life miserable. Admittedly "terrified" of parents, she has little contact with them about discipline problems. Classroom management quickly becomes inseparable from teaching. Jan just can't figure out what to do when teaching/disciplining: "I do a lot of just recall, which is terrible and I hate it, but a lot of times it's the only thing . . . that will work with those crazy kids because they just refuse to think a lot of times. . . . I get so frustrated but after a point . . . I give up." After workshop training during the year on critical-thinking skills and higher-order questioning, Jan likes even less the fact that she has students "regurgitating history facts," but believes they can handle little else. She describes herself, by year's end, as having been in a constant battle with students and hoping that they learned critical thinking in another class. Despite her confession that she was often but one step ahead of the students in terms of their reading assignments, Jan feels that her most effective professional trait is her knack for "getting across information to my students" and notes pleasure with their district test scores.

Although "nothing was really particularly a breeze" about her first year, Jan calls it "pretty great" overall. Disregarding "inept" administrators, she feels fortunate to have the colleagues she does: "I just really lucked out in getting the people that I had to work with in my department, because they were so helpful and very supportive of me." Jan feels some confidence with a year's experience behind her.

Job-Related Autonomy. In its report, the National Commission for Excellence in Teacher Education (NCETE) (1985) comes at teacher autonomy in a manner different from that of the Holmes Group, though with no more specificity. For the NCETE and Jan, autonomy joins salary, status, and working environments, among other factors, as "conditions in schools" that "work against lifelong commitment to teaching as a career" (p. 20). Highlighting the distinction between the job and the work of teaching, the group recommends that "teachers' responsibilities and working conditions should be commensurate with the requirements of the job." They continue: "Teachers have limited autonomy and decision-making authority to produce the kinds of *services that students need*" (emphasis added). Not only do most teachers lack phones, offices, or secretarial support; some don't have chalk, books, or toilet paper in the bathrooms. In short, the sort of autonomy the NCETE refers to deals directly with "the physical and professional circumstances in which teachers work" (p. 21).

To change teachers' job-related autonomy requires change by others within the institution, including principals, who, along with school superintendents, "are responsible for developing and promoting the environment for professional growth of teachers and for establishing a collegial environment in which teachers are viewed as partners in efforts to improve instruction" (National Commission for Excellence in Teacher Education, 1985, p. 21). Like the Holmes Group, the NCETE points out that "teaching must be viewed as a teacher's primary responsibility," adding that "other activities should be assigned to qualified support personnel." Unlike the Holmes vision, however, the NCETE future is one in which "teachers' participation in making decisions for their schools also should be expanded, and the overall teaching conditions should be significantly improved" (p. 21).

Differing from its Holmes and NCETE peers, the Carnegie Task Force on Teaching as a Profession (1986) gives considerable attention to teacher autonomy from the perspective of teachers' work and jobs. This report places teacher autonomy squarely in relationship to classroom teaching— what it calls "the crucial function of the teacher." It assumes, as did the NCETE group, that teachers must be continuous learners who, as the Holmes Group notes, make critical independent judgments. At the same time, the Carnegie group severely criticizes the bureaucracy that controls how the job of teaching is done:

Teachers work in an environment suffused with bureaucracy. Rules made by others govern their behavior at every turn. . . . The text and the scope-and-sequence of the curriculum define in detail what they are supposed to teach. Decisions made by curriculum supervisors, teacher training experts, outside consultants and authors of teachers' guides determine how a teacher is to teach. Teachers who choose to work together as professional colleagues must constantly fight the natural tendencies of a system based on very different principles. (p. 39)

The Carnegie group does not in the end suggest expanding teachers' autonomy to include issues shaping their job (institutional) environment except to the extent that these can be understood in relationship to their work (classroom) environment. With this enhanced accountability comes concomitant responsibility:

Teachers should be provided with the discretion and autonomy that are hallmarks of professional work. State and local governments should set clear goals for schools and greatly reduce bureaucratic regulation of school processes. Teachers should participate in the setting of goals for their school and be accountable for achieving agreed upon standards of performance. (p. 56)

Two points deserve note. First, much of this exercised autonomy will be "guided" by colleagues designated "Lead Teachers" (a point we will discuss further in the next section). Second, teachers' professional autonomy, as understood in the Carnegie proposal, begins and ends at the institutional door:

Within the context of a limited set of clear goals for students set by state and local policy makers, teachers, working together, must be free to exercise their professional judgment as to the best way to achieve these goals. This means the ability to make—or at least to strongly influence—decisions concerning such things as the materials and instructional methods to be used, the staffing structure to be employed, the organization of the school day, the assignment of students, the consultants to be used, and the allocation of resources available to the school. . . . This autonomy will work only if the school staff work collaboratively, taking collective responsibility for student progress. (p. 58; emphasis added)

In sum, reform-related autonomy seems to be most clearly understood as teachers' professional freedom (and responsibility) to make work-related decisions that distance institutional bureaucracy from the classroom. And while these reforms urge important changes within the bureaucracy itself (many of which address management/administrative practices), only the

NCETE suggests that teacher autonomy include the broader context of "working conditions."

Slightly more than four years after graduating from Justin High School, Rita returns to join the faculty there. Her year begins badly: "You were a student for 16 years of your life, and now you're standing at the door greeting your students, and you're sort of dumbfounded. What do I say? You stand up there, and they're all looking at you. They don't want to be there, they're just like, 'Oh, Okay.'" Within weeks Rita is already awaiting next year, when she'll have experience in beginning the year, establishing discipline, and contacting parents with problems. By the time the first six-week grading period arrives, Rita characterizes teaching as "a 24-hour job for me."

Autonomy, whether confined to classroom decisions or encouraged in the broader, job-related sense, is a prerequisite for professional practice. Yet Rita's worries as a rookie teacher have little to do with issues regarding the nature or extent of her autonomy: She quickly realizes that she doesn't actually know how to teach, in general, or teach Algebra I or Informal Geometry, in particular. (Throughout her first year she speaks little of her sophomore geometry class, in large measure because this is her "best" class, with students who are more mature and successful.) She spends nearly 10 hours a day at school, then comes home to briefly relax before tackling grading and the next day's plans. Rita sees early in the year that she's "not as prepared as I'd like to be. I don't have enough self-confidence." She is shocked to learn that a new student can be assigned to any of her classes on any day of the week, requiring Rita to determine whether the student belongs in her class (all of Rita's algebra students are tracked) or in another one. For this rookie teacher, who is so unsure of what she's doing anyway, such job-related responsibilities create major hurdles.

One of the more troubling of teaching's mysteries is knowing what students can "handle." Rita understands that good teaching includes "knowing what to expect from my kids, knowing how they're going to react . . . [or] think, or the problems they're going to run into on a certain topic." No less important is "knowing how high I can set my expectations, because you want to have high expectations." Yet she knows *none* of this. What she does know is that her algebra students find her classes frustrating, that she teaches mostly through lectures, and that she's begun to question her expectations of students.

High standards and expectations enabled Rita to graduate second in her class from Justin, to be recruited into the Bridenthal Internship program, to receive additional scholarships while at Central, and to complete a mathematics major and almost complete a science major. Rita's own standards and expectations are what allow her to continue to feel different—

special. Yet despite her individual freedom to set academic standards within her classroom, she sees this specialness endangered as she encounters problems with student motivation and discipline—problems that, for example, lead her to decide not to introduce an innovative unit to her students and not to continue trying to employ more cooperative strategies in her teaching.

She also learns that with most students, one call to their parent(s) will result in changed behavior and greater respect in the classroom, though she is amazed to find that for other students, calling their sports coaches works even better. "And it's kind of sad that the kids respect their coach but they can't respect their teacher in the classroom." By mid-year Rita describes her typical handling of discipline problems as follows: "I've had a lot of kids smart off to me. So I would take them out in the hall and say, 'I am the teacher here. I am older than you. I am certified to teach this. I do not deserve to be treated like this. You don't treat your coach like this.'"

The last thing on Rita's mind throughout her first year is autonomy. In fact, what she wants is help and advice. She seeks out colleagues, particularly her department head, who can help solve immediate teaching problems. Yet Rita gets little help from her assigned buddy teacher and is frustrated that veteran teachers cannot readily empathize with a rookie's concerns. She also remains troubled by the fact that everyone seems so busy that neither she nor her colleagues can talk readily or often. Beyond seeking help, she stays in her classroom most days and makes few friends.

Most of the advice Rita does get has to do with her levels of intensity and academic expectations: "I know that you're young, you're eager to make changes, but you need to just try and survive your first year," one colleague offers. "It might be to your benefit to be an easy teacher rather than a hard teacher," another suggests. Her main support person and best source on such matters, though, proves to be her department head, who Rita says "helps me learn what I need to teach. At times I didn't particularly care for her advice, but for the most part she was helpful with my planning. If I had a class bomb a test or a quiz, she would examine my test or quiz. Usually, according to her, they were too hard. Sometimes I think they weren't too hard and the students just didn't try hard enough." What Rita also learns from this woman is to plan in smaller steps, so that changes can be made more quickly and with less long-range impact. More importantly, Rita learns how to orchestrate her classes so that the students do more work from "bell to bell" while she does less: "Get kids to do as much work as possible." With her departmental leader's help Rita manages to realize some success with this approach by May.

Rita develops a love/hate relationship with her algebra classes—a fact she has to admit following a visit to one "bad" algebra class by her department head: "She gave me direct feedback: I was too tense, and they could see it. I was unsure of the material, and they could see it. I didn't like them and didn't want them to be there, and they could tell. And there was tension. She told me about that." Rita often appeals to the algebra students by explaining that "you have to be in here, so just do the work and get out, and don't worry about next year. Why waste your time failing when you'll just have to take it over?" In contrast, she enjoys her geometry sophomores because they are more like she was in high school: "I had my stuff out, I was paying attention to the teacher."

In short, Rita's deep, recurring struggle has to do with the nature of the bond she establishes with students, wanting to be an authority figure, yet seeing herself sometimes as "one of them"; wanting to be in charge and in control, yet knowing that she must find a more nurturing balance point. We see this turmoil in a story Rita offers about an especially good day when an unannounced evaluation took place during her geometry class:

> My best class. The kids are very bright. . . . I'm more relaxed in that classroom because they identify with me and I identify with them. . . . I [taught] closer to them. Usually I'm at the overhead, and it's sad to say that I [worked closer to the students] because [the evaluator] was there. I would go up to the students and touch them and . . . encourage them. . . . It worked wonderfully.

She tells how much like a team they've grow into over the year, noting how the same strategy would never have worked with her other (algebra) classes.

Teaching concerns aside, the amount of bureaucratic paperwork and reports (not to mention grading) grows large, prompting Rita to exclaim during the year that all teachers should have clerical help. After settling her initial panic of not knowing quite how to go about the work of teaching, she learns about the district tests: "I'm in a panic! I need to teach them so much stuff because we have to teach information that they're going to be tested on. . . . Trying to get that material done on time, that's my only problem."

By year's end Rita sees herself "changing a lot" with regard to how she is organizing her teaching and handling problems. In algebra, students now spend the first part of class getting settled, followed by a review of yesterday's work or a lead-in activity for the day's work. Rita always has an assignment on the board when class begins, "to get them doing something so that I can collect my thoughts." Her lectures are shorter, and students do a good deal of their homework in class—which allows Rita to grade previous papers: "I've learned to bring less paperwork home. . . . I've gotten a lot more sleep. It's helped my attitude." She also walks around the room on occasion, checking progress as students work. Though troubled and still second-guessing herself, Rita has lowered her standards for the algebra students. She finds some pleasure is knowing that her students' test scores seem fine and that she has the fewest number of failures for Algebra I students in the department. When asked about problems in the waning weeks of school, Rita proclaims: "Not any more. You just learn to deal with it. Lately, I've put off a lot of things. I just haven't had the desire to do anything with school at this point. It's kind of like burn-out."

Rita closes out the year with her feeling of "specialness" intact. This former honor student with an intellectualist orientation, who returned to teach as a Bridenthal Intern, has learned that "teaching is not teaching any more. You're trying to discipline the kids, but it's not your responsibility, I don't think. They don't work, they don't apply themselves, and they're rude and disrespectful. And the parents . . . don't know how to handle their kids."

Year one in a classroom has given Rita a new perspective on the relationship between teaching and the "public-at-large," prompting her to note how impossible it really is for nonteachers to ever appreciate that "the paperwork is incredible" or "how many lives you affect daily. You could make or break a student. . . . They don't look at the 160 lives you have in your hands for nine months." Rita has survived the year, but is less sure than ever about the importance of autonomy or the essence of professionalism.

Stratification: The Structure of Reform

All efforts to professionalize teaching found within the major reform reports are guided by the desire to enhance the image of the job so as, in part, to attract and retain better teachers. The creation of clear, vertical career stages for teachers, so the argument goes, will do just that. Moreover, this stratification of teaching will create new structures within which many of the other proposed changes (stronger service ideals, greater autonomy, etc.) will be defined and played out as cultural changes in teaching and schools.

The Carnegie Task Force (1986), for example, proposes "that districts create positions for a group of . . . Lead Teachers in each school . . . to guide and influence the activity of others, ensuring that the skill and energy of their colleagues is drawn on as the organization improves its performance" (p. 58). The authors envision the following four-tier career ladder for teachers:

1. Licensed Teachers (those newly graduated from teacher preparation programs who have passed the National Board for Professional Teaching Standards' basic, general knowledge tests)

2. Certified Teachers (those who have passed the National Board's examination to become certified)
3. Advanced Certificate Holders (those with considerable experience who have passed a more advanced version of the National Board exam)
4. Lead Teachers

These positions would be tied directly to differentiated salary levels derived from four dimensions: job function, level of certification, seniority, and productivity; all but Lead Teachers will hold 10-month contracts.

Lest this be interpreted as mere bureaucratic growth, the Carnegie reformers emphatically note that "Lead Teachers must create communities, not additional layers of bureaucracy to clog the system and frustrate their fellow teachers. Lead Teachers would derive their authority primarily from the respect of their professional colleagues" (p. 58). The primary work of teachers under this new staging remains focused on the classroom, though Lead Teachers would assume other responsibilities, such as serving as adjunct faculty in schools of education that use the teachers' job site as a "clinical school" for the preparation of new teachers. "What is central," according to the Carnegie thinkers, "is that, by vesting responsibility for instruction in Lead Teachers, schools will capitalize on the knowledge and skills of its most capable staff and create a career path worth pursuing" (p. 60).

Although they make the same arguments for why the teaching career appeals to so few (inadequate salary, limited advancement, etc.), the National Commission for Excellence (1985) stops short of recommending a more clearly staged career, developing instead a vision of institutional change wherein school administrators would function as instructional leaders who create "conditions for professional practice for teachers" (p. 21). In these schools, "teachers are viewed as partners [of administrators] in efforts to improve instruction," and everyone works together within a "collegial environment" (p. 21). Again, this absence of recommended additional hierarchy underscores the NCETE's position that structures should be altered to enhance teachers' ability to do their own work (teaching); everything else should be handled by qualified support personnel and management.

The number-two goal of the Holmes Group (1986) reads: "*To recognize differences in teachers' knowledge, skill, and commitment, in their education, certification, and work*" (p. 4, emphasis in original). Like its Carnegie counterpart, the Holmes Group begins with the assumption that all who enter the classroom are equally competent. Those at entry level, Instructors, are expected to be "beginning teachers whose job would last only a few years"—Wright's Peace Corps approach to teaching. (Ironically, given the argument that some of the best people leave teaching because of its career "flatness" and that this newly staged career will retain greater numbers of highly qualified people, the lowest rung on the career will be occupied by temporary career visitors.) The majority of the teaching work force is comprised of Professional Teachers: "people who have proven their competence at work, in rigorous professional qualification examinations, and in their own education" (p. 8).

At the apex of the Holmes hierarchy of teachers stand the Career Professionals—that 20% of teachers with a need to move beyond the classroom context into

> jobs in which fine teachers can use their pedagogical expertise to improve other teachers' work, as well as to help children. It means jobs in which teachers can become experts in a specialized area, such as curriculum development, teacher evaluation, or school management. It means jobs in which real leaders can exercise the responsibilities and reap the rewards of serious professionalization. (p. 8)

As in the Carnegie vision, the Holmes' Career Professional Teacher would become involved in institutional duties: "Remediation and the improvement of teaching, for example, would be efficiently handled through the constructive supervision that specialized, differentiated roles in schools would make possible" (p. 37). Left unstated among the other reports is this group's dream that these Career Professional Teachers will become "practitioners who can *lead their field to improvement*" (p. 8; emphasis added).

Lucy begins her career with a strong focus on *teaching*, though in time she will develop an inescapable desire for the kinds of professional stratification and leadership responsibilities just discussed. Lucy's ideal teaching environment requires not only administrative support but respect. Although she talks now and then of related aspects, virtually all of her thinking and attention centers on her work.

Important is Lucy's attention to students' learning potential in light of characteristics such as "ability," "motivation," and "hard-working." She believes that most discipline problems stem from overenthusiasm and learns to judge her teaching accordingly. Early in the year Lucy lists her two primary teaching goals as improving student self-esteem and keeping students and their parents constantly updated about academic progress.

By mid-year Lucy identifies her "major concern about teaching" as "the individual welfare of my students," noting that she seems to feel this concern more than her teaching peers. She has begun to learn about individual

students' family backgrounds and how socially and psychologically complicated the lives of sixth-graders can be. She also develops concerns about the
ways students treat each other in school, and their involvement "in the
clothes, music and attitude of the drug culture (even though they may not
realize what they're doing). I want to change them," she notes. Lucy keeps
in relatively close touch with many of her students' parents, yet finds some
of these contacts frustrating. In the spring, she has a "letter to the editor"
published in one of the city's major newspapers in which she scolds parents
who "shelter their child from the consequences of his or her behavior."
"When a teacher tries to teach a child to be a better person," Lucy writes,
"that teacher should not have to struggle with parents."

Working with students in her "basic" class becomes Lucy's "major
accomplishment" as a new teacher. She sees innovation as one of her true
strengths, employing not only lectures but class discussion and questioning
strategies as teaching styles: "I've written poems, made up skits, and drawn
notes like pictographs. The more effort I put into a lesson, the more the
kids seem to enjoy and learn from it. . . . I like teaching. The only really
hard part is being consistent with discipline. The rest is fun!"

In addition to the work of teaching, Lucy learns much about the job
demands of control, "paperwork," and performance expectations. Early in
the year she voices discouragement in her journal with being expected to do
"*so* much and *never* make mistakes." This entry comes after relating several
instances where she is "talked to" about misspellings on worksheets, turning
reports in on time, and using incorrect duplicate forms when making a
report. "There are so many hassles!" Lucy also learns the ropes around
teacher evaluations, realizing that these reports have little to do with being
the kind of "good teacher" she wants to be. Good teachers in her district are
defined largely by these evaluations, which "just test if you can teach a
certain way (and most people can, with practice). I still want to be an
excellent teacher," she writes; "now I know more specifically what is required to do so."

Key to excellent teaching, for Lucy, is careful planning and support
from her superiors. Lucy finds personal and professional strength in being
highly organized and procedural regarding her teaching. She carefully ties
her planning to the district's curriculum guide, formulating "specific questions" during the process, which she presents to her teaching colleagues.
With their feedback in hand, Lucy then decides "what to use, what to
change, and what to invent. The more specific my plans, the more confident
I feel." Times when she did not follow this procedure "are so *awful* that I
try to avoid them whenever possible."

As the year passes, Lucy develops an appreciation of the ways in which
her environment, and especially the leaders in her school, help to make her

work as good as she feels it is. She describes the school climate as cooperative. The four members of the science teaching team talk a great deal about their students, respect each other's academic freedom, and share ideas: "They would feed me worksheets and give me their whole curriculum notebooks." Within this context "lesson planning wasn't a problem," Lucy notes. "I do what I want."

Most of her end-of-year reflection, however, revolves around the support she receives from her department head, Jean Hawkins, who teaches her more about "the system" than anyone else, and the school counselor, who "always took action when I had a concern about a student." Lucy describes her assistant principal as a woman "who always backed me up when I had a discipline problem—even though sometimes I didn't deserve it." But it is Mr. Lahand, the school principal, who proves to be an especially important supporter of this first-year teacher.

Lucy knows that Lahand lobbied hard within the district to get her at Jack Simper Middle School. What she appreciates most is the freedom and respect he gives to teachers. Lucy develops the sense that a principal makes a big difference in teachers' lives, not only through policy but through less obvious forms of support and encouragement—like her principal's enthusiastic funding for teachers to attend various workshops. In Lucy's eyes, Lahand respects her and wants her to succeed.

He also becomes her strongest cheerleader. After several evaluation visits, Lucy notices that Lahand rates her higher than do other evaluators and encourages her to continue stretching herself in terms of innovative teaching, despite the obvious trade-offs she must make with classroom control. He praises her organization, too, as well as her efforts to stay in touch with parents. Lucy knows that this attention and praise is not exclusively hers: Lahand is no less supportive and encouraging with the other new teachers in his school. It's just how he is.

Of three first-year teachers at Simper, Lahand nominates Lucy for the district's "Rookie Teacher Award." Already fulfilling her dreams of working in a place where people want and respect her and of being publicly recognized for her work, Lucy calls it "a good year, considering that I didn't have any experience. But I was very lucky."

AUTONOMOUS TEACHERS AND CULTURAL CHANGE

Mattingly (1987) argues that the work of teachers in this country has been formed and defined throughout the past two centuries by larger forces that have worked to shape the job of teaching. The cultures of teaching in the United States originally took shape through the work of male ministers in the seventeenth and eighteenth centuries who, as teachers, understood their job as a largely moral one. Their professional autonomy stemmed from respect as "virtuous" and "educated" men in a world that valued both traits. Yet as society changed, so too did these teachers and their work. Following the American Revolution, teachers' autonomy slowly began to diminish as they remained responsible for schooling's moral agenda while relinquishing their power over the very content and purposes of their work. As nondenominational and nonpartisan groups took greater control of schools, "the teacher became saddled with an insupportable burden: the set of public expectations that proper instruction would not only shape the character of each individual but would provide, in Horace Mann's resonant phrase, 'the balance wheel of the social machinery'" (p. 41).

Westward expansion, growing immigration, and fluctuating economic conditions created the need for an increasing number of teachers who could move more freely from school to school or region to region. Moral character became a less critical attribute as nonclergy took teaching positions. During this period, "schoolmen" found themselves embracing bureaucratic structures in order to distance themselves from increasing pressures between conflicting public desires. And with the arrival of the War Between the States teaching opened its gates to a flood of women, which "testified as much as any single factor to the paternalistic place of education in the hierarchy of Robertoian values" (Mattingly, 1987, p. 42).

With the feminization of the work of teaching firmly established through the development of normal schools for the preparation of women teachers, educational leaders (virtually all men) set out to recruit men who could not only teach women how to do their work but act as their managers on the job. New social and economic forces (e.g., industrialization, emancipation, and woman suffrage) influenced educational leaders (still "schoolmen") and helped to broaden the gender divide among educators, forming divisions not only of autonomy and power but of salary and knowledge as well. With the arrival of the twentieth century, schools had become work places divided against themselves—the work and job of teaching as clearly distinct as the prestige, power, and career differences between teacher and administrator.

Bureaucratic Impediments to Autonomy

External forces throughout this century, including the situating of teacher preparation within universities, world wars, political struggles between liberal and conservative federal policies, and major social-change efforts such as the civil rights movement, have continued to work in ways that diminish the autonomy of teachers' work. Coupled with the increased bureaucratization of schooling, it should surprise no one, according to

Mattingly (1987), that teachers have so little autonomy. Few people who work within bureaucracies that are largely shaped by changing social forces do.

Gene expected bureaucratic problems long before he met his first class of students. He waited out most of the summer following graduation from Central before taking the only job he was offered—at Justin. From Justin's opening in-service session to the school's habit of moving students from one class to another during the first six weeks ("That infuriated me!"), Gene knew that this job would bother him continually.

Gene spends the first week "just letting students know I am serious about my rules and I cannot be manipulated for their own specific desires." Students not in their desks at the bell are tardy, and when they reach their desks, they often find work awaiting them. All students sign a paper acknowledging Gene's class rules and can always see the "little chart above my blackboard that has a little progression of offenses." No one doubts who's in charge in this classroom.

Gene finds teaching "exciting." As an intellectualist, he brings a thematic approach to his history class and spends much time in discussion, striving for higher-order thinking and reasoning. Even with his "regular" economics classes he often employs various activities to address different learning styles and enjoys using debates and oral reports. He believes that "most learning takes place in controlled chaos" and tries to foster such an environment. This belief affects his planning as well: "My teaching style is sort of like surfing. When something new comes up I'll do it. I seldom plan more than four days in advance. . . . My teaching style is flexible. . . . Sometimes I'll drop what I have planned to apply the day's news to what we have going."

"I think the thought that motivates me most," he writes that fall, "is a sense of mission." Gene's mission is intellectual: "Knowledge is valuable for its own sake," he declares. In most cases, however, Gene feels that his is a mission impossible:

> With very few exceptions I'm seeing my students as they will be for the rest of their lives. Occasionally I can effect a change in one or two.
> . . . The vast majority have already been warped. There's not much I can do. There's not much anybody except for their parole officer can do. The good ones are going to be good anyway. But I just have to keep staying in there . . . a positive example for the occasional one that's kind of straddling the fence, and hope that they fall on my side of the fence.

Given this perspective, the more "realistic" work at hand is "to prepare my students . . . for life in the job world or life in college," which he does by focusing on accountability: "I do not baby them. . . . I believe that students should accept responsibility for their actions and that schools baby them too much." He offers one personally bothersome example:

> I send out progress reports to students every three weeks. Now, I don't require them to be signed by parents because I don't believe in that. I think my students should be responsible enough to handle that themselves as juniors and seniors. Evidently, my administration thinks that if students are failing, a progress report isn't good enough and that I need to call parents. . . . My students are 16, 17 and 18, and I shouldn't be changing their diapers for them!

Despite teaching a schedule that many veterans only dream about, Gene recognizes numerous forces within his immediate and surrounding environments that work against him. Gene is deeply concerned about the state curriculum standards, which shape what he can and cannot do in economics. "I don't think I should be locked into any rigid . . . pile of garbage that they call curriculum," he steams. Given his habit of presenting considerable amounts of information and differing points of view, Gene doubts "that the state curriculum qualifies as education. I think it might be more appropriately called 'indoctrination.'" In time he simply ignores these guidelines, maintaining only a vague awareness of them as he creates his own curriculum.

Ironically, his comfortable pride in deciding to ignore state guidelines and create his own version of a good economics curriculum is not matched in his European History situation. Gene knows that these "gifted students" await a test in order to receive International Baccalaureate or Advanced Placement credit for the course, yet "I don't know if I am teaching the right material for the test."

Gene's sense of intellectual isolation becomes an issue that affects his teaching as much as bad curriculum and looming tests (though all of his advanced students did fine). As discussed in Chapter 8, he finds literally no support from master teachers, visiting Central faculty, or departmental peers (his colleagues teaching economics "are pretty much out of touch with what economics should be when teaching kids who are going to be living in the twenty-first century").

Gene becomes physically sick and exhausted about midway through the year, in part because he feels so unorganized. "But the administration certainly didn't help. . . . They kept changing the rules! Every few weeks they would come up with a new form to replace an old form that I had just learned about."

"Paper work, discipline, and administrators" are Gene's windmills. By mid-year he considers his primary responsibilities to be "administration and control." He resents the complete absence of power he has over his own classroom, for example, when he is told to remove a Renaissance poster because of nudity, to be less demanding with students (some of whom complain about the work in Gene's course and have themselves transferred out of it), or to use a school-specific code when entering grades in his gradebook.

Time-consuming administrative tasks are no less bothersome for Gene, who feels far from professional when he finds himself doing parking-lot duty ("I was to get names and license plate numbers of students who were speeding. I was also to hurry students to their classes from the parking lot"). Yet what proves most disturbing is the "system": Everything must be done with a certain procedure and a particular form. He recalls, "I had a student who wasn't disciplined once because I did not sign his discipline notice. My name was on it, but I hadn't put my signature in the signature part, so an administrator refused to discipline the student. And when I finally signed it they *still* refused to discipline him because they said it was too late!"

The intersection between administration and discipline may be the most troublesome spot in Gene's apprentice year. Gene, like his father, believes that the administration does not support teachers in their efforts to dispense discipline because the administrators fear parents. Gene struggles with the administration's seeming acquiescence to parents all year. He feels that teachers ought not to be constrained in their work (i.e., should be able to remove disruptive students from their rooms or assign a failing grade) by administrative rules that require continuous parental contact or consent. School administrators ought to create environments that permit teachers to teach, free from nonacademic, community constraints: "In the end I think that is what teachers resent most. They're expected to do so much, but they're given so few tools and so little autonomy to do it."

At the close of his first year Gene acknowledges that "I don't stay up until 1:30 A.M. any more. I manage to get most of my imposed paper work done during my off period." He also talks of his early visions as a Bridenthal Intern, "of being influential in the educational reform movement . . . able to change some of the egregious inequities within the system." For his final journal entry he writes:

> I thought that teachers who were demoralized or lazy would see me do-
> ing my job, and doing it well, and shore up their resolve or their stan-
> dards. Little did I realize that most of my colleagues wouldn't give a
> damn about me or would even bear animosity toward me for maintain-
> ing high standards. Nor did I expect them to tell me that the reason I

worked so hard is because I am a novice, and that soon I would get the "hang" of it and stop taking work home and stop coming up to school. Nor did I expect the administration to move students to teachers who maintained lower standards at students' request. How can I maintain my high performance expectations when everything about this medio-cre place—the administration, the curriculum, the parents, and my col-leagues—hope that I will be a failure as a teacher?

Gene's first year illustrates the seemingly inescapable tensions and con-tradictions between teachers' work and job as well as between professionals who perform a service and workers who are held accountable as bureau-cratic employees. Densmore's (1987) research on first-year teachers ex-plores these very intersections.

Framing her study with the work of Braverman (1974), Johnson (1982), Larson (1977), and White (1983), Densmore describes the subjec-tive experiences of two first-year teachers in relation to their "objective" working conditions. Densmore uses these cases to argue that teachers have little autonomy because, like other professionals, their work has been prole-tarianized:

> Proletarianization refers to certain tendencies in work organization and work processes under capitalism: an increased division of labor; separation of con-ception from the execution of tasks, including the tendency to routinize high level tasks; increased controls over each step of the labor process; increased volume of work; and the downgrading of skill levels. (p. 135)

Clearly, few professionals would describe their work in these ways, and fewer still would welcome the thought of having those outside of their profession exert primary control over the work they perform. Yet this is what has happened to the work of teaching.

Citing the work of Derber (1982), Densmore explains that proletarian-ization occurs in both technical and ideological ways. Technically, proletar-ianization occurs as managers exert greater control over the shaping of professionals' own goals and objectives as well as the ways in which profes-sionals accomplish their work. Professionals are encouraged to see them-selves as more highly skilled and valued and to become more autonomous within a decreasingly complex work environment—Friedman (1977) calls this "responsible autonomy." Ideologically, calls for greater professionalism under these circumstances serve to avert workers' focus from the reality of their work situation to the goals and objectives of bureaucratic managers. From this perspective, as teachers increasingly lose autonomy and control to outside forces they will seek to (re)construct greater professional autonomy over what little they can. This strategy thus succeeds not only in creating a false consciousness about teachers' overall labor situations, but in constricting teachers' sense of efficacy and professionalism to the confines of their classrooms.

The processes of proletarianization can be seen most obviously in the various tensions and contradictions of teachers' work. Contemporary reform agendas represent fine examples of efforts to create, for example, more specialized and technical subject matter (pedagogical content knowledge and instructional practices), or to view teachers' work in light of external goals and outcomes (raising test scores to better compete with the scores of students in other schools here and abroad). Although the obvious contradiction between calling for teachers to develop their own goals while simultaneously holding them accountable to the outcomes of the bureaucracies within which they work persists, "appeals to professionalism continue to characterize the occupation" (Densmore, 1987, p. 144).

These "appeals to professionalism" create their own conflicts, which tend to be shaped and resolved by the bureaucratic culture of teaching. Teachers are asked to take more of a professional role in restructuring schools, for example. Although such actions are most routinely accomplished through collective action, efforts toward collective action, especially by those who embrace their individual autonomy, seem all too unprofessional. Teachers are also asked to exhibit greater professionalism by taking on more work and job responsibilities while such intensification tends to provide the schools with "free" labor and greater productivity. Further, these additional responsibilities for teachers seldom include

> a role in making significant determinations about the education they are providing. Their pace and work volume, instead, create duties in addition to their instructional responsibilities. The quantity of work performed by teachers does not tell us anything about the quality of that work; typically, a high work volume increases their dependence upon prescribed materials. That is, they simply do not have the time to create many of their own lessons or do much beyond distributing predesigned curricular materials. (Densmore, 1987, p. 149)

Collective Efforts Toward Change

Densmore suggests that teachers can extricate themselves from this self-defeating process of proletarianization by shedding their emphasis on individual autonomy and choosing to understand their objective work situation in a more realistic, critical, and collective way. Collectively, they can learn to recognize that their problems and concerns as well as their joys and triumphs are shared by all teachers; that their sense of powerless isolation reflects bureaucratic cultural forces that have been collectively shaped and must likewise be addressed and reshaped; and that their work can be better and more gratifying through such means as team teaching, interdisciplinary curriculum building, and community building within the school itself (Densmore, 1987). Roberto's second year as a teacher proved "better and more gratifying" for these very reasons.

Roberto returns to King-Jackson with his deep commitment to students and an ulcer he developed during year one. His district is focused on cooperative learning for this school year, so he is, too.

Roberto shares his room with 29 fifth-graders this year, "a good heterogeneous group" including several mainstreamed special education students and four members reading well below grade level. He refuses to read their files before schools starts, preferring to learn about them in his own way and through his own eyes. During the year he works to integrate computers into the teaching he does and the learning they do, largely through writing activities.

Again Roberto reports no discipline problems. This year he is more confident with his teaching, bolstered by last year's good feelings and reports and confident that his particular values and beliefs complement his growing skills in planning and delivery. He notes feeling little anxiousness prior to any of his four formal evaluations and considerable pride following each. This year his mandatory teaching evaluations "finally showed me that I'm a little bit more comfortable with teaching." As the school year ends, Roberto has become certain that he can do his work and do it well.

During year two Roberto's understanding of his job has evolved from "trying to teach kids subject areas and the basics" while "just staying in those four walls" to a role far more complicated. Teaching now includes attending to students' personal needs, working with parents, and "how to work with the profession itself." He believes that teachers who work in isolation lose a tremendous amount of experience "and they're probably hurting the kids that they're with."

Significant to this broadened perspective are changes in Roberto's work place in general, and in his fifth-grade colleagues in particular. He spent a good deal of time over the summer working with his new partner, Mrs. Justice, on an interdisciplinary program designed to run through much of the school year. Roberto shares ideas and contacts he's developed over the past two summers while working with Latino teens in a similar, city-sponsored program. He is excited to find a teaching colleague willing to invest so much energy in a program targeted for low-income students, and his respect for Mrs. Justice grows as the year passes, as does his realization that he's an equal participant in the project.

Roberto works much harder as an equal this year to maintain and enhance King-Jackson's special environment. Though he understands that he was "allowed" to do less last year as he got situated, he also knew enough at the close of the year to turn down Ms. Lillian's suggestion that he become fifth-grade chairperson: He knew that he would still be learning his job "and felt that [this responsibility] would be too much for me." Nonetheless, he spends this year serving on the school's curriculum-development committee and beginning graduate studies in educational administration at Central. Though glad to be more involved with the overall school, he admits to being less creative in his teaching this year than last.

As for the state tests, Roberto discovers that others find these exams problematic too. Beginning early in the year, the fifth-grade teachers work together to develop ways to better handle the test and its preparation. Despite some arguments against it, the team decides to "teach the test" to fifth-graders by having them come to school 30 minutes early during the weeks prior to the testing date. This program, called "Start Time," is their way "of focusing on the testing areas and try[ing] to really avoid taking school time to teach students what the objectives were going to be on this test." Roberto adds, with second-year certainty: "If your test scores are not good enough, then something is going on with the type of teacher you are and the type of school you are."

He also participates more this year in the many Alliance School responsibilities. On top of this, the entire school is immersed in preparations for a state accreditation visit. Roberto participates in countless committee and whole-faculty meetings and spends hour-upon-hour with colleagues preparing written responses to questions asked by past accrediting teams throughout the district and sharing these with the entire staff. Ms. Lillian is often there sharing "effective schools research and telling us what, basically, [the accreditation team] would be looking for and some of the questions that we might expect . . . making sure that we know where our curriculum guides are and how to use them."

Ms. Lillian's expectations for him are understandably higher "now that I've kind of gotten my wings." What he's noticed this year, though, similar to Densmore's (1987) point, is the degree to which the collective faculty shape much of what takes place at the school. "We put a lot of pressure on our principal sometimes," he says, when the group arrives at a decision that differs from their principal's. At the same time, Roberto notes how interesting it is for him to watch this group of selected veterans, each with a strong will and voice, negotiate among themselves toward consensus or respond to the principal's efforts to have them see things her way. "They're all leaders," he claims, wondering "how do you get all these leaders to all of a sudden be followers?"

Becoming an empowered team member shapes Roberto tremendously. As the year winds down, he draws parallels between his experience with the King-Jackson team and the Bridenthal Interns to illustrate his points. Both groups were "assembled" to work toward common goals, yet a lot of the interns "never really wanted to take it beyond whatever was the simplest thing they had to do to get through." He notes a similar situation at another Alliance School, where some of the hand-picked faculty "bought into the alliance and some did not. And that school is kind of split in that way right now."

At the end of two years Roberto has begun to "really feel like a teacher." He is less focused on "knowledge" and more on teaching "a lot of values. . . . I want a whole person. . . . I want to give [students] a whole, totally different perspective on things," noting that for the economically poor Latino students he teaches, "there's too many things out there they could miss out on." He sees teaching as "a very fine craft. You almost have to know who you are, like most artists, and just kind of be in tune with yourself and decide where you're going to shine." With this perspective Roberto now understands that with curriculum, textbooks—with *every-thing* he learns about and works with—he must "make it more me than anybody else. . . . You always have to find a way to make it more you. . . . Otherwise . . . it won't work, and the kids pick up on that real quick."

But he also sees that context is just as important as commitment. He knows that his presence at King-Jackson enables him to be the kind of teacher he's always wanted to be. Further, with the support of his colleagues and his principal he's come to appreciate his role as a participant and decision maker in school policy. Recalling how shy he was until his induction into the Bridenthal program, he's struck, now, with his ability to recognize and state how he's developing into a school leader: "I've had to start being more assertive and voicing my opinions a lot more, because they tend to be ones that need to be heard, at least, if not followed." As always, those opinions had to do with the welfare of students.

Failing at "Hybrid Introduction"

Despite Roberto's success and Densmore's (1987) guarded optimism regarding the possibility for changing the culture of teachers' work through reshaping the culture of teachers' jobs, the fact remains that like all cultures, teaching "tends to attract and hold people who are initially disposed to value what the work has to offer and to be able to cope with difficulties the work presents" (Feiman-Nemser & Floden, 1986, p. 512). The job of teaching, as shaped by the institutional and bureaucratic cultures of schools, has an enormous effect on even the most idealistic and committed teacher. The beliefs, language, and practices that sustain the cultures of schooling will eventually influence and change the work of all but the strongest and most deeply committed teachers.

Though we can only "see" cultural change through actions, these new behaviors reflect largely subliminal, quiet, internal, and laboriously slow changes in beliefs, values, and attitudes, which serve as the essence of cultural identities. When new teachers resist elements of the cultures of schooling and teaching (Zeichner & Tabachnick, 1984), they do so because what they value and believe stands in conflict with the established cultures. This teacher resistance "will be subjected to intense selection during the individual's first few years of teaching. Individuals who do not fit the norms of the continuing teacher population will exit to alternative careers" (Ost & Ost, 1988, p. 53).

Proposals to change teaching cultures through behavioral and structural alterations, while important, ignore the deeper nature of the cultures themselves. Discontinuity is more profound, in this case, at the level of belief, thought, and values. Ost (1989) sees this discontinuity as an important and powerful avenue for cultural change in the same ways in which these cultures obviously change their newest members. Because cultures provide identities for people and enable individuals to avoid anxiety and uncertainty, changing them will require altering their natural selection processes. One example of this is "hybrid introduction," described as "the process of selectively filling positions with persons who are familiar with the culture but whose personal assumptions are somewhat different from the mainstream culture. These [people] must be provided with support systems that will facilitate change in the organization" (p. 175). Of course, they must carry with them values, beliefs, and visions of a better culture.

In some respects the Bridenthal program reflects a sort of hybrid introduction, especially with interns like Rita—who had never imagined classroom teaching as a likely career and who brought high standards with her to work. Though she continued to praise the support she found available through her second year (largely provided by the intern group and Wright), her lack of a guiding vision of change allowed various forces to reshape the way she understood her work.

Rita has "no doubt about earning your three months vacation" after her difficult first year of teaching:

> During the summer, I was like, no, I don't want to go back because [last year] ended on a sour note. But now, I've got different ideas, I've got one year experience, I've got my files, I've got my notes. I just have to learn how to expand on that and be more creative, and experiment

with my classes. . . . I've talked to a lot of teachers as far as their focus now in mathematics on group work and collaborative learning,
and critical thinking. And I thought I was the only one afraid to do
any of this new stuff. But, I'm not! . . . I went to a cooperative learning workshop [over the summer], so, I've got something visible that I
saw that worked and I could go and put it in my classroom and try it
with one six-week grading period.

Rita thus begins year two with new confidence, new plans, guarded
optimism, and revised memories of last year as actually going pretty well,
"a lot better than some second-year teachers." As evidence, she notes that
within the first weeks of this school year several former students visited her,
indicating that "some of my kids liked me." Another reason for Rita's
outlook has to do with the fact that she again has her own classroom
(many Justin teachers must change rooms during the day) and the same two
subjects as last year. Finally, she has only *two* classes of freshman algebra
(last year's "worst" classes) and three of sophomore Informal Geometry
(last year's "best" class). The only additional responsibility Rita takes on is
sponsor for the Marine Science Club.

At various points throughout her second year Rita reflects on how
difficult it is for her to teach mathematics. She worked most of last year
trying to learn to teach Algebra I and has accumulated sufficient worksheets, quizzes, and ideas to enable her to feel somewhat better prepared
for this year's two classes. With multiple geometry sections this year, however, she labors equally hard with this content. She now second-guesses her
decision to switch from science to mathematics at Central, noting that "even
though I made it with decent grades [in math], high B's, I realized that I
struggled a lot. And was I really having fun? I don't know. Some people
loved what they were doing. I couldn't say I loved it." She admits that
"math was good and I learned a lot. But I don't feel like that's my forte. . . .
I don't have the enthusiasm or the joy . . . about math." When asked why
she decided to pursue mathematics teaching certification rather than some
other area, she notes that "it's just easier to get a teaching job. That's
probably why. And . . . it's pretty impressive to have a math degree." She
ponders her own situation in this light: "I never did realize that until after
the fact, and I was already into it and going through it. Mathematics is
interesting to me, personally. It's just that kids aren't interested in math.
Maybe for kids who are taking a foreign language, it's an elective they can
choose to be in, and that might make a difference."

Year two makes Rita more certain than ever of the relationship between teaching success and students' interest in subject matter. It doesn't

take her long to realize that this year's Informal Geometry students are "a different type of student [than I had last year]. They're not motivated, and that sort of gets you down":

> I feel sorry for them. I feel bad for them, but I have the hardest time motivating them or getting them to do anything. . . . They're mostly minority students. . . . You think, well, these students are less intelligent or not so skilled in math. Oh, I don't want to teach them. They're discipline problems. I go in there with that type of attitude and that's wrong, that's not good.

"They're not *real* discipline problems," she explains. "The problems that I have are talking while I'm lecturing and just getting them to do their work diligently instead of working and talking and working and talking." Rita describes these classes as "a lot of memorization and basics of geometry, most of which you should have learned in probably seventh grade." Most members of her department don't feel any better about teaching students "who can't handle regular math" and, like Rita, see Informal Geometry as a "filler class" and "a waste of time for some of my students, especially the ones that keep talking about going to college."

As an intellectualist and "new breed" of teacher, Rita feels helpless. "I don't know how to help them," she offers. "They're real good, they come up for extra help, they're sincere, but they just don't have the math skills. And I feel just like saying, 'I would like to transfer some of my brain to you.'" At another level Rita understands that the prescribed content for these classes leaves much to be desired in terms of stimulating, challenging learning opportunities, yet this awareness results in guilt of a different sort: "Well, I could supplement, but that's a lot of extra work. I'd have to come up with more creative things for the students to do rather than just book work. It's just that I didn't take the time over the summer to do it."

Her daily challenges and feelings of inadequacy lead Rita to describe teaching this year as "very difficult." She admires teachers with "very high expectations. They respect themselves and they demand respect from their students and their administrators." She admires one colleague in particular who is often assigned the "worst" groups of students because everyone knows she has "total control. . . . And that's what I want to be like . . . because I can't stand an uncontrolled classroom and that's what brings me frustration each week. My expectations are so high, and I'm such a perfectionist that it bothers me."

Yet when pressed to elaborate on these expectations, especially in light of how she might see them next year, Rita can only add: "I know I am very intense on learning the material, but I would also like to teach students about expectations, about working hard, about putting forth the best effort that you can. And I would do that through my expectations." When asked what she would do if a student who has worked hard, never missed or been late for class, and sought extra help scores 68 percent on a test, Rita says that she would assign an F grade, "because to be successful, . . . no matter how much you're on time, no matter how hard you try, if you can't get the job done you're going to be fired."

Rita is aware of the forces shaping her teaching thoughts and practices as well as she is aware that she often finds herself taking opposite sides of an issue like the one noted above. Parents comprise one such force. On the one hand, Rita enjoys knowing that, in many cases, one call to parents can literally change a student's attitude and behavior overnight, and Rita relies heavily on this tactic in year two. On the other hand, Rita also suspects that parents have too much control over the administration: "There are four thousand students and the administrators have no control over them. They're wild. And [administrators] jump at any parental request. They're manipulated by the school board and they give in." She has seen examples of this kind of parent "control" with her own geometry classes:

> A lot of my students are too smart for this class. They're just taking the easy way out. Or maybe they really can't handle regular geometry. . . . [Counselors] just let them do what they want. And, if the parents see that their child is struggling, and the parents want them to go down to a lower level, [counselors will] listen to the parents. They're very afraid of parents.

Rita becomes more jaded, overall, about the school and its policies and rules, some of which "basically tie our hands." For example, her hands are tied when it comes to decisions about what she can and cannot "grade." In this case, Rita requires all students to keep a notebook, "which teaches them organizational skills and responsibility. But we cannot . . . *require* them to have a notebook or give them a grade for their notebook, because it's not tied to the [state's basic learning objectives]. . . . I have my kids keep a notebook, but I don't take a grade on it. I've just decided not to worry about that."

A more powerful example of the strange effects external forces have on her work can be seen in a story Rita shares in November. Acknowledging that her Informal Geometry classes are boring, she suggests that students must "make it fun inside themselves and say, 'I've gotta learn this.' That's the way I did it":

> I made it fun for myself because the teacher can't make it fun all the time . . . because it's the basics. And it takes a lot of prep time to

make it exciting, and entertaining every day. That's something that I'd like to work on, if I had more time, like during the summer, to expand my lessons. Right now, all we try to do is survive day to day. And get the material across to them so that when it comes time for the test, they can take the test.

That's what one of my students brought up in fifth period: "It's so boring, you're teaching us to the test." And I said, "I know." "But that doesn't mean we're learning," he said. And I said, "I know." "Then why are you doing it?" he asked. I said, "You have to pass the test. If you don't pass the test, you don't pass the class and you don't graduate." "But Miss," he says, "it doesn't make any sense, if we're not learning anything." I said, "I know." Then he goes, "Can't you do anything? Can't you go to the school board? Can't you change the system?" And I said, "It takes changing the entire society, the entire state in order to get this kind of change."

Rita no longer sees herself as much of a reformer: "I've never thought about it. I've been probably very apathetic to it because it's impossible." She knows that her state teacher organization lobbies the legislature but has not kept up with these issues "because it's just a bunch of politics and I don't like politics. . . . I do a lot of complaining but then I don't do anything about it." As a two-year veteran teacher she goes so far as to suggest that her legislators might want to rethink their approach to educational reform: "Content, content, content. What students know. But it becomes irrelevant when they know so much, but then they can't cooperate with other people and get along in an environment where they're dealing with other people, or be polite and courteous, or follow the rules."

Rita would like more support from the administration next year with respect to her expectations for students, yet she adds that "you can't just demand it, but ask for it nicely." She's suffered several denials for requests she's made and ideas she's shared with her department head, who often claims that they're not what the principal wants: "That's it. End of story." When reminded that several years ago she had low regard for docile, apolitical teachers who didn't seem to be doing anything to reform schools, Rita admits: "I sort of became like this. Nobody ever listens."

Just before school ends Rita talks about her ability to withstand another year with a sense that she's done pretty well. She doubts that high school teachers are important in their students' eyes and is demoralized by her students' disrespect. "I'm more successful this year at math," she observes, "but it's the disrespect that's getting to me." She tells of a colleague talking of becoming a trash collector, because "trash won't talk back to me." At the same time, Rita continues to feel respected for her membership in the Bridenthal program (especially from colleagues at Justin). Yet while her identity as a Bridenthal Intern remains strong, she will no longer speak to high school students about becoming teachers: "No. I'm too negative right now, and I wouldn't want to turn off somebody that really would be excited."

STRATIFICATION AND LEADERSHIP:
THE PROMISE OF EVENTUAL CHANGE

We have shown thus far that the cultures of teaching—or how teachers understand their work—are shaped in large part by the bureaucratic cultures of schooling (the "job" of teaching) in ways that make problematic the hopes for professionalizing teaching and reforming teacher education. Indeed, it is the recognition of the symbiotic relationship between schools and teachers' work that prompts reformers to call for partnerships between schools and teacher education institutions, like Wright's Alliance Schools, in the restructuring of U.S. education. The need to retain successful teachers compels reformers to argue for a more staged or differentiated career structure wherein teachers' salaries and work responsibilities can grow commensurate with their experience and expertise. Yet, in our opinion, these new stratification schemes are as likely to hurt as to help the work of teachers and the cultures they tenuously sustain.

How Teachers' Thinking Is Changed

To the extent that teachers control their work, they do so within the confines of their classrooms. Here they can usually understand and exhibit individuality, freedom, creativity, and a sense of personal and communal mission in ways that are seldom understood and exhibited outside their doors. They can have a say. They can make important decisions. They're in control. They can close their doors to the bureaucracy, at times, filtering job-related pressures and tasks whenever possible, orchestrating institutional invasions when necessary, and seeking support when desired. Inside classrooms, teachers privately manage the tensions and contradictions of their work and job cultures in ways that suit them best.

Reform proposals like those of the Holmes and Carnegie groups would change all of this. Despite hopes to the contrary, the stratification of teachers will result in a new layer of bureaucratic oversight, which will bring the institutional culture further inside teachers' classrooms. As we have seen above, those who reach the upper tiers of the teaching strata will not be engaged in the reshaping of school culture or improving teachers' working conditions; they will focus on teachers' work: improving instruction, evaluating performance, and overseeing the development and performance of new teachers. In short, despite their enhanced status, salary, and responsibility, these "top teachers" become an extension of management, who will finally succeed in extending its bureaucratic tentacles into the heart of education — the classroom — and recreating the world of teachers' work.

The issue here is not so much the infiltration of former colleagues now "working for the boss" as one of cultural change. As we have seen, the bureaucratic culture, which is manifested in the job of teaching, maintains powerful influence over teachers' work, yet teachers continue their struggle to maintain their own work culture — to do what they think is best in ways that they find useful. Many teachers believe they succeed at their work despite the managerial and institutional pressures brought to bear on them. Creating new positions of leadership among their ranks will allow their own colleagues to reframe discussions, rename their discourse, and redefine their work in ways that accommodate the needs of the institution, thus further limiting teachers' individual autonomy and control.

Popkewitz (1991) describes a study (Popkewitz & Lind, 1989) that illustrates this sort of influence and the ways in which teachers' work is shaped by bureaucratic power. Working in committees along with administrators, school board members, and university consultants, teachers in three school districts set out to develop programs that addressed their working conditions. Their original proposals included ideas such as release time, sabbaticals, team teaching, and the like.

However, their deliberations were shaped by goals and language of "reform" that differed from the values and patterns of teachers' work. Thus, "certain assumptions about the organization of reform emerged in the ongoing practices across school districts" (Popkewitz, 1991, p. 204), while other common assumptions emerged concerning the goals of reform. In all cases, the language and practices adopted proved to be more alike than different, more administrative than normative, more directive than reflective. When completed, their projects shared four elements: (1) the assumption of a common framework of teacher experience and goals; (2) an intensification of work; (3) the increased monitoring of teachers' work through new evaluation schemes; and (4) a limiting of teacher autonomy. In short, teachers' original concerns were reformulated to intersect those of management through newly established hierarchies that promote the growth of organizational culture (and its language and practices) in ways that will remake teachers' work. During her second year, Lucy exhibits some of these very shifts in attention and language. Her exposure to organizational culture helps her to develop ways to understand both her work and her job.

The importance of students and innovative ways to reach them appear essential to Lucy's image of good teaching throughout her second year. Inspiration and self-esteem vie equally with knowledge and skill transmission as central to her work, especially with sixth-graders "because they're so formative and they're searching and they're looking for role models and they're curious and enthusiastic. It's not too hard to do [all] that—not really to mold them, but to watch them change and grow and learn new things. That's what teaching is." Lucy again finds working with the students in her basic science class a challenging joy: "They're just more interesting, more fun. They don't fit into the mold of a good student," she says, adding that this year's group is "20 times harder" to teach than last year's. Lucy sees this as the result of having several "learning disabled" students and three limited-English-proficiency students added to the routine mix of "at-risk" and repeating students in class.

What emerges during Lucy's second year of teaching is her tendency to discuss students with passion and warmth one moment and a language of control and management the next. Indeed, she characterizes her most important lesson of year two as the realization that teaching involves a good deal of the latter. "I just thought I'd spend a few minutes planning and then get up and teach. You know, just *do it*," she says with a laugh. Now she's "more aware of the management parts of teaching": administrative forms, professional development workshops, contact with parents and colleagues.

This new awareness can be seen in some of the ways Lucy approaches her work differently. For example, she decides to have each student in all six of her classes take turns developing a project that she or he would "teach" to the rest of the class. Though excited about the idea itself, Lucy's enthusiasm wanes when

> I realized that I would have to make up a different test for every single class. . . . So I watered it down a lot and made up real general questions [to use with all six classes]. That was a practical problem I didn't see because I was all caught up in the philosophy of [having students get] these new experiences in front of the classroom and planning and researching and stuff like that.

Lucy has even minimized the number of "unusual ideas" she tries in class after finding that students' grade averages have dropped. She knows that each of her six classes is different from the others, and that each student in any one class is unique, yet her creativity comes largely from a "trial-and-error" process of teaching the same lesson six times each day: "It always progresses throughout the day that I get more and more specific and more detailed with my instruction because I just realize they're going to have problems with this, so I might as well say it in the beginning and get it over with so they won't have to ask questions about it."

Beyond her specific classroom teaching duties, year two finds Lucy with several additional responsibilities, including serving as the school's "wellness advocate" and sponsoring the Young Astronaut Club. Though not especially pleased about the extra time commitments, she enjoys her new leadership roles. She also sees herself in a kind of self-appointed leadership role of being a "positive force" among her colleagues. "They need some idealism to rub off on them, some fresh ways to do things," she claims. "Maybe it's because of the person I am. Maybe it has nothing to do with the fact that I'm young." By year two, "making a difference" has become Lucy's theme.

Although in terms of teaching Lucy is "doing the same thing" as last year, her approach to classroom discipline has changed considerably. Having attended a Lee Canter workshop called "Beyond Assertive Discipline" over the summer (at her principal's suggestion), she now believes that her teacher preparation only taught her the right "attitude" about discipline ("You can do it; you'll handle it"), whereas the Canter workshop taught her "exactly how to handle it . . . the steps. Exactly how it was supposed to work." Thus she begins the year "trying to be more structured. I give much better instructions and plan my time much, much better." Tying teaching to discipline she continues: "Last year I didn't teach bell to bell very well, but this year I do a much better job and that cuts down on discipline problems a lot — just keeping them busy, making sure they know what to do."

As the year unfolds, however, her "how-to" faith in discipline procedures falters as Lucy finds herself giving more and more student detentions. Her discipline workshop doesn't help when it comes to school policies and practices. Under a new system of discipline reports and conduct referrals, teachers must record discipline infractions daily, though they cannot send students to the office for minor infractions without parents' permission to do so. Once a student's conduct referral sheet "fills up," the student *must* be sent to the office, at which time parents are notified that their daughter or son has a "record" of discipline-related infractions. Last year Lucy simply called parents following the first infraction and obtained their permission to send students to the office thereafter, but she is reluctant to do so this year, given the new and somewhat unusual system in place. She admits distancing herself from parents, recalling once when an angry parent phoned about her son's grade. Though she handled the situation well, Lucy did not fill out the requisite form for receiving parent complaints "because I was afraid that [the principal] would call me in."

This new discipline policy and her related concern with parent contacts reflect a larger situation Lucy now sees involving Mr. Lahand. This year, Lucy must reconcile the fact that a lot of her teaching colleagues don't like working there because of their principal:

> He says some dumb things. Like one time he said, in a faculty meeting, "You can't fail a student because of their homework. If they don't do their homework but they still pass the test, they master the concept and they should pass." All the teachers said "That's ridiculous!" and just went on and on about that. That was . . . probably something that a parent got him to say. . . . He makes some things harder than they have to be.

As Lucy's knowledge and awareness of her work-place culture matures, what she doesn't need is a more difficult job. She's begun to feel "settled" at Jack Simper and to recognize her multiple roles there as she slowly accepts additional responsibilities and minor leadership tasks. She's almost convinced herself that she can pay less attention to the "natural" aspects of teaching (caring for students, teaching in innovative ways, and the like) and concentrate more on management aspects, which "in a lot of ways [are] a real rewarding part of my job, too":

> I think I always knew how to teach [and I looked forward to] just being where I naturally felt good. . . . I think teacher preparation programs should prepare teachers for the management part of it, because you are really a manager more than a philosopher. . . . You have to manage a classroom; you have to manage your paperwork and your responsibilities; you have to manage the parents.

This developing importance in management stems in part from Lucy's satisfaction with several workshops she has attended during her beginning years of teaching, which have helped her learn do things better and more efficiently. Additionally, she has a second successful teaching year despite additional responsibilities, including "unofficially" mentoring a new first-year teacher: "I've enjoyed doing that. I thought it was fun to be a leader!" Lucy exclaims. She is now convinced that even her success as a student in high school, and especially college, was due to good management: "I just went to class all the time . . . and I take good notes. . . . Good management skills."

Her growing awareness of the positive force of management skills is also linked to the fact that Lucy has begun work on a master's degree in educational administration. Taking one class each semester, she credits her early coursework with having a direct and positive impact on her teaching, noting time management, priority setting, and stress-management skills as examples of this. She tells how her own assistant principal, "fresh from the classroom," sees herself not as an administrator so much as a teacher "teaching some real important things" to the teachers she sees every day. Management and leadership meet teaching, for Lucy, at the crossroads of administration.

Lucy is invited, during her end-of-year conference with Mr. Lahand, to teach eighth grade next year, but she declines, reckoning that "it would be totally different. I'd have to retrain myself and I'd have to use totally different methods with those kids." She does agree to the possibility of assuming additional leadership responsibilities in the role of "head teacher" among her sixth-grade colleagues if the current head teacher moves into administration. "I could see myself doing that," Lucy notes, "I could even see myself being a department head."

Talk of Collective Support

Following year two as a teacher, Lucy writes that she wants to become an administrator who is "highly respected" and a "leader in the field." Her new dream is "to have an impact on education. Some day (before I'm 35) I would like to be in the position to make teachers happy and fulfilled. I know this would result in better education for their students."

These shifts in Lucy's language and reform vision represent just one concern with the stratification of teaching. A second ironical promise for a more staged career in teaching is that such stratification can allow top teachers to actually help create community and promote collegiality within their schools. Teachers who reach this career zenith will be, according to reformers who promote differentiated staffing, teachers who have derived their authority not so much from their new titles as from collegial respect. Freed from some amount of their traditional work load (i.e., classroom teaching), they will be better able to develop a shared sense of community among their peers; to provide help, support, and guidance when needed; and to work to strengthen the collective culture of teachers' work.

New Friends, Same Context. At least three problems accompany this assertion. First, this scenario assumes that through structural change the nature of a culture can be changed. Elevating someone within a community and then making that person responsible for "community building" is not likely to change an intensely individualistic culture. Some research suggests that such teacher leaders actually end up distanced from their colleagues (Smylie & Denny, 1989), in part because helping each other is not a part of the culture (Little, 1987). And even when teachers acknowledge their preference for being directed toward change by "one of their own" (as opposed to a full-time administrator or outside consultant), they continue to need an environment that not only welcomes and invites interpersonal dialogue and communication but is structured to promote it (Fullan, 1991). As Fullan (citing Fullan & Hargreaves, 1991) puts it:

> The implication is that teacher-leaders should be working on improving the professional culture of the school—helping to make teaching more public, encouraging norms of improvement, helping teachers examine the consequences of instructional practice for students, etc. It will require confronting norms of isolation, while at the same time avoiding the imposition of solutions, premature forging of consensus, and failure to take into account the personal situations of those with whom the teacher-leaders wish to work. (pp. 139–140)

No Need for Contrived Collegiality. Another problem with elevating someone from the teaching ranks to build collegiality and community among teachers has to do with the nature of the collaboration that is most likely to result from such arrangements. Little (1990) discusses the relationship between collaboration and culture, noting that some forms of collaboration, such as sharing and helping, are essentially superficial in nature and form "weak ties" among people. In contrast, deeper forms of interaction, such as joint planning and experimentation, require what she calls "joint work" and depend on fundamental structural changes within teachers' environment. These distinctions bear a resemblance to the Fullan and Hargreaves (1991) notions of "contrived collegiality" and "collaborative cultures." In the former we find bureaucratic structures, like mentoring programs, and specific job descriptions, like "support teacher," all of which require contacts seen by many teachers as encroachments on their valuable time. The latter, collaborative cultures are those in which contacts with colleagues represent interactions central to teachers' work. Both Hargreaves and Little insist on noting in their work that those who would reform teaching must always be wary of assuming that collaboration is uniformly good in light of institutions as well as individual teachers. Nonetheless, their caution remains strong that the nature of collaboration is central to efforts for successful cultural change.

Though she never saw herself as "one of the gang" of Bridenthal Interns, it was Jan's attachment to her departmental colleagues that made her feel most positive about returning to a second year of teaching at Justin High.

Jan spent the summer developing plans for a "more-take-charge" approach to discipline—labor she feels was well spent, especially after learn-

ing that this year two of her five American history classes are "fundamentals." Justin tracks students, and those in the fundamental classes,
according to Jan, were students with reading levels at or below third grade:

> A lot of times it's the students that have finally given up on school.
> They failed the class so many times and [the administration] just sticks
> them in there. They don't give a darn about the whole thing anyway,
> and they're going to drop out when they turn seventeen. They're not
> motivated at all. . . . It's going to be a lot more difficult to control
> them than it was to control my regular students. And it's going to be a
> lot tougher because I've never worked with the fundamental students.

On top of a new kind of teaching challenge come new regulations and
job-related responsibilities, including bus duty and a new administrative
policy that requires teachers to keep track of student absences and send
notification to students' homes at various intervals. Jan isn't thrilled about
more paperwork.

The occasional Bridenthal gatherings make Jan thankful for the friends
she's made among her teaching peers. Because she places such a high pre-
mium on experience, she sees her colleagues as good teachers who assure
Jan that with experience, she'll get better at her work. Queried about this
group's collective energy toward educational reform, she admits that "although they're very wonderful people they're very [pause] negative, maybe;
not lazy, but they won't get together to make changes. They're really great
about complaining about changes all the time, but actually trying to work
together to make a change—that's a different story." Like last year, year
two finds Jan seeking continuous advice from her friends in the department
because, once again, Jan's trying to survive as a teacher.

"I don't know why," Jan offers in the fall, "but I don't have quite the
same attitude I had about teaching last year. . . . I don't feel as positive. It
wasn't long after school started before I started feeling this way." Several
factors bring this about. First, Jan finds herself no better organized for
handling the grading of the dozens of worksheets and quizzes she routinely
collects than she was last year. Second, she knows early that her standard
teaching style is no more innovative than it was last year. "I've gotten kind
of in a rut lately," she muses at year's end when talking about her reliance
on worksheets, "because it's what the students want." She tries several
innovative ideas offered by her faculty friends, but with no apparent success:

> I would have students read the section of the book and they had to tell
> me about it. And then we would have a quiz over it at the end. And

we did that for one chapter, and I thought they were going to kill me
when we were finished. They hated it! They hated that they had to be
responsible for the material; that I wasn't just spoon feeding it to
them.

She is uncomfortable with her teaching and knows that it bores both her
and her students, yet she is tired of fighting to have them accept something
different. To make matters worse, these students' test scores are nowhere
near as high as those of last year.

A third factor affecting Jan's teaching is discipline. She has little luck
with parents, now believing that 75 percent just don't care. She theorizes
that basic to problem students is "a very poor family life. And then they get
here . . . and they rebel against all their problems that they try and leave at
home." This theory helps Jan see why discipline problems arise with students in all tracks and in all schools, though she lays considerable blame at
the feet of the administrators who put certain combinations of students into
these tracked classes. At no time, however, does Jan question the tracking
system itself.

To make matters worse, she discovers early problems with the school's
"disciplinarians":

They seem to back the student more than they back the teacher. If I
would send down a discipline form, I would have to be prepared to
[further] defend my position, whereas I kind of felt that if it was serious enough for me to write the kid up, then the kid deserves whatever
punishment is warranted. I shouldn't have to defend my position any
more than I have on my discipline report.

Refusing to defend her discipline decisions in this manner, Jan decides in
October not to send another student to the office unless the offense is purely
procedural (cutting class, being tardy, etc.). In effect, Jan traps herself
within a discipline nightmare, helping to explain why at year's end she says,
"If I had to teach the same kids . . . for the rest of my life . . . I would go
crazy. . . . All of them are nuts." She tries everything, from warnings and
"heart-to-heart" talks to keeping them after school. In the end what worked
best was measuring the amount of time a class wasted and keeping them
after the bell for the same amount of time: "It's not the most positive
approach and it makes some kids suffer, but it's been the one that's most
effective."

Jan's most significant problem, however, is her students' low motivation and apparent apathy. Asked at year's end about classroom discipline,
Jan quips: "Who cares about that any more? I just care about trying to get

them to do anything. Even if they're acting poorly, it's trying to get them to write their name on a sheet of paper that I have trouble with now." Five classes of freshman American history, two of which are "fundamentals," leads Jan to realign her notions of the teacher's role:

> I think that obviously a big part of teaching is going to be getting information across to your students that they need to carry with them. But I think also something that I've found to be important these last two years is working to motivate students to do *anything*—even if it's not [related to] history: to brush their teeth in the morning or to graduate so they can get a job.

Jan finds some comfort when other teachers tell her that they, too, share her concerns and that this apathy she recognizes is apparent throughout much of the ninth-grade class as a whole. This is just the sort of thing Jan finds so endearing about her workmates and makes her feel so lucky for having ended up at Justin.

By year's end Jan knows that she'll be leaving to follow her fiancé to his new job, and despite her bad year she believes that if she weren't moving she "would probably stay because of the friends I've made within my department [more] than because I would enjoy what I was doing." Once again, her luck held out:

> I still think that the people I work with [pause] I'm very lucky. The students I work with are a different story. But I think that . . . I'm very lucky to have the people that I work with. I'm going to be leaving the school this year and that really upsets me. That I have to leave those people. Now, the students—you can throw them out the window. . . . I'm not going to miss them.

It is difficult to imagine how the creation of an internal hierarchy for teachers could lead to the sort of collegial bond Jan finds naturally among her peers. Thus we suggest that a third problem with reform efforts that create formal leadership hierarchies has to do with their need and function in the first place. The work of Rosenholtz (1989) helps us to better understand this concern.

The Power of Natural Leadership. In her superb study *Teachers' Workplace*, Rosenholtz (1989) describes quite different conceptions of teacher leadership within environments that ranged from collaborative to isolated in their overall nature. Teachers in virtually all of the "collaborative" schools identified leaders among their colleagues, while fewer than half of the teachers in schools characterized as "moderately isolated" did so, and only one-sixth of teachers in "isolated" schools recognized colleague leaders.

More to our point is that none of these schools formulated a structured, identified "role" called teacher-leader. Rosenholtz's work has shown that educators who work within a collaborative environment readily recognize leaders among their ranks and see in them colleagues who share concerns for the work of teachers. This is not to suggest that these "naturally identified" leaders ought not to be recognized and rewarded for their important work through salary stipends or career differentiation. Rather, this research helps us to understand the relationship between the institutional culture and the ways in which it shapes and is shaped by teachers' work. How much more efficacious might these natural teacher-leaders be if they could work with their colleagues to literally reshape the organization and rules of the institution itself? If they could create an environment in which teachers' work had a fair chance to challenge and change teachers' jobs? If the respect and professional power they enjoyed from their teaching peers proved influential with school administrators and board members?

That we can feel so sure of the kinds of leadership to result from reforms that create new teacher-leaders stems from several sources. To begin, the culture of schools as institutional bureaucracies prompts an industrial orientation to leadership (Marshall, Otis-Wilborn, & Sears, 1991). Industrial leadership works best in structures that are hierarchical; environments that are bureaucratic, task-oriented, and routine; and value systems that promote a priori knowledge, expert authority, and systems maintenance. Such a culture works to prohibit the emergence or introduction of characteristics such as the shared authority or facilitative structures of human relations–oriented cultures or the flattened structures and mediated understandings of knowledge found in transformative cultures.

Reform-proposed leadership strata stand in stark contrast to the kinds of natural or emergent leadership that currently exist among teachers. As envisioned, these appointed leaders will enjoy increased autonomy at the expense of their former teaching peers — autonomy that comes in service to management as opposed to students. Without the realization or felt need and desire to see larger changes in the overall social and political discourse that shapes the very ways in which we understand schooling and teaching, and without the means to alter the structures and functions of schools as they currently exist, these new teacher-leaders will be left with mid-level management roles in the never-ending game of "piecemeal tinkering." Unfortunately, for them and their teacher peers, their realm of power and authority will be restricted to tinkering with those pieces that largely constitute teachers' work and culture.

NEW VISIONS FOR NEW PROFESSIONALS

"Good ideas and missionary zeal," writes Sarason (1971), "are sometimes enough to change the thinking and actions of individuals; they are rarely, if ever, effective in changing complicated organizations (like the school) with traditions, dynamics, and goals of their own. To change complicated settings requires, initially at least, a way of thinking not the same as the way we think about changing individuals" (p. 213). The "way of thinking" represented in most contemporary education reform reports is hardly different from the way we've always thought about educational change. As before, these reports operate from the perspective that teaching, teachers, and the schools in which they work are largely the same—or at least alike enough so that we can talk about change in unspecific, generic terms. As we have shown in this chapter, and as most educators will tell you if asked, change is always site-specific—and lasting change results from the involvement of everyone concerned.

Talk of changing or improving teacher education must, therefore, be tied to talk of changing schools—not simply changing teachers' work but changing the job of teaching by restructuring and reevaluating the school culture. Change of this sort recognizes the importance of teachers as participants in, not merely recipients of, change. Change of this sort recognizes the need to see change within its broader historical, social, and political contexts—contexts that have shaped the very language and understandings we presently have about education. Indeed, change of this sort requires genuine new ideas—not mere variations on old and usually bureaucratic ones.

Further, the process of becoming a teacher would change dramatically, as the places where teachers are taught experienced cultural change. Preservice candidates would learn that their future career is nothing short of a life's work that, while rooted in the classroom, requires them to take their energy, intelligence, and wisdom as educators well beyond classroom walls. These future teachers would recognize the absolute necessity of developing and evolving a genuine social vision to guide their work and would learn to see that their rewards are to be measured not in test scores and college-bound graduates but in the kind of society their students help to shape and build. Most importantly, people who enter teaching that is genuinely reformed will come to understand that their work, like that of all others, shapes and is shaped by political, social, and economic forces at every turn, and that in order to maintain a balance in this cultural dynamic they must actively and intelligently participate in representing their profession in this exchange.

Though Gene exhibited a sense of social vision during his student days at Central, it doesn't seem to have carried over to his life as a teacher. Nor does he exhibit much faith in his ability to successfully struggle with the forces that shape his teaching conditions.

Gene finds himself with another appealing schedule for his second year. He spent his summer reading and preparing for his two history classes, anxious to get back to teaching despite his visit to school in late summer to get his room readied:

> I walked into the office of the vice-principal and he looked at me. At first he didn't recognize me because I'd grown a bit of facial hair, so I took off my sunglasses. He said, "Oh! You're not going to keep that [beard] into the school year, are you?" It wasn't, "Hi. How are you doing? Did you have a nice summer?" . . . I told him, "Yes. It's nice to see you, and it'll stay on at least a month."

In some respects Gene's second year mirrors his first. His work schedule is no less demanding than last year's. He maintains his "in-charge" approach to teaching and repeats his role as intellectual model, distanced from but also personable with students. This year more students confide in him about their personal lives (drug-abusing parents, abortions, etc.) and he even shares a bit of his personal life with students: "Usually, though, not until after the first six weeks. Then I let them know I was in a fraternity in college . . . something out of Animal House. I act like I let it slip, but I don't; it's all calculated." This year, too, he worries about students who are either underprepared or intellectually unable to handle the work in his classes. In part because of this, Gene remains "innovative" in his teaching methods, recognizing this as an area of creative strength and self-doubt: "I'm not very confident of my methods because my curriculum at Central, I don't feel, was very strong in methods."

Knowledge and learning maintain their inherent value for Gene in year two, though his idea of both good teaching and teaching focus change. Gene's ideal teacher continues to be someone who is challenging, who sets high standards, and who has sufficient knowledge to see things from many perspectives. New to this mix is the teacher's primary role "to facilitate learning"—a realization Gene suspects took this long to formulate "because the methodology class [at Central] didn't come until the third year," by which time he'd established a different, content-oriented mindset. "When I came into Justin last year I thought of myself as more of a scholar and less of a teacher. It was the second semester when I started thinking about how I could get the material across better than I was. This fall I've done more of that. I've seen a need to use more creative methods." As a partial reward for his continued belief in and pedagogical attention to students' learning, Gene boasts throughout the year of students "coming back to me" to talk, seek advice, or just say, "You know, you were right," or "I really understand what you were saying."

Perhaps students know what Gene is saying, but his peers and superiors remain uncertain. Gene continues his sparring with the bureaucracy on issues such as showing "X-rated foreign films" to his European History class. With his deepening interest in teaching for better learning, Gene finds the variety of forces within his school culture to be even more constraining than last year. He is now vehement in his belief that "paperwork is inhibiting me from doing my work. You reach a point where you do so much paperwork that you don't have enough time to spend on what you should be doing—teaching and designing innovative lessons to interest your students."

But it's not simply paperwork that wears Gene's spirits. School has become "just a machine" that, unless a parent complains or a crisis occurs, functions with little concern for education or people. While *he* tries to remain focused on the intellect, "principals and vice-principals focus on efficiency. They don't worry about educating the kids, they just worry about numbers. . . . I'm not sure what [counselors] worry about." Gene offers one example:

> I attended something called the New Jersey Writing Project over the summer and learned how to better apply writing in my classroom. But when I tried to do it, I started having students bail out . . . of my class into classes that were less demanding. I only had 11 kids in the Asian History class, and that class just barely had enough to make a class. [The counselors] let three kids drop from it, and then I had my butt chewed off by the vice-principal because I had a class that was too small. . . . And the guy down the hall shows the films *Top Gun* and *Platoon* in class instead of teaching economics. I require papers. I started out with 32 kids [in my economics class] and I'm down to 20.

Gene's second year embellishes his original sense of despair and cultural deprivation at Justin. He's lost all respect for colleagues, including his department head, who "has not bought any new materials for the department in three years." Despite a system replete with master teachers, supervisors, and the like, Gene is alone: "I'm not getting support from the administration who asks me to be innovative and creative, and then are unwilling to help me out. I'm not being supported by the rest of my colleagues that I have not managed to change, like the one that shows *Top Gun* down the hall."

As we described earlier, job-related cultural forces have affected Gene's characterization of his work as a second-year teacher:

When I came into this [Bridenthal] program, my idea was that I was going to be a teacher, but I found out that I'm going to be a parent and a social worker. . . . To expect a teacher just to teach the material is like expecting a doctor only to do surgery. But teachers aren't expected just to teach the material. They also—unlike doctors—have to scrub the patient and the room before and after surgery. And they have to do all the paperwork with the insurance company, and so forth and so on.

What makes this observation even more dismal for Gene is his growing professional concern for his classroom work:

I'm not sure that I can even address diversity in my classroom. A professional can . . . but a civil servant can't. A professional can treat each student as an individual, but a civil servant has to treat all of them the same. If a teacher in the present system does not treat all the children the same and one child complains about getting a different sort of treatment, the teacher will not be backed up in the office. For example, I try to give a girl a break every once in a while for not getting to school on time. I suspect that she is living out of her car. So a parent called last week and said that I was giving certain students special treatment in my class. Now, he hasn't complained to the administration, but I have a feeling he will because I think his son's going to fail my class.

Gene elaborates on teaching as civil service:

You are told how much paperwork you have to have, how many grades to have, and what types of assignments are acceptable. If a parent doesn't agree with the assignment, the parent can take a child out of your class. . . . Why is it that parents can second-guess the professional judgment of a teacher who has been trained to do this? Every parent thinks he's a teacher!

At the close of year two Gene becomes reflective about leadership and change. Noting that "institutions like schools don't change very quickly," he does recognize some change he's fostered at Justin. He's added materials to the library as well as to his own department's collection, and a few colleagues try some new ideas he has introduced. However, he expects that "the machine will keep going the way it's been going" as teachers continue to accumulate more chores without input into what he calls "high decision-making." He warns that the powerlessness he feels is enough to send most idealistic, change-oriented new teachers fleeing from schools and suggests that teachers entering schools with master's degrees might be more successful at reform, because they will have more clout than his undergraduate degree gives him.

For Gene, recruiting high-ability young people into teaching is no longer about changing the system, developing leaders, or affecting the conditions of teaching, but about providing a service to students. He suggests something like a Peace Corps model in which energetic young people, whom we can expect to more easily and quickly get "burned out," can at least serve as he has: "I've been able to use what I know, and I've been able to impart that as well as some of my understanding about what the world needs to my students." Part of why he has lost faith in making larger change comes from his newly developed realization that school environments can alter even change zealots like him. "Retention is not workable," Gene declares.

LIKE NOVICE TEACHERS in general (a group not hoped to be comparable), these Bridenthal Interns spent their first two teaching years struggling to survive the overwhelmingly complex conditions of schools. Coping with various contexts, they virtually abandoned earlier dreams of "making a difference" for hopes of "making it through." Yet obvious differences seem clear. Ranging from an Alliance School to the cold, sprawling halls of Justin High, school cultures relentlessly affected their sense of efficacy and worth. And ironically, perhaps, Lucy and Roberto—the interns most comfortable with their initiate years—have already begun to climb the school administrator's ladder.

CHAPTER 10

Finding One's Place: Past Promises and Future Decisions

Career adjustment represents the interaction between individuals and organizations as they negotiate ways to meet their respective needs. The success attained through adjustment influences the length and nature of the relationship between the person and the institution (Lofquist & Dawis, 1969).

From its inception, the Bridenthal program set out to successfully prepare high-ability students to become career teachers. Through a liberal arts education; a focus on educational issues within the context of reform; an accent on field-based, "practical" knowledge; and an emphasis on beginning teacher seminars, the program sought to recruit, prepare, and retain these interns in the teaching profession. In the process, Wright hoped that these intern-teachers would empower their veteran colleagues, thus creating "an enhanced sense of professionalism and, ultimately, better teaching" throughout the school organization (Lichtenstein, McLaughlin, & Knudsen, 1992, p. 38). As we have shown in Chapters 8 and 9, along the way the interns' beliefs about power and their role as "catalysts for change" was transformed as their "teacher" identity gradually eclipsed that of intern while the school culture overpowered that of the university and the Bridenthal program. In short, what empowered them as interns did not necessarily empower them as teachers.

In this chapter we discuss these changes in light of career adjustment and from the perspectives of those responsible for helping these new teachers adjust. Specifically, we examine others' evaluations of the interns' effectiveness as school leaders and classroom teachers.

229

IN SEARCH OF SATISFACTION

A report by the Carnegie Foundation for the Advancement of Teaching (1988) found over 75 percent of teachers "satisfied" with their jobs in public schools. Another report, however, found more than 50 percent of teachers frustrated with educational reform and feeling "powerless" and negative about the conditions under which they worked. The majority of teachers gave school reform a grade of C or less (Olson, 1988).

In light of contradictions like these between expressed satisfaction and frustration, teachers must find other aspects of their jobs that are meaningful and rewarding. Chapman (1982) has identified certain aspects that distinguish individuals who remained in teaching from those who did not, among them the extent to which teachers feel their skills and abilities are used in their work and the value they attach to interpersonal rewards such as recognition and approval of others. Later studies (e.g., Chapman, 1984; Chapman & Green, 1986) related these factors to teachers' professional and social integration in their careers.

The interns demonstrated professional and social integration in their careers with varying degrees of success. Expecting that their academic abilities and knowledge of subject matter and policy would be employed, their reform-oriented values desired, and their experience-based awareness of classroom life respected, they were routinely disappointed with having to tolerate and negotiate their chosen career paths.

The Value of Special Abilities

A significant part of the interns' preparation for their role as change agents was devoted to building and enhancing their knowledge base—a cornerstone of the Bridenthal program. They studied education from all directions and became especially well versed in their specialization areas as well as in general educational reform policy. The value of this approach to teacher preparation is supported by one study that found three sorts of knowledge requisite for teachers who wish to change their profession, their schools, and their own classrooms: knowledge of the professional community, knowledge of educational policy, and subject-area knowledge (Lichtenstein, McLaughlin, & Knudsen, 1992).

Knowledge also served as a cornerstone of contemporary educational reform. As the Holmes Group points out in *Tomorrow's Teachers* (1986), "the past century has seen the most amazing explosion of knowledge in human history" (p. 37), and teachers bear responsibility for bringing this knowledge into the classroom. Modern-day reformists, however, present a contradiction. On the one hand, policy reports criticize the "tell-me-what-to-do" attitude of teachers and emphasize the need for them to take more control over aspects of their work. On the other hand, these same reports promote the creation of a more highly bureaucratic context that becomes increasingly more procedural and prescriptive. Gene certainly experienced this contradiction.

As a teacher of honors courses, co-director of a special mentor program, teacher of gifted and talented students, and coach for the "Odyssey of the Mind" program, Gene found himself in an anomalous position as a beginning teacher due to circumstance and opportunity. While Gene filled a number of needs for the high school, his assignments filled many of his own needs as a self-identified intellectual. This match, however, was not without its problems. On a number of occasions, Ms. Weller (Gene's area supervisor) and the principal discussed their concerns with Gene regarding his high rate of student failures and withdrawals. By year two, according to Weller, Gene had pushed his principal to the brink:

> You have, on the one hand, teachers like Gene who have very high expectations for their students, and on the other hand you have this administrator who's saying, "Look, if you fail 50 percent of your students, we're not going to be able to have a job for you next year." So, he was very obviously angry about that. I just talked with the principal this morning . . . and he kind of shook his head. . . . "He's done annoying kids in that honors class." And, I said, "He's getting better, he's getting better." He looked at me like, "How do you come up with that assessment?" I said, "Well, because he's worried about it. Last year he wasn't worried about it; this year he's concerned about it."

In his second year, Gene found himself with only 10 students compared with other honors courses touting 75 students. This caused Gene to rethink not only his recruitment strategies but his strict entrance and grading criteria. Eventually, he adjusted his standards in order to maintain enrollment in his honors class.

Gene's knowledge was a commodity for only a select group of students who reflected his own high ability. Ms. Weller noted that his rapport with the upper-level students was generally better than with the regular track students because of his high expectations for scholarship. "He doesn't relate to kids that just want to get out of high school and just want to get the job done," she offered. This helps to explain her surprise when she learns that Gene plans to stay at Justin beyond the program's two-year teaching requirement. In defense of all similarly bright, young teachers like him, Ms. Weller supported Gene's potentially *short* tenure at Justin: "For whatever time they put into public schools, they're valued as an intellectual model for others. Gene . . . [has] a respect for intellectuality in a teacher. If you can have a valuable person for one or two years . . . then it would be a missed opportunity not to attract them to Justin."

As with Gene, Rita felt her subject-matter knowledge was her greatest asset to teaching. While mathematics admittedly was not Rita's favorite subject, she excelled in it during her student days at Justin. In contrast with Gene's beginning teaching experience, Rita's hard-earned mathematics degree brought her few dividends as a new teacher.

Even though Rita was not able to pass on her extensive knowledge in mathematics and physics, she could pass on her beliefs about hard work and high expectations. Cecilia Sanchez, Rita's supervisor, noted how troubled Rita seemed when students did not take mathematics, her course, or their grade seriously:

> She sets very high goals for herself and for her students, and therefore becomes very frustrated sometimes when those goals are not attained. . . . I think she finds it easier to manage the algebra classes, which everybody would generally, because your on-level students are those who are going to be on track and are going to have a little more self-confidence.

Ms. Sanchez attributed Rita's difficulties to an absence of pedagogical knowledge and skill:

> She knows her subject area so well, and is so frustrated because sometimes it's hard to express that to the students. It's not her knowledge of the subject area that causes her problems, it's her ability to relate on a lower level sometimes. In other words, she knows what she's trying to teach, she knows the concept, but sometimes she can't get down on the level that the student is on to explain it in such a way that it becomes a concept they can deal with.

For Ms. Sanchez, Rita reflected the problem of Central's overemphasis on content at the expense of everyday teaching knowledge and skill.

> That's the big paradox that we fight within the field of education. Because I think we go from one extreme to the other. In many places, they stress that we must teach more subject matter. . . . You have more math classes to be able to teach. Then, on the other end of the spectrum, there are those who say your knowledge of the subject area of course is necessary, but you've got to be able to give that to the stu-

dents. You can know everything there is to know about math . . . just because someone is an A student in math does not mean they'll be a good math teacher.

Rita's integration into the social context was not a priority; she was too busy. She continued to work on her relationships with students, an aspect of teaching that had concerned her during student teaching. Ms. Sanchez also noted that Rita made attempts to become more involved and show an interest in her students outside of the classroom. Though not involved in after-school clubs, Sanchez pointed out, Rita attended football games during the fall season:

> I think that's important to the students to know that you care. . . . As a veteran teacher, you have a tendency to watch your students. You get to know them and they become almost a part of your family . . . you tend to follow what they do in school and their involvement in other things. And I thought that would come for Rita, as she got more experienced in teaching.

Although Rita communicated with Ms. Sanchez regularly (three to four times a week in the beginning) on issues of teaching, school policies, and discipline, her interaction with other teachers remained limited. According to Ms. Sanchez, Rita

> seems to get along well with the other faculty and is doing more now as far as spending time with them. As I mentioned before, in the beginning of the school year, she didn't eat lunch often, stayed in her room and graded papers to be with students who needed the extra tutoring. She does come out now and eat lunch with the other faculty, which I think is very important for her, just to know them and to be on a social level.

Ms. Sanchez noted a couple of instances in which Rita demonstrated initiative outside of her regular teaching duties. In her second year of teaching, Rita collaborated with another new teacher who graduated from Central a year ahead of her on a math curriculum for a basic math class. Additionally, Rita once volunteered to attend a seminar on working with students for whom English is a second language (ESL) with another teacher in the department. For the most part, however, Rita remained a loner in her supervisor's eyes.

Finding Common Ground

Sara Lawrence Lightfoot (1986) believes empowerment is present in the "goodness" of schools. Goodness is a manifestation of a school's ethos, the elements of which include its people, structures, relationships, ideologies, goals, intellectual substance, motivation, and will. In Lightfoot's "good schools," teachers are active players in conceptualizing and shaping the educational environment. There is a balance between teachers' individual development and the development of the broader school community. Lightfoot notes, "Good schools are places that recognize the relationship between the learning and achievement of students and the development and expression of teachers" (p. 25).

Achieving goodness in schools requires that the values and needs expressed by the organization and its participants coincide. Working together to create and sustain this match empowers the community and fosters adjustment by reinforcing the critical needs and values of individuals. Thus, not only are individuals allowed and encouraged to use and develop their abilities, they are reinforced in doing so. As beginning teachers, some Bridenthal Interns found themselves in contexts that conformed to their own values and needs for rewards while others found discrepancies.

What Roberto needed and valued was apparent from the beginning of the program: to be important and influential in children's lives. But Roberto also needed to be nurtured and a number of individuals fulfilled this need throughout the Bridenthal program. Eventually, Roberto found his voice as a professional peer in King-Jackson Elementary School—an ideal environment for a beginning teacher like Roberto.

Ms. Lillian, his principal, shared information about him through what she called "Roberto stories." These stories served as evidence of his impact on students:

> One of his students . . . spent his entire year with his desk next to Roberto's desk. He was just difficult to work with. He had kind of grown up not working very hard, and he was planning to do that in fifth grade, too. Roberto stayed after him all the time. Last week that young man came back to see Roberto. He likes sixth grade and he's doing well. That's kind of a success story. . . . Last year, with some of those boys, Roberto went to their baseball games, got them involved in Little League. None of their parents were there to see them, but he was there. He's a very significant other in these children's lives.

Roberto's rapport with students impressed not only Ms. Lillian but other teachers and parents:

Roberto had a very gentle child, a very sweet child who had a lot of learning problems . . . [her] father is an obstetrician . . . the mother is a nurse. . . . They weren't feeling like everything was being done for her so we had a [team meeting for referral for special education] early in the year with the resource teacher and Roberto. Roberto, a brand new teacher, asked in a soft but authoritative voice, "What's going to happen in this meeting?" I was a little bit worried sitting in there. . . . As the meeting continued, I became very impressed with him and they were, too. He had insights into that child.

King-Jackson turned out to be just the place where Roberto could be personally nurtured. In a sense, Professor Wright, who had mentored Roberto through his years at Central, had passed him on to Ms. Lillian to continue the grooming process. According to Ms. Lillian, Roberto holds special status in their school because he's the only male and, as she stressed, "I think in terms of nurturing a young teacher . . . it was very fortunate for him to be here with the supportive faculty."

Roberto taught alongside different teachers his first two years, each facilitating his development in very specific ways. Ms. Lillian described his first colleague, Ms. Justice, as similar to Roberto: "Peggy just kind of nurtured Roberto along. She very quickly became fond of him. I think Peggy and her husband have gone out to dinner with Roberto and his fiancee. They became very good friends, and they did all their planning together. She shared techniques. . . . Peggy was very encouraging of anything that he wanted to try." In contrast, Judy Haley, Roberto's "tough" second teammate, emphasized the importance of classroom management and clear behavioral expectations for students.

Roberto's image of himself as a leader grew throughout his years in the Bridenthal program. Both Lillian and Wright encouraged Roberto to continue to think about "leadership" in education. Lillian views all three of the interns she hired as "the leaders of tomorrow. They're bright, articulate young people." As noted before, following Roberto's second year of teaching, Ms. Lillian again asked him to become a grade-level chair, and this time he took the job. Like her friend Don Wright, she too encouraged Roberto to become an administrator. She offers yet another "Roberto story" to illustrate: "He was joking with me on Friday at our conference. We were talking about our counselor and how she's been a great support to him. I said, 'Roberto, when you're a principal, you need to have a counselor like that.' And he said, 'I'm going to take that one . . . she's going to work with me.'"

Lucy expressed needs somewhat different from those of Roberto. Professionally, Lucy was looking for opportunity and recognition—consistent themes in her life. While the Bridenthal program fulfilled these needs during her college years, Lucy successfully found ways to satisfy them in her role as a middle-school teacher. She worked at being a better-than-average first-year teacher and searched for opportunities that would bring her attention.

At Jack Simper Middle School, the principal, her colleagues and students, and parents thought well of Lucy—a teacher who went "above and beyond" what was expected. Mr. Lahand explains: "She works more closely with the sixth grade unit . . . they're all together, but she has a good relationship with them. If there's an idea she hasn't tried, she's willing to try it out to see if it'll help her. She uses their experience, but at the same time, she has a lot of unique ideas that she shares with others."

Others saw in Lucy a number of strong teaching qualities, including her willingness to try new instructional ideas and her rapport with students. However, she particularly impressed Mr. Lahand with her intelligence. He understood that "high ability" was a criterion for participation in the Bridenthal program and felt it made a difference in the way that Lucy could "show relationships between concepts" in her teaching. He felt this discipline-based orientation contributed much to her ability to work with middle-school adolescents. Lucy's relationship with the administration was equally as good in Bob Lahand's eyes: "No problem whatsoever. We enjoy her. We love her. She does a good job. When she has a problem, she's not afraid to come and ask us about it. She's very responsible as far as getting grades in on time or meeting deadlines for reports and all that kind of stuff. She's always very friendly. . . . She's just a good teacher."

In her new role as teacher, Lucy actively seized opportunities to be recognized as "a model." In her first two years, she published an article in *Better Teaching Magazine* describing a communication program with parents, contributed a letter to the local newspaper warning parents of "overprotecting" their children, and was nominated for the district's beginning teacher award. Lucy had begun to build a legacy with expectations of notable performance. Mr. Lahand predicted a bright future for Lucy: "I can see her as a grade-level leader. I can see her as a department head down the line. We have several of our science teachers that make presentations at conventions; I can see her getting involved with that and sharing some of those ideas that she has with others. I can see her continuing publishing articles."

In this flurry of professional activity, Lucy kept in focus her need for stability. As her formal commitment to the Bridenthal program came to an end, she was still successfully constructing a life that she could be pround of sharing with her son, Daniel.

JOINING IN THE FUTILITY

Educational policies vary in the extent to which they infringe on a teachers' work and limit opportunities for teachers to use their power to initiate change. The amount of personal control one has over aspects of the work place correlates with one's work-place commitment (Rosenholtz, 1987). The more control the "system" exercises over the work of teachers, the weaker the perceived and hence the actual link between what the individual does and the outcomes of his or her work. When this occurs, teachers lose their "internal motivation" and their sense of teaching efficacy declines. Jan's experience illuminates the control that the context and policies created and enforced by the "system" exert over the role teachers develop for themselves, in turn influencing their sense of teaching efficacy.

A number of factors created stress within Jan's environment. Jenny Kelly, Jan's supervisor, described the context in which Jan taught:

> Justin, as a large school, experiences a lot of the growing pains that large schools do. Fifteen years ago, we were a rural school district. We had a graduating class of 30 or less. We now have a graduating class of more than a thousand. So we have severe growing problems right now. This [lower] campus has been added in the last three years. We're still trying to work between the two campuses. Jan has had to work in an environment where a lot of things are experimental and they're not working very well. And, she's dealt with them very decently.

Jan expressed concern with Justin. Frustrated because the state competency tests did not reflect what she taught, worried that teachers who were assigned "fundamentals" classes (like herself) were being punished, and bothered by the lack of administrative support in her building, Jan turned to Jenny for emotional support. Ms. Kelly shared that Jan has "cried on my shoulder . . . but I just say, 'That's the system.'" During Jan's second year, she experienced health problems about which Ms. Kelly speculated: "I think the system is strangling her, like it is a lot of young people coming out with all their ideas about what they can do. Then they're crammed in a square hole; but they're round!"

Jan often found it easier to follow suit. She went out of her way, for example, to avoid talking with administrators but continued to bring her concerns to Ms. Kelly: "Jan's concerns were legitimate, I mean she should be able to go [to the administration with them]. As a new teacher, she still experiences that, 'I don't want to cause any trouble' kind of attitude. She hasn't gotten over that yet."

Jan demonstrated a more flexible response to her job than did other interns, finding it easier to give up control and follow a path of least resistance. Consequently, she grew to believe that aspects of teaching outside of her control, such as school policies and students' background experiences, controlled her teaching effectiveness.

Jan found satisfaction in meeting the technical aspects of her job and developing a social network of teacher friends rather than a sense of teaching efficacy. Power and control for Jan was within her classroom. Based on her student teaching experience, Jan understood the importance of establishing classroom control. And, though Jan confided that she was usually just "one step ahead of the students," Ms. Kelly's impressions were that she also had control of subject matter: "Jan had no trouble relaying subject matter to the students. . . . [Often] that's a problem, bringing information down. She doesn't have any problems with that."

Jan quickly adjusted to Justin's culture. Supervisors complimented her for calling parents according to school policy, teaching to the test, and participating in writing goals and objectives. She also plugged into the social context, according to Kelly: "She came right in and settled in and she is very well liked in our department." Although other Justin teachers (including Rita and Gene) shared Jan's frustration with "the system," she tolerated those aspects over which she felt she had no control and drew satisfaction from aspects of teaching that fit her social needs. No one encouraged Jan to revolutionize teaching at Justin, and from her earliest days as an intern Jan never promised to be on the forefront of educational reform. As the other interns assumed their roles as "a new breed of teacher" and broadcast their mission as "catalysts for change," Jan's response then was much the same as her response now: She would be satisfied with control of the technical aspects of teaching, students dutifully working in her classroom as she enjoyed the support of a select group of teacher friends.

Pondering what Jan might be doing in five to seven years, Kelly offered.

I don't know what the system's going to do to her. If she gets in a school system or if the reform movement continues to change and open and move towards teaching as a craft rather than just another profession, then she might stay because she'll get some self-satisfaction out of it. Right now, she feels like many of the others, that she's beating her head against a wall. And that's unfortunate.

VIEW FROM THE ORGANIZATION

An individual's tenure in a job or career is a function not only of career satisfaction but also of an employer's satisfaction with the individual's job performance. Loftquist and Dawis (1969) refer to this aspect of career adjustment as "satisfactoriness"—that is, an individual's ability to fulfill the task requirements of the work environment. Satisfactoriness is an external indicator or others' perceptions of an individual's successful adjustment. Traditionally, performance evaluations are used to measure satisfactoriness. The degree to which an individual meets the employer's performance expectations impacts further development and employment in a particular job or career. While teachers' work is primarily directed toward students, they must satisfy three other constituencies or "stakeholders": the school (organization), educational reform (policy), and society at large.

For the schools, measurement and recognition of teachers' developing competence is operationalized through teacher evaluation practices:

> The purposes of teacher evaluation are often described as dichotomies between assessment and assistance orientations, formative and summative evaluation, employment and dismissal decisions, and qualifying and not qualifying for merit pay or career ladder advancement. . . . Teachers tend to support systems that primarily support professional growth and do not force comparative decisions. On the other hand, less support and acceptance are evident when the system provides information for career ladder placement and incentive pay decisions. (Andrews & Barnes, 1990, p. 570)

The induction period coincides with the early "probationary" period wherein future employment rests with performance as evaluated by supervisors and administrators. Here evaluation is more often summative than formative. The power relationship is clear: Evaluation facilitates the organization's abilities/capabilities in meeting its needs by determining the extent to which the teacher contributes. For most beginning teachers, evaluation is an "early teaching" concern and most expect performance evaluations to be more negative than they turn out (Fuller & Brown, 1975; Marso & Pigge, 1987).

According to Stodolosky (1985), several major assumptions undergird the current educational reform context regarding the evaluation of teacher performance: Good teaching can be defined (valid); and teaching effectiveness is stable, repeated by a teacher over time and in different instructional contexts (reliable). Additionally, such evaluations assume that a "generic" set of observable behaviors exist that constitute good teaching and are somehow linked with research. Medley (1982), however, contends that the only generic set of skills that meet the criteria necessary to develop a research base are those associated with the maintenance of a learning environment.

The recent frenzy in developing alternative teacher evaluation and assessment practices seeks to develop valid and reliable measures of teaching performance that are efficient and practical. The variation in instrumentation, however, makes achievement of valid and reliable measures difficult. Instruments vary not only on the basis of assumptions regarding the observability and measurement of teaching performance but on assumptions tied to specific theoretical frameworks or models of teaching. Different instruments, in fact, can yield different views of a teacher's performance, as can the perspectives and biases that evaluators bring to the evaluation process.

The interns' first two years of teaching were formally evaluated according to a summative instrument, the State Teacher Appraisal System (STAS), used statewide for career ladder decisions, staff development, and contract renewal. At least two different professionals (one of whom is the beginning teacher's immediate supervisor) observe the novice four times a year during both scheduled and unscheduled visits. The observer rates four "domains" of teaching behavior:

1. Instructional Strategies—provides opportunities to participate actively and successfully; evaluates and provides feedback on student progress during instruction
2. Classroom Management and Organization—organizes materials and students; maximizes amount of time available for instruction; manages student behavior
3. Presentation of Subject Matter—teaches for cognitive, affective, and/or psychomotor learning; uses effective communication skills
4. Learning Environment—uses strategies to motivate students for learning; maintains supportive environment

Points are awarded based on observable evidence of specific teaching behaviors or "indicators" demonstrated at an acceptable level of quality and consistence. Teachers can also earn exceptional quality performance points (EQ's) for teaching behaviors within each of the categories. A total of nine EQ's is possible on any one observation.

We used the Teacher Performance Appraisal System (TPAS) to gather independent teaching data characterizing the interns' work as teachers across four teaching episodes—two during student teaching and two during the latter part of the interns' second year of teaching (see Chapter 7). These data were ultimately synthesized to formulate a level of performance for each of five functions and an overall level of performance on a six-point scale, ranging from "Superior" (consistently outstanding and at the highest level of performance) to "Unsatisfactory" (consistently inadequate/unacceptable teaching performance that requires considerable improvement).

These two sets of standardized observation data serve to complement comments from the interns' supervisors, department heads, and/or principals—those individuals responsible for ultimately judging the interns' adequacy as classroom teachers. Further, these individuals highlighted the interns' teaching strengths and compared them with typical first-year teachers. Taken together, these data create a detailed picture of the interns' teaching performance.

All interns, according to scores earned on the STAS, met the minimal criteria for "acceptable" teaching performance. In fact, most were judged to have "exceeded expectations" by their second year of teaching. They seldom lost points and on almost all evaluations received from one to nine EQ's. The domains in which most lost points were Management of Student Behavior and Management of Instruction, while every intern earned EQ's in Learning Climate. Jan, like the others, performed well.

Jan: Contradictions

Jenny Kelly, Jan's department head, considered Jan an unusual case. Impressed with her "confidence from day one" and her classroom management skills, Ms. Kelly compared Jan favorably with other beginning teachers. She also expressed "no doubt" that Jan could teach children "at all levels." In her opinion, Jan displayed the intelligence to teach honors courses ("where smart kids will learn on their own no matter what") and the pedagogical skills to teach the "fundamental" classes.

Jan's formal STAS evaluations revealed a similar picture. Four different people evaluated her over the two years. While she lost points from time to time (in three of eight evaluations), it was most often for missing a step in the "lesson-cycle" or not obtaining participation from every student in the class. Justification for her EQ's for "creating a supportive environment" included:

> "Pleasant classroom climate. Lots of encouragement. Excellent rapport."
>
> "Teacher was courteous even when students did not meet expectations. She even encouraged a student whose English proficiency was not fluent."
>
> "Teacher smiled. Teacher kneeled next to desks to assist group work."
>
> "She passes three students, pats arms as calming effect."

Jan provided organized instruction, in terms of her ability to direct and manage class activities, and she provided explicit directions (with dates assignments were due and chapters to read). On one occasion, the observer praised her for having students' names for groups on an overhead and in different colors.

However, independent evaluations on the TPAS over her first two years placed Jan's overall performance somewhere between "below standard" and "at standard." The very behaviors that Jan was praised for by her own supervisors and administrators were observed by an outside expert and educational practitioner to be "below standard," including her management of instructional time, instructional presentation, and instructional monitoring of student performance. Nonetheless, Ms. Kelly viewed Jan in terms of her performance as a second-year teacher as: "very unusual. . . . About the third year is when they begin to come out of their shell so to speak, and they feel confident about the material that they're teaching. Jan's had confidence from day one."

Jan's view of the purpose of her evaluation was that it was to meet another school policy—one she may have complained about, but in which she was required to participate. In the same way she mastered the teaching routine, she mastered the evaluation routine. In fact, her teaching style nicely fit with the lesson-cycle formula on which the evaluation tool was based. Gene was a different case altogether.

Gene: No Compromises

Justin administrators, like most school-based practitioners, placed great importance on the ability to use what are identified as "generic" pedagogical teaching skills measured by most standardized evaluation instruments. Research on effective teaching becomes codified in lesson-cycle models that prescribe specific teaching behaviors that are expected to be present and accounted for, regardless of the subject matter. Gene found such prescriptives at best troublesome, and at worst insulting.

Gene's first two years were rebellious. According to Amelia Weller, "Gene came in with some preconceived ideas that 'There's a lot of administrative garbage and I'm not going to like it.'" Fighting this "garbage" every step of the way, he found the state's formal evaluation process neither threatening nor valuable. Ms. Weller noted that compared with other first-year teachers, Gene "has a lot of confidence in himself as a presenter, as a leader of instructional activities. He has not been overly caught up in the evaluation instrument; he has not gotten bent out of shape."

Also, as one might expect, Gene's teaching evaluations demonstrate that he had his own style, which would not be compromised by something as simple as the lesson cycle. His scores indicate a consistent absence of a review statement at the beginning of a lesson, a purpose or objective, and a summary of the major lesson points.

Gene, however, was skillful in other aspects of his instructional presentation. His strengths included posing appropriate-level questions, offering relevant examples and demonstrations to illustrate concepts, and providing feedback to students throughout his discussion-focused classes by continually probing students' knowledge. In short, Gene wrestled with students over academic content and issues. Our independent evaluator wrote, "Overall rating was 'above standard.' I rated him above standard in two important areas, management of instructional time and instructional feedback. If Gene had incorporated review and summary into his lessons, he would have earned an 'above standard' or 'well above standard' for his instructional presentations."

The complex relationship between Gene and Justin is best characterized by mutual disdain and mutual need. Justin needed someone with Gene's intellectual and subject-matter background to teach "bright students," and Gene needed to fulfill his scholarship requirement and save money for his future educational pursuits. Perceptions of Gene's satisfactoriness at Justin High School, while based on his teaching, become tainted by his intellectual arrogance.

THE POWER OF PUBLIC POLITICS
IN EDUCATIONAL REFORM POLICY

Policymakers' dissatisfaction with the outcomes of schooling in the early 1980s resulted in mandated observable competencies for all teachers. Teachers were held responsible for the declining achievement of youth across the nation based on data that called into question the quality of practicing teachers and those preparing to teach.

In an effort to address the public's concerns, teaching competence was closely linked with subject-matter knowledge. The Holmes Report, the Carnegie Report, and the NCETE all called for the recruitment of individuals with outstanding, above-average academic ability. However, realizing that the link between subject-matter knowledge and teaching can produce results that are ineffective, they prescribed better evaluation of teaching performance. In this regard, the Carnegie Task Force (1986) emphasized that while the teaching work force needed "people of substantial intellectual accomplishment," these new teachers also needed to be able to "communicate what they know to others" (p. 25).

Attempting to balance subject-matter competence with teaching performance, the Holmes Group (1986) offered the following teacher competency description: "Competent teachers have knowledge, skill, and professional commitments that avoid the problem of 'bright person' versions of the teaching-learning process" (p. 29). These bright-person models are teachers who can present a substantive body of knowledge or, preferably, present knowledge *and* keep order, or, ideally, plan well, present knowledge, *and* keep order.

Lucy: A Model of Reform

Of the five interns, Lucy most closely reflected the teacher characterized by educational reformists. While bright, she worked well with students
(including those classified as "low ability") and demonstrated a desire to
move up the new career ladder. She also impressed her supervisors, including Bob Lahand: "I would say she's above most of our first-year teachers so
far." He attributed her teaching success to a number of factors: "She does
unique things in class with the kids to help them learn the concept. It's not
just out of the book or just little things. She shows relationships a lot
between different concepts. I was always very impressed when I'd go observe her."

The exceptionally high scores Mr. Lahand gave Lucy on the STAS
evidenced his evaluative seal of approval. Over the two-year span, he conducted four evaluations. Only once did Lucy lose points; in December of
her first year Lahand wrote: "Several students rested heads on their desks
and were not redirected." In his opinion, Lucy's only problem came at the
beginning of her first year, in the area of student discipline. However, she
changed her approach and gained better control.

Scores from her outside STAS evaluators also reflected a positive view
of Lucy's teaching. She gradually grew from receiving three to all nine EQ's
during her second year. Lucy was elated: "Few beginning teachers received
nine EQ's."

According to Mr. Lahand, Lucy's teaching abilities distinguished her
from not only other beginning teachers but also many veterans:

> In her presentations in classes, she offers more than a lot of veteran
> teachers. Sometimes they may be set in their ways, and they don't like
> to deviate from that. She makes her classes very interesting; brings in a
> lot of different items, approaches kids in different learning styles. It's
> not all lecture and discussion, but she'll have models that they'll look
> at or work with. . . . She tries to find what interests kids by going be-
> yond "the book."

In contrast, after observing Lucy teach four science lessons from student teaching to her second year in teaching, the independent evaluator
using the TPAS concluded:

> Lucy's teaching was a genuine enigma. The first two observations [dur-
> ing student teaching] were rated as "at standard"; the second two ob-
> servations [as a second-year teacher] were rated as "below standard."
> The expectation is that after one gets out in the field and gains addi-

tional experience, one's teaching expertise becomes better instead of worse.

Lucy received an overall combined evaluation of "below standard" on the TPAS. Problem areas included: making maximum use of instructional time, managing students' behavior, monitoring instructional performance, and providing adequate feedback. Evaluator comments from her final lesson document these difficulties:

Lucy did not appear to have procedures and rules for student participation clearly established. Sometimes students raised their hands, other times they spoke randomly. She did not respond promptly and consistently to students who were talking when they should have been concentrating on their tasks and who were out of their seats when they should have been seated.

The areas in which Lahand gave Lucy the most credit (explaining difficult concepts and creating interesting lessons) were not consistently evident in the collection of observation data from Lucy's first two years of teaching. Often she spent minimal time on didactic teaching and maximum time on independent student work.

Rita: One Image Lost, Another Found

Rita demonstrated problems with behavior control from the beginning; however, her supervisor, Ms. Kelly, characterized Rita as "a very dedicated teacher who really works hard for what she feels is best for her students." The problems that she experienced were typical of most other beginning teachers and her handling of them improved with experience: Rita became more confident in dealing with classroom behavior problems, more knowledgeable and adept at following school policies (e.g., communication with parents), and more flexible in dealing with students' math difficulties.

However, Rita's formal teaching evaluations on the STAS did not illustrate experiential growth. All but two of her eight evaluations awarded her all points possible, including EQ's ranging from one to five points; the behavior problems so apparent to Rita and Ms. Kelly were never noted by outside evaluators, who found instead "an excellent climate of courtesy; Good positive respect in the classroom; Excellent rapport with students; Very positive classroom atmosphere." Kelly, who observed her twice, wrote on Rita's last evaluation: "I think it's a shame that you may not be with us next year but the experience of working abroad will be invaluable. I wish you the very best!"

According to the alternative TPAS instrument, Rita's teaching strengths were Instructional Monitoring and Instructional Feedback—both rated "above standard." Her mathematics lessons were structured with teacher-student problem solving and oral and written "products" for evaluating student performance. Our independent observer wrote: "Overall rating of 'somewhat above standard.' . . . Management of instructional time, management of student behavior, and instructional presentation rated as 'above standard.'"

During her second year of teaching, Rita began working on new knowledge and skills as well as a new career image. She began Japanese language classes and applied for an international program to travel to her mother's homeland and teach English in Japan.

Roberto: Straddling Agendas

Two years of formal evaluation evidenced Roberto's teaching effectiveness on the basis of criteria set by the STAS. Ms. Lillian's evaluation at the end of year two concluded that Roberto "exceeds expectations." On all but one of eight occasions, Roberto received all possible points, with from four to five EQ's earned for providing students with feedback, student involvement, organizing students and materials, and managing behavior. On every evaluation, Roberto earned EQ's for creating a supportive environment.

While Roberto always scored well on evaluations, Ms. Lillian recalls with astonishment how grateful he was, viewing mistakes as an opportunity to learn:

> He was observed last year by our language arts consultant in the district. And he had a terrible time while she was in there, on classroom management. It's terrible, but she had to give him zeros in that area. And normally that's very upsetting to a teacher, and can create a very antagonistic conference. And Roberto's response to her—and I was present—was, "I saw what was happening and I was so glad you were there because I know I need some help with that." Well, she was so impressed with him, she arranged for him to go to the reading in-service for a week.

Ms. Lillian identified Roberto's strengths as developing rapport with students and gaining insight into their needs. While she credited Roberto's personality for his teaching competence, she also believed his preparation in special education helped him.

Roberto's teaching, as determined by the TPAS instrument, reflected similar strengths. In instructional presentation and management of behavior he was rated well above standard or superior. In all other areas he received above-standard ratings. The only teaching behavior identified as inconsistent was "communicating standards/expectations for student performance." The independent evaluator wrote: "Overall rating is well above standard. Roberto is an excellent teacher who will only get better as he gains additional experience."

Other information about Roberto's teaching philosophy and practice paints a picture of an individual concerned about his students within their individual social contexts. Issues of family background and support are important to Roberto, who operates from a framework of direct experience. A member of a minority, Roberto understood the struggles that his students will encounter.

FUTURE STEPS

Chapman (1983), in testing his model of teacher retention, proposed the following hypothesis based on Holland's Trait Factor theory: "One would expect that individuals leaving a profession would be characterized by a different set of competencies and values than those remaining in that profession" (p. 45).

Within Holland's framework (see Chapter 3), teaching is described as requiring competencies, activities, and values associated with social, artistic, and enterprising (SAE) work environments. Using responses to the Self Directed Search (SDS), we categorized the interns in their first year of the program and recategorized them after two years of teaching. Their self-assessed competencies, activities, and values reveal some interesting changes.

For example, the "Mavericks" became less social. Rita, whose first-year code of ISC (I = Investigative, S = Social, C = Clerical), matched jobs such as a public-health microbiologist, scientific linguist, and mathematics teacher. She was fairly consistent in her self-assessment in year six (ICS). Her match to an investigative-type work environment was better than her earlier match to the social context most commonly associated with teaching. Rita would not teach public school the following year.

> Well, I don't think I'm going to stay [in teaching]. . . . If I didn't have this program and I just decided to go into teaching, I would have quit probably after six months my first year because of the stress and the discipline. I didn't want to deal with these kids. But knowing that you're not the only one has helped me a lot personally. And, the obligation to pay back the money is a big factor there.

In the spring of her second year, Rita interviewed with the Japanese Consulate to teach English in Japan for one year. "If it doesn't happen, I'll be in line for an insurance company . . . and it strictly has nothing to do with teaching. It would be an actual, real job."

Gene's original score on the SDS indicated he was comfortable with social and artistic environments (SIA) and matched occupations such as clinical psychologist and school psychologist. As a second-year teacher he had become less comfortable with social aspects and better matched with careers like economist, market-research analyst, or art appraiser (IAS). Gene would teach one more year before departing for graduate school:

> There have been mixed responses to my leaving. The IB art teacher was really sorry. My co-worker in the gifted and talented program said it's probably good that I leave now before my brain turns to mush in the public school system. Other colleagues have said that it's good that I'm getting out now; but most of these colleagues that I've talked to generally have spoken out of bitterness. As far as administrators, I know they're not happy with my leaving. A lot of it has to do with their trouble recruiting people who would be willing and able to teach my European History class. The principal still talks like I'm going to be there forever. I don't want to burst his bubble just yet. . . . My mother really doesn't want me to go to school again. She wants me to settle down and teach for the rest of my life. My father thinks that it's a wonderful idea that I'm going back to school and pursuing my graduate work.

Jan, the only "Traditionalist" among these five interns, changed in terms of visions of herself in a "social" environment like that of teaching. Jan's code in her first Bridenthal year (S,A/E [scores for artistic and enterprising environments were equal], I) was closely aligned with teaching. In year six, however, while her code remained similar in form (S/A [scores for social and artistic were equal],C,E), the weight given a social environment dropped significantly. In the next year, Jan planned on marrying and moving to another city where her future husband worked. However, she speculated on what she would do if she were to stay in the city: "I would stay at Justin, probably more out of laziness or inability to find another job if I weren't moving. . . . I would probably stay more because of the friends I've made within my department than because I would enjoy what I was doing."

Lucy, a "Reservationist" about teaching early on, and Roberto, a "Convert," maintained the best match with a teaching environment. Lucy's first-year and sixth-year codes (SEI) were identical. This code corresponds to a variety of careers associated with leadership, such as director of guidance, executive director of a nurse's association, president of an educational institution, and school superintendent. Lucy would remain at the Jack Simper Middle School as she pursued her graduate degree in educational administration at Central. Three years down the road, Lucy expects to have her master's degree and be eligible for the career ladder, "and that's a bonus that might keep me in." She knew she wanted to remain in education, and although she liked teaching, she liked leading more.

Roberto, one of only two "Converts" among the 17 original interns, was coded SIA in years one and six, though measurable increases exist in the year-six scores for each letter. Occupational matches included clinical, school, and counseling psychologist. Becoming a child psychologist was Roberto's original career choice—one he maintained until his senior year in college. While deciding to pursue a master's degree in educational administration, he contemplated going to school full-time, but decided to teach another year and go to school part-time. Projecting a future that includes a doctorate in education ("hopefully [to] give a lot back to education"), Roberto plans always to be near the classroom and to teach.

While aspects of the work environment may contribute to retention in teaching, they may also be constrained by personal and historical factors that individuals bring with them to the context of teaching. The variables most powerful in discriminating between individuals who remain in teaching and those who leave are initial commitment to teaching and early teaching experiences (most notably, student teaching). Thus, decisions the interns made regarding their plans to leave or remain in teaching lend support to Chapman's (1983) conclusions.

Did the Bridenthal program empower the interns? The scholarship money they received enabled them to attend Central College, an opportunity Roberto, Lucy, or Gene would not have been able to afford. The program convinced Roberto, Rita, and Gene to pursue teaching, a career they would otherwise not have considered. The program gave Lucy the push she needed to pursue teaching and eased Jan's entrance into a career that she had always wanted.

On the other hand, the program prohibited Rita and Roberto from following careers in which they indicated an interest from the beginning of the Bridenthal program (Rita in foreign language and Roberto in psychology). While teaching generally is viewed as a "stepping-stone" to other careers, the impact of delaying a known career direction (in Rita's case) or altering a previously considered career choice (in Roberto's case) won't be understood until later in the career-development cycle.

Teaching provided Gene the chance to save enough money to go to graduate school and complete a career he planned from the beginning of the program. Ironically, the Bridenthal program, followed by additional scholarship support from Central for a master's degree, cut short Lucy's commitment to the classroom by facilitating her move into administration. Recognition and leadership, Lucy determined, were best found within school administration. And Jan, while demonstrating an initial desire to teach, was never personally or professionally empowered by the Bridenthal program. Never given the opportunity to confront power, authority, or control, she relegated teaching to one of life's routines.

THE DISEMPOWERMENT OF TEACHERS: RETHINKING THE BRIDENTHAL PROGRAM

Truth is a thing of this world; it is produced only by virtue of multiple forms of constraint. And it induces regular effects of power. Each society has its regime of truth, its general "politics of truth": that is, the types of discourse which it accepts and makes function as true; the mechanism and instances which enable one to distinguish true and false statements, the means by which each is sanctioned; the techniques and procedures accorded value in the acquisition of truth; the status of those who are charged with saying what counts as true. (Foucault, 1972, p. 131)

While Ashcroft (1987) defines power as capability/ability in action, Foucault refers to the "manifestations" of power, which result in the imposition of one person's (group's) will over that of another (Ashcroft, 1987). One might take the view that contemporary educational reform created its own regime of truth whose discourse was of failure and blame; whose mechanisms included legislative and policy mandates; whose techniques were of management and control; and where status was attributed to "task force reports," experts, and tests. Giroux (1988) refers to this regime as the "discourse of domination which manifests itself in forms of knowledge, school organization, teacher ideologies, and teacher-student relationships" (p. iii).

One of the "truths" that the second wave of educational reform handed down is that "the behavior of teachers needs to be controlled and made consistent and predictable across different schools and student populations" (Giroux, 1988, p. 92). Accountability and evaluation processes are the mechanisms for achieving this truth. The power relationships between teachers, schools, reform, and society create a series of cunning responses that enhance the power of those defining the knowledge or truth and diminish the power of those who must accept and be controlled by it.

Today, teaching quality is defined (evaluated) by preparation institutions, school districts, states, and standardized instruments (e.g., National

Teacher's Exam)—with nationwide professional measures just around the corner. However, teachers teach to these evaluations in the same ways they teach to the test. Evaluation becomes "pseudo-evaluation" in the same vein as the Holmes Group (1986) defines "pseudo-credentialism": going through the motions is equivalent to achieving the goal.

A second "truth" handed down in educational reform is that there is power in integration. The formal and informal mentoring processes for beginning teachers illustrate this truth. Integration implies incorporation of the part into the whole wherein the whole has to make accommodations or shifts in order fit its new part and vice versa. Integration, thus, suggests a natural give-and-take until neither the whole nor the part is the same as before; each has to change within the relationship. However, when power is manifest as control, the individual accommodates to an unchanging whole.

Such is the integration of many new teachers into a schooling system that sees management and control as the way to achieve truth. Though constantly changing, schools are seldom transformed because the lenses through which their leaders view the world never change. If anything, their optical prescription becomes stronger and more focused, regardless of vision problems. Thus, too few teachers transform. They work, instead, and are rewarded for striving to meet unchanging organizational goals.

Giroux (1988) writes about reformulating the role of teachers as those who must rethink the broader questions of purpose and process for schooling. His reformulation includes viewing "teachers as intellectuals" who work to change the discourse of domination to one of democracy and who recognize the various ways power creates and distorts truth. He charges:

> Teachers as intellectuals will need to reconsider and, possibly, transform the fundamental nature of the conditions under which they work. That is, teachers must be able to shape the ways in which time, space, activity, and knowledge organize everyday life in schools. More specifically, in order to function as intellectuals, teachers must create the ideology and structural conditions necessary for them to write, research, and work with each other in producing curricula and sharing power. In the final analysis, teachers need to develop a discourse and a set of assumptions that allow them to function more specifically as transformative intellectuals.
>
> As intellectuals, they will combine reflection and action in the interest of empowering students with the skills and knowledge needed to address injustices and to be critical actors committed to a world free of oppression and exploitation. Such intellectuals are not merely concerned with individual achievement or advancing students along career ladders, they are concerned with empowering students so they can read the world critically and change it when necessary. (p. 122)

Don Wright had hoped that the Bridenthal program would help to transform the schools. Ironically, though, almost none of the interns understood reform as something highly complex, structural, and political in nature. They learned, instead, to believe that academically knowledgeable teachers could improve students' learning, which would, in turn, improve the quality of schools; they saw themselves as improved pieces of this amorphous schooling phenomenon. Demonstrating little understanding of the underlying nature and assumptions of reform, leadership, or school culture, the interns began teaching with narrow conceptions of their role as change agents within schools, but big ideas about reform—ideas that were quickly lost or set aside as they struggled to simply survive as beginning teachers.

Transforming Catalysts into Survivalists

With her limited understanding of the complexity of schooling and change, Rita had to question the conventional wisdom her special preparation set out to instill. She now admits that as Bridenthal Interns: "[We] are realizing how hard it would be to change the education system. I think that it needs a total overhaul . . . and the only way you're going to get that is to get mass support—and that costs money."

Roberto offered a somewhat more optimistic, though equally industrial analysis:

We [interns] came in right under reform and it was a very negative time. Everybody was just looking at the criticism; that was the main reason reform was around in [our state], to fix everything. . . . Now, I think, as time has passed, finally we've dealt with *A Nation at Risk*. . . . People . . . [are] still not that observant of what teachers are doing but I think they're now seeing that without teachers we're going to have too many people that we're going to have to support, whether through social welfare programs or things like that.

He also noted with little pride that teachers themselves often "cut their own throats. They're the first ones to start complaining about [their] situation, and people hear that and then you have disunity within your own ranks."

Roberto remains certain that he will not be one of these "throat cutters" because he believes he is making a difference in his school and its population. He will become fifth-grade chairperson as a third-year teacher and continue serving on the curriculum committee. In his words: "I've been able to be a decision maker. I've had a voice in my school."

In contrast, Gene believes — despite two years of struggle, grief, and the realization that his voice was seldom heard by his professional colleagues — that he, too, has made changes: "I think I've been a pacesetter within my own school. I know that, having looked at the body of, say, economics curriculum and materials and methods that existed before I came, there was next to nothing. After I came, we have different methods that we're using now. I'm still developing new ones." At the same time, he agreed with Rita that Justin will not have changed substantively after he leaves:

> I think that the only reason why some of those methods have changed is because I am there now and I talk to the other teachers in my department and I bring current events in to them down at the teacher's lounge, because that's where they sit . . . around and chew the fat . . . before school in the morning. They don't do any work in their classrooms. I think the machine will keep going the way it's always been going. I made a momentary . . . and very fleeting change: I'm in a machine.

Rita felt she's made a difference "for some students. As far as challenging things in the system, no." Again, she returns to the theme of the importance of teachers, echoing the very concern that motivated the creation of the Bridenthal program in the first place — a poor public image of teaching: "I think the community also needs to be aware of the difference that teaching makes in society. We definitely need more support and attempts to understand the situation of the school, the situation of the teacher, instead of constantly criticizing and saying that the teachers aren't doing a very good job."

For Gene, improving teachers and their public image was not enough; the answer to badly needed systemic change will come from above. Thus, like his friend and mentor Don Wright, Gene now believes in five-year teacher preparation programs that culminate in a master's degree because with such a degree "you'd probably be able to move up quicker within the ranks — maybe become a department chair faster." Yet, in the next few breaths, he admits that even with the added "clout" of a graduate degree, "there is no way the university can prepare me to fight this machine." Gene's paradox lies in his belief that reform comes from administrators, yet "I think I would be soiled if I went into the administration. . . . The only leadership I can exercise is by example."

The interns based their view of how change occurred on their observations of Wright: the wheeler-and-dealer for foundation monies, the consummate debater over educational issues, and the frequent delegator of menial day-to-day responsibilities. The relevance or application of this leadership model to public schools was not discussed during their formal seminars or informal chats between the interns and Wright or in their unevenly scheduled beginning-teaching seminars. Within their leadership repertoire, both human and technical skills were noticeably absent as the interns reentered public school.

Were Roberto, Jan, Lucy, Gene, and Rita reformers? Are they showing signs of leadership? The answer, of course, depends on who is asked and how one defines reform and leadership. The institutional structure, the environment in which they worked, and the organization's values made a major difference (as they do for all teachers).

While the interns' leadership styles varied, none of them had the institutional support (at either Central or in their school) to fulfill Wright's dream of their becoming "catalysts for change." None of the interns emerged, as they had repeatedly described themselves, as "pacesetters for a new generation of teachers." Rather, their successes and failures as teachers and, more importantly, as leaders, were largely determined by the dimensions of school culture (structure, environment, values) and their personalities and life experiences. Contradictions between the school and leadership culture to which the interns had been exposed, and their own force of leadership, created barriers to their functioning as "change agents."

Gene remained as professionally aloof and intellectually self-assured in May of his second year of teaching as he had been when he entered Justin two years earlier. Like his mentor Dr. Wright, Gene adopted the role of "high priest," believing that other teachers could learn from his example; administrators, mired in the technical and human relations realms of leadership, were simply ignored. Unfortunately, Gene, unlike Don Wright, had little institutional credibility and no resources to command the attention, if not the respect, of those would-be followers. Moreover, despite Gene's positive assessment of his teaching abilities, his inability to grapple with the technical and human relations aspects of being a teacher meant that he failed to inspire his students intellectually or emotionally.

In contrast, Rita moved quickly into the technical realm, acknowledging her lack of preparation in this area by Central. Rita's overriding concern with issues of classroom management and the presentation of herself in the classroom left little time for her to collaborate with colleagues in professional ways. Desperately seeking to lead herself out of logistical and administrative dilemmas, Rita was never in the position to lead others toward a vision of public school renewal; Rita never moved beyond the technical realm of leadership.

Jan, of course, never truly bought into this reformist vision of high-ability students as teacher-leaders. Content with her new circle of teacher friends, Jan settled easily into the bureaucratic routine that marks teaching.

While Gene, Rita, and Jan worked within a large high school whose structure, environment, and values fit well within an industrial orientation, Roberto's selection as a fifth-grade teacher in an experimental school opened up a variety of leadership opportunities. Taken under the wings of an exclusively female workforce, Roberto cultivated his natural teaching abilities as he observed a principal whose leadership orientation was more human relations than industrial. Lucy's environment fell somewhere between the industrial environment of Jan, Rita, and Gene and the human relations orientation present in Roberto's setting. She strived for organization and consistency in her teaching but also demonstrated a rapport and flexibility with students and colleagues that reflected her human relations leadership style.

Recasting the Mission

For most of the interns the Peace Corps model articulated by Wright, rather than the program's original goal of retaining teachers in public schools, holds the most salience. As Gene notes:

> I've been able to do something I wouldn't have been able to do had I not been a teacher: I've been able to do a service. I could have done a service in the Peace Corps or I could have done a service for the Red Cross. But, not only have I been able to do a service [as a teacher], I've been able to tie that with my love of the material and the subject which, for me at least, is more rewarding than just helping a community build some sort of center.

Recasting the Bridenthal program as a domestic Peace Corps for high-ability students attending an elite private college contributes to the successful image of the program and its participants. Of course, it conveniently bypasses the question of the model's effectiveness in retaining high-ability students in teaching and fails to examine alternative approaches to teacher retention and the development of leaders for public school reform.

Had there been better preparation of these interns on the more mundane aspects of pedagogy and leadership, would the program and its interns have been more successful? The answer to this question depends on the leadership orientation one believes most appropriate for school reform. Outside the everyday world of public schooling, the Bridenthal program appealed to reform-minded foundation directors, status-conscious Central administrators, starry-eyed interns, and the dilettantes of the education profession. Who could resist 17 bright, energetic, articulate college students primed for educational reform?

The program's architects and advocates, however, failed to consider the context in which these would-be teacher leaders would work. Not surprisingly, difficulties related to the interns' understanding of the social context of schooling and educational reform as well as the personal lived experiences of teachers and students with whom they worked emerged. The interns had little respect for the pedagogical, technical, or human relations leadership skills needed to effectively confront such difficulties. Most of the interns never perceived shortcomings in their leadership skills, choosing instead to blame others — the bureaucratic "system," the unmotivated students, the unconcerned parents — for their professional ineffectiveness and their personal anguish. A few, like Roberto, spent much of their first two years overcoming their leadership deficits through the assistance of a supportive school staff.

Certainly, those favoring the human relations and transformative orientations would argue for a substantially different structure, environment, and set of values. Persons supporting either of these alternative orientations would be bothered by the type of students selected to become Bridenthal Interns: academic high achievers, a disproportionate number of whom were female, white, and middle-class. They would undoubtedly find a particular irony in the belief that this was the best pool from which to recruit persons as teachers and educational leaders of twenty-first-century public schools primarily populated by cultural and racial minorities.

In short, both orientations would underscore the fundamental social contradiction of the Bridenthal program: the development of reform-based teacher education programs modeled on industrial concepts of teaching, learning, and leadership to work in a near-future postindustrial world in which the process of teaching, the conceptions of knowledge, the types of students, and the roles of leaders will be radically changed. Despite certainties of changing school demographics and global economies, corporate-funded reforms of the 1980s like the Bridenthal program and state-sponsored reform efforts like *A Nation at Risk* were based on traditional premises of leadership and pedagogy. As we move into another decade, the consequences of these failed premises (e.g., increases in the high school drop-out rate, decreases in standardized test scores, and centralization of educational decision making) have become apparent and so, too, will the need to rethink these premises, to ponder the question, "Why not the best?" and to acknowledge those circumstances when best doesn't equal good.

Epilogue

A FINAL CONVERSATION WITH THE INTERNS

At the close of their second year of teaching we invited the 16 graduates of the Bridenthal program to return to Central's campus and discuss the program, educational reform, and their professional futures. Among the interns who participated were Jan, Roberto, Lucy, Gene, and Rita. What follows are excerpts from the group's discussion.

Getting It Right the First Time

RITA: It's really sad when you come out of the Bridenthal program with very high expectations . . . with other people that have high expectations and that's what you've been taught, to have high expectations. Then you get knocked down for what you've done and you get chewed out for something that all your life you've been taught to do; you've grown up with that same ethic. It's very discouraging. Your hands are tied and it's basically because of the administration and not necessarily the bureaucracy.

JAN: And, how do you balance all of the demands? I find that I can only spend so much time worrying about parental involvement, worrying about my psychological needs, and my students', and worrying about if I can teach every bit of this material that I have to cover all in the same day and in one hour.

RITA: So, maybe since Central took so much time in selecting us, selecting the brightest, maybe we still need help to get us placed in selective schools or maybe we should go together into one school.

GENE: But then you run into this kind of elitism. There are a lot of kids out there that need changers and movers in the schools, and if we're all in one school that's specializing for that one school or school district.

RITA: Yeah, that's wrong. . . . Well, wherever these new teachers go, I think they need a really good support group. Someone with experience to help them deal with situations that they face. You can really face bad problems—but as long as you have a support group or someone experienced that can help you deal with your situations and correct them before they get out of hand.

LUCY: What's wrong with the concept of a "teaching school," like they have "teaching hospitals"—you know when a nurse or a doctor is just first out there they go to a teaching hospital. I think that everybody should go into an ideal situation first, maybe they're not ideal kids, maybe it is an inner-city school. But, have the administration supportive and open. And then maybe limit their time. Maybe they see the ideal world there for a little while—get on their feet and see how it can be and then go somewhere else.

GENE: But, then you're just delaying what we've been going through. Instead of after two years people thinking about leaving, you have people thinking about leaving after four. They stick around in this model school for two years and they go out into the real world and teach two years and then they're fed up. It's an extended student teaching.

JAN: But, isn't it the hope that they can see in this great school that there is some light at the end of the tunnel, somewhere?

GENE: I didn't really have a lot of choice; I was only asked by one school. There wasn't a lot of self-selection.

JAN: I don't really feel like I had "self-selection" either. I think that just the way the outside system is, there's no self-selection involved. If there is a job, then you take it. I think the Alliance School program may help. So you might need something like that if you want to have the support.

Prospects for Reform of the New Program

GENE: I think if you want to recruit people into teaching, you should improve the conditions of teaching and at the same time, by retaining the good people, the good people stay in as an example. And that is the best way to recruit other good people.

LUCY: Now, how do you identify the good people?

GENE: See, I can't do that. Like the Supreme Court uses for obscenity, I know it when I see it. But, that's about all I can give. I can't give you scientific criteria to use.

LUCY: When I was planning to be a teacher, I had the opinion, oh yeah, we need bright teachers, we need innovative teachers, we need smart teachers. Now that I'm a teacher I look around and I say, "Well, the teachers aren't that bad; at least where I am." The teachers aren't that bad, but they need some inspiring once in a while. So, I think some of the money should go to teaching old, maybe burned out teachers, or those who have just gotten into routines.

GENE: Recycling teachers!?

LUCY: Yeah, teach teachers how to do their job better. Give them more tools and more options and more inspiration. There are, however, some who don't want to change.

ROBERTO: We are dealing with a lot of people who are just in there to retire. They don't want anybody to rock the boat. They just want to get through to their pension and that's it. And it's real hard for new people like us to come in to change it completely because we're basically a threat to them.

RITA: I think that brings up a very good point about retention: that just because we don't stay here, or stay in teaching, that this program has been a failure. A lot of it has to do with situations—where you're at and how positive an experience you had. So as far as a program, I think the problem would be, how to better retain teachers in the profession. They've got to be sure to get them in a decent and positive situation. Because a lot of my experience was negative, and I think that has a lot to do with what I want to do next year or the year after that. You've got to base your future on your past experiences, and since my past experiences weren't all that positive, do I really want to come back and face all this again?

LUCY: You said it's not necessarily you as a person, but I think it is. Because if you weren't the person that you are, you wouldn't have been through Central. My father always said, "Lucy, whatever you do you're going to be a success because you've always been a success." And that's true of almost everybody around this table. . . . that a certain kind of person is successful at whatever they do.

Plans for the Coming Year

GENE: I'm going to teach at Justin next year. And I've really mulled this over in my head. . . . I'm changing everything again next year. I did that last year. And one of my goals is to raise hell next year. So what I'm probably going to do is just speak up on a weekly or bi-weekly basis. It will be my last year. But there are some things that . . . Justin could be doing better, and if I say something about it and if I go through the proper channels first and then they don't do it, which they won't, then I'll go through improper channels. They won't do anything, but at least my stomach won't be churning as much as it is right now. . . . Because I have had the vice principal use the Bridenthal Internship program against me. She said, "You have to teach two years, but not here." That has kept me with my tongue in my mouth this year but next year it won't. They've handed me my renewal contract and once I sign it, I know I'm not coming back, and barring any extreme indiscretion, they won't fire me in the middle of the year. So that's what I'm doing next year. And in the meantime, I'm learning a foreign language so that I can move into graduate school, because I will need a reading knowledge of a foreign language to go on and get a Ph.D. in history. . . . They turned Bridenthal against me, and now I'm going to turn some things around against them.

RITA: Well, I'm off over the ocean next year. I'm going to go to Japan and be an English teacher. I'm going to be on my own in a foreign country. But it will be exciting. It's an interest that I gained when I was at Central College. . . . My interest has shifted toward foreign language, whether that would be in the education field or not, I'm not real sure yet. I'll decide when I come back next year. I might even consider ESL. I've dealt with students coming from South America or Mexico . . . Hispanic students that are just placed into my classroom with no English background. . . . I don't know how to teach them but I find that helping them is much more rewarding to me. There's a language gap, and these students need me more than any of the other students . . . so maybe I'll teach ESL or something in the foreign language area . . . [where] students really appreciate you.

JAN: I'm moving to Dallas, Texas, getting married, and I hope I will be teaching. I'm attracted to districts that are more "professional" (she emphasizes by gesturing the quotes). I'm looking right now at about five districts; the ones that are the best in Dallas. If I can't get in, I want to go back to school. I'm so afraid that I can't make a difference in the schools. Maybe I can make more of a difference in some other area of education because everything gets pushed down to us and 100 of us can't necessarily speak out. Maybe I'm wrong. So maybe I can think about some other level in education.

LUCY: I always wondered when I was growing up why actors and actresses always wanted to be directors; that was supposed to be a promotion. I didn't understand that, until I figured out that the directors are the bosses; they're the ones that set the creative mood and they tell people what to do and how to do it. And I'm kind of seeing myself in that role now. I'm a teacher, and what I'm doing is important, but now I want to be the director. I want to be the administrator . . . the person behind the scenes that's more in charge . . . that has more control . . . that sets the mood for the school and tells people how they can do things better. That's why I'm in the educational administration program. I'll be there for at least two more years until I get my degree. I think it will take me longer than just getting a degree before I have enough experience to be credible as an administrator. But, probably by 30, 31, or 32, I'll be applying for an administrative position, and I hope there will be one around, and there won't be another bunch of people in front of me. But I would consider changing schools or changing districts if it meant I could be more in control. Because I know that there are a lot of people at Northside who are ahead of me that have more experience and better qualifications.

ROBERTO: I'll be at King-Jackson next year. I'd like to be there as long as I can because I really like this school. I like the chance to participate in the groundwork of everything. I want to finish my master's degree, but I don't want to leave things hanging at King-Jackson. So, I may take a leave of absence for a year just to finish my degree up and go right back. I want them to hold my job. I've said many times that my ideal situation is to take on the role of administrator but to stay in the classroom also. I want to have a situation where I can still teach kids; at least one class or something. Next year, I think there will be a lot more responsibility, a lot more pressure, but I think it's good because I've seen myself grow; I think I'll be ready for it. They offered me the job as fifth-grade team leader last year, and I could honestly say that I was not ready. They asked me again this year for next year, and I said, "I'm ready." I'm looking forward to being team leader; seeing myself take on that role, see how I do. I know they'll [colleagues] be right behind me, helping me out.

THREE YEARS LATER

As the writing of this book comes to a close (three years following the final group conversation and five years after their graduation from Central), we find the Bridenthal Interns dispersed and pursuing a variety of career paths. Recall that one of the original interns left the program in preparation for law school, leaving 16 of the original 17 interns to complete their degrees and teacher certification. All 16 completed their two-year teaching commitment; 7 interns have begun their fifth year of public school teaching, while several can be found in graduate programs—not all related to teaching. Two other interns are teaching in private schools. A number of women are raising families with no inclination to return to teaching in the near future. Others have found their way into careers like computer technology and medicine.

What about the five interns that are at the centerpiece of this book?

Gene (a Maverick) began a graduate degree in history after his third year of teaching at Justin High School but eventually became discouraged with his university advisor. He is currently in the process of applying to doctoral programs in Educational Administration. In his opinion, this is the only way that he can have the "power to make changes in education."

Rita (another Maverick) is in a period of transition. After completing two years of teaching, she thought she had fulfilled the obligations attached to two scholarships that supported her college education at Central. She went to Japan, where she taught English for three years. However, although she had satisfied the BIT requirements with her two years at Justin, Rita returned from Japan to discover that she owed one more year of teaching for the scholarship she received from the state. She currently teaches middle school students in what Rita staunchly asserts is her "last year of teaching." Her future career plans will focus on becoming a Japanese language interpreter or starting a travel agency that provides services to Japanese visitors to the United States.

Lucy (a Reservationist) is completing her fifth year of teaching at Jack Simper Middle School. She recently earned her master's degree in Educational Administration from Central College and intends to begin soon the search for an administrative position. While Lucy admits that such an opportunity may not come immediately, it may be sooner than she thinks due to a number of positions opening up in the district.

Jan (a Traditionalist) moved to Dallas, Texas, after getting married. She has completed her third year of teaching tenth-grade world geography in a well-respected suburban school district serving middle- to upper-class students. While she likes the students better than those in her first two years of teaching at Justin, the camaraderie with her colleagues does not compare. Jan still plans on getting a master's degree, maybe even a doctorate. So far, educational administration, in her mind, is the most logical choice. To date, however, she has not started taking coursework.

Roberto (a Convert) remains at King-Jackson Elementary School as a fifth-grade teacher. He remains the grade team leader and has taken on other administrative jobs, including summer school coordinator (in his third year), mentor teacher, coordinator of practicum experiences for student teachers (from Central College), and coordinator of the bilingual program. Roberto thinks these responsibilities give him a "jump start" on administration. Having just finished his master's degree, he already is looking toward a doctorate. Central College will once again provide him a "unique" opportunity for this degree as it pursues a partnership with a major state university in order to offer the doctoral degree to a select group of graduate students. In the meantime, Roberto has applied for the district's administrator training program (required prior to taking an administrative position). Additionally, after two attempts at winning the "Top Teacher of the Year" award from the district (he was runner-up both times), Roberto has set his sights on winning it this year.

SOME FINAL THOUGHTS

Education professors like Don Wright and institutions of higher education such as Central College are rare to teacher education. Traditionally, there has been little active recruitment of teachers. Most institutions have relied on the traditional student simply to walk through their ivy-covered revolving doors. Aside from a personal sense of mission held by certain individuals, institutions rarely have viewed the recruitment of outstanding teachers as important. Too, there has been little incentive for teachers and counselors in secondary schools or colleges to recruit high-ability students into the teaching profession. Consequently, few of these students have seriously considered public school teaching.

Once considered a noble or at least respectable profession, teaching has lost much of its historical status, and the attractors for teaching (e.g., positive community attitudes, relative classroom autonomy) have declined (Kottkamp, Provenzo, & Cohn, 1986). As a result, the teaching profession has lost many of its more traditional students and has become progressively less appealing to the few "brightest and best" who did enter. Today, Teach for America and President Clinton's college loan forgiveness program, like the Bridenthal program, seek to capitalize on a reservoir of social commitment and young people's penchant for fostering change by channeling their talents—albeit temporarily—into social and community services.

Although originally the Bridenthal program sought to "retain high-ability students," the retention model gave way to a Peace Corps model as most of the interns left public school classrooms. While the proportion of interns remaining in teaching was about the same as for other high-ability students not participating in such an incentive program, these interns have departed at a *slower* rate than other high-ability teachers (Darling-Hammond, 1984).

Ten interns returned to the public school classroom for one year beyond the two required by their scholarship, and five years after graduating, seven interns remain teaching in the public schools. Understandably, Wright claims success. These returning interns demonstrate the successful accomplishment of the original program's goals: the recruitment, preparation, and retention of high-ability persons for the teaching profession.

But what about those interns who continued teaching beyond the two-year requirement? How many of the ten interns returned to the classroom a third year because, like Roberto or Lucy, they had an intrinsic commitment to teaching? How many were more like Gene, taking advantage of a rare opportunity for a revolutionary swan song? And how many are really like Jan, who found teaching to be a convenient profession that enabled her to pursue her family and social interests?

The yardstick of "years in teaching" to judge the program's success is, of course, problematic as suggested in questions such as: Is three years a sufficient indicator of retention? Are the interns who continue to teach those who had expressed an interest in teaching prior to their enrollment in the program? How effective are these returning interns as classroom teachers and professional colleagues? Though these and other such questions were addressed in Chapter 10, it is important to emphasize that among the five interns selected for their representativeness among the larger group, neither of the Mavericks (Rita and Gene) stayed beyond three years (and only one of the five Mavericks is still teaching in public schools); both Roberto (Convert) and Lucy (Reservationist) are pursuing administrative certificates; and only Jan, the Traditionalist, appears to have settled into the life of a classroom teacher.

Addressing such questions, of course, makes the issue of retention more problematic than the unequivocal statement that ten interns continued to teach beyond their two-year commitment or that seven interns remained in teaching after five years. It is the simplistic power of such a "numbers" statement that will insure debate among many readers of this book.

There are other questions that should be addressed in evaluating the effectiveness of programs like Bridenthal. First, can such programs squeeze out of the profession other students, possessing less cultural capital but likely to teach for a longer period of time? In this scenario, as programs like Bridenthal become more widely adopted, the value of teaching will rise and the supply of a satisfactory pool of teachers will dwindle due to the increasing difficulty for a high school senior possessing a strong desire to teach but scoring 900 on the SAT to quality for admission (Weaver, 1984). While this has particular implications for the preparation of minority educators (Raizen, 1986), to date this phenomenon has not occurred.

Second, can high-ability students enhance the status of teaching or the quality of learning experienced by their students? They may not be willing to work within the excessively bureaucratic and intellectually stultifying context of public school teaching. They may find themselves isolated or simply incapable of restructuring the teaching field. As we discussed in Chapter 8, educational research has consistently demonstrated that the intrinsic considerations that bring people into teaching often lead to frustration when they confront institutional and contextual barriers that makes effective teaching more difficult (see, for example, Darling-Hammond, 1984; Goodlad, 1984). As we have demonstrated in case studies of five interns, these intrinsic factors are particularly relevant for academically talented persons (Smith, 1986). Only Roberto, working in an Alliance School, did not endure the everyday frustrations and barriers experienced by most classroom teachers.

There are, of course, other explanations for the departure of high-ability teachers from the classroom. One is that these persons are, in general, simply not effective teachers with students other than those who, like themselves, are academically able and motivated (Villeme & Hall, 1985).

Given that few beginning teachers have the opportunity to spend most of their classroom day with the school's "brightest and best" students, it was not surprising that interns like Rita experienced personal frustration and witnessed poor student achievement. It was surprising that Gene, despite his envious teaching placements, found himself on the verge of reassignment by the school principal and that Jan, an intern who never felt she fit into the Bridenthal group, developed close working relationships with her less academically talented colleagues.

With the exception of a few interns like Gene, most of these high-ability recruits had to deal with other than the most sought after students; a few directed resentment toward those "less able" students with whom they worked, and most held unrealistically high expectations for what their students could accomplish. Further, as Gary Sykes (1983) suggests, "to lure academically capable people into the field via fellowship money, then coerce a grudging proof of service, is not likely to yield excellent teaching" (p. 117)—a fact borne out by independent evaluations of these interns' two years of teaching. This group was quite comparable to other groups of non–high ability students as beginning teachers. The interns represented the spectrum of teaching abilities found among novice teachers. Some, like Roberto, were quite talented; others, like Jan, lacked many initial basic classroom teaching skills.

Another, more policy-based question, is whether we should use public monies to subsidize children of middle- and upper-middle-class families to enter public school teaching. Embedded in the question "Why not the best?" is a meritocratic ideology in which the academic playing fields of schools become social tournaments in which all compete for status, power, and money within a society stratified by social class and fractured with racial and gender divisions.

Participants in the Bridenthal program were disproportionately drawn from the Anglo middle-class. Like children of other middle-class parents, these interns could not have reasonably expected to attend Central without such a scholarship program. The class-based composition of the Ivy League curriculum and its student body was well documented in a study of the enrollment patterns at elite institutions during the late 1980s:

> Those who make it through the highly competitive admissions process of the prestigious universities are considered "the best and the brightest," those qualified, perhaps even destined, to have the most prized careers. Often overlooked, however, is the fact that the student bodies of these institutions are drawn heavily from affluent families . . . the elite private institutions appear to remain linked to an upper-class constituency within this putative meritocratic order. (Lewis & Kingston, 1989, p. 28)

Noting that while increasing financial support for academically successful middle- and low-income students might result in a more diverse student body, these researchers cautioned that without concomitant changes in institutional definitions of "high ability," the "two-tier" system in higher education would continue:

> If the very selective private institutions remain committed to the conventional measures of "merit"—high scores on standardized tests, well-balanced interests, special skills—in their admissions decisions, any increase in aid is likely to have only a slight impact on the social background of their students. Most students who are meritorious in the conventional sense come from high-income families where they have enjoyed special opportunities; children from lower-income families acquire relatively fewer linguistic and cultural skills—a decided disadvantage in their school work. (Lewis & Kingston, 1989, p. 32).

While programs like the Bridenthal Internship in Teaching made available an elite education to a number of talented, middle-class students, most policies and programs designed to recruit the best do little to resolve the expected teacher shortage and promote the retention of good teachers. In fact, such programs exacerbate the problem by channeling scarce available resources to a relatively small group of prospective teachers who are unlikely to remain in teaching, while at the same time elevating academic standards to a level that few minority students with teaching aspirations can meet. Providing scholarship funds to students who already have amassed a significant amount of "cultural capital" (i.e., the knowledge base, values, and language of the controlling cultural group) and who will undoubtedly do well without any such support depletes resources for others who lack such capital and further reinforces the "bright students equals good teachers" premise. As these resources are depleted, no scholarship programs for "low-ability" students who evidence qualities of a "good teacher" are developed (Sears, 1990b).

The Bridenthal program, supported by private monies from a tax-exempt trust, allocated hundreds of thousands of dollars to this "demonstration project." A critical factor in the successful recruitment and retention of high-ability students who had not considered teaching is a loan/scholarship package. If this project moves from demonstration to widespread application, the expenditure of public dollars (in direct grants or in tax subsidies) would be significant: $50,000 per high-ability student turned teacher. While such an expenditure pales in comparison with the costs for educating doctors, the fact that fewer than one-half of the interns who had not seriously considered teaching taught for more than a few years questions the efficacy of public policies that encourage such investment.

In a world of nearly unlimited resources this ought not to be an issue.

After all, some high-ability students *can* become good teachers, and having such persons in the school—if for only a few years—certainly would be desirable. However, in the world of global economic competition, trillion-dollar deficits, and reduction of social services, the desirable is not feasible. Asking "Why not the best?" means posing difficult questions such as "Who really benefits from the recruitment of high-ability students?" Documenting "When best doesn't equal good" means acknowledging that there are other young people, particularly from diverse backgrounds (e.g., persons of color, working class) who may not score high on traditional academic measures but who would make good teachers (positive role models, effective instructors, and long-term teachers). Following a decade of reform-inspired reports and programs, it is time to judge the wisdom of the seemingly innocuous question, "Why not the best?" Following this longitudinal study, it is time to ask teacher educators as well as policy makers if we have the clarity, conviction, and courage to acknowledge that teaching is, in fact, one of those professions where the best doesn't necessarily equal good.

References

Abelson, R., & Friquegnon, M. (1987). *Ethics for modern life* (3rd ed.). New York: St. Martin's Press.

Adler, M. (1982). *The paideia proposal: An educational manifesto.* New York: Macmillan.

Altenbaugh, R. (Ed.). (1974). *John Dewey on education.* Chicago: University of Chicago Press.

Altenbaugh, R. (1989). Teachers, their world, and their work: A review of the idea of "Professional Excellence" in school reform reports. In C. Shea, E. Kahane, & P. Sola (Eds.), *The new servants of power: A critique of the 1980's school reform movement* (pp. 167–175). New York: Greenwood.

American Association of Colleges for Teacher Education. (1985). *A call for change in teacher education.* (ERIC Document Reproduction No. ED 252 525)

Anderson, C. (1989). The role of education in the academic disciplines in teacher education. In M. Reynolds (Ed.), *Knowledge base for the beginning teacher* (pp. 88–107). Oxford, England: Pergamon.

Anderson, L., Cook, N., Pellicer, L., Sears, J., & Spradling, R. (1989). *A study of EIA-funded remedial and compensatory programs.* Columbia, SC: South Carolina Educational Policy Center.

Andrews, T., & Barnes, S. (1990). Assessment of teaching. In R. Houston, M. Haberman, & J. Sikula (Eds.), *Handbook of research in teacher education* (pp. 569–598). New York: Macmillan.

Anrig, G. (1986). Teacher education and teacher testing. *Phi Delta Kappan, 67* (6), 447–451.

Apple, M. (1974). The process and ideology of valuing in educational settings. In M. Apple et al. (Eds.), *Education evaluation: Analysis and responsibility* (pp. 3–34). Berkeley, CA: McCutchan.

Applegate, J. (1986). Undergraduate students' perceptions of field experiences: Toward a framework for study. In J. Raths & L. Katz (Eds.), *Advances in teacher education, volume 2* (pp. 21–38). Norwood, NJ: Ablex.

Armstrong, W. (1944). *The college and teacher education.* Washington, DC: American Council on Education.

Ashcroft, L. (1987). Defusing "empowering": The what and the why. *Language Arts, 64*(2), 143–156.

Ashton, P. (1992). A teacher education paradigm to empower teachers and students. In L. Katz (Ed.), *Advances in teacher education, volume 4* (pp. 82–104). Norwood, NJ: Ablex.

Ashton, P., & Crocker, L. (1987). Systematic study of planned variations: The essential focus of teacher education reform. *Journal of Teacher Education, 38*(3), 1–8.

Association for Student Teaching. (1968). *Internships in teacher education.* Washington, DC: Author.

Ayers, W. (1990). Rethinking the profession of teaching: A progressive option. *Action in Teacher Education, 12*(1), 1–5.

Bacharach, S., Bauer, S., & Shedd, J. (1986). The work environment and school reform. *Teachers College Record, 88,* 241–256.

Bagley, W., & Learned, W. (1920). *The professional preparation of teachers for America's public schools.* New York: Carnegie Foundation for the Advancement of Teaching.

Bailey, L. (1982). The relationships of career development and career education assessment and evaluation. In J. Krumboltz & D. Hamel (Eds.), *Assessing career development* (pp. 3–17). Palo Alto, CA: Mayfield.

Ball, D. (1990). The mathematical understandings that prospective teachers bring to teacher education. *The Elementary School Journal, 90*(4), 449–466.

Ball, D., & McDiarmid, G. W. (1990). The subject-matter preparation of teachers. In R. Houston, M. Haberman, & J. Sikula (Eds.), *Handbook of research on teacher education* (pp. 437–449). New York: Macmillan.

Barnes, H. (1989). Structuring knowledge for beginning teaching. In M. Reynolds (Ed.), *Knowledge base for the beginning teacher* (pp. 13–22). Oxford, England: Pergamon.

Behymer, J., & Cockreil, I. (1986). *Financial aid attracts students into teacher education.* (ERIC Document Reproduction Service No. ED277 649)

Beigel, H., & Willcox, I. (1953). Motivations in the choice of teaching. *Journal of Teacher Education, 4*(2), 106–109.

Bell, D. (1966). *The reforming of general education: The Columbia College experience in its national setting.* New York: Columbia University Press.

Bennett, W. (1983, February). The shattered humanities. *American Association of Higher Education Bulletin,* 3–5.

Bergsma, H., & Chu, L. (1981, April). *What motivates introductory and senior education students to become teachers?* Paper presented at annual meeting of the American Education Association, Los Angeles, CA. (ERIC Document Reproduction Service No. ED 202 818)

Berlak, A., & Berlak, H. (1981). *Dilemmas of schooling.* London: Methuen.

Bethume, S. (1981). *Factors related to white females' choice of education as a field of study during college: An analysis of the national longitudinal study of the high school class of 1972.* Unpublished doctoral dissertation, University of North Carolina at Chapel Hill.

Beyer, L. (1984). Field experience, ideology, and the development of critical reflectivity. *Journal of Teacher Education, 35*(3), 36–41.

Beyer, L. (1987). What knowledge is of most worth in teacher education? In J.

Smyth (Ed.), *Educating teachers: Changing the nature of pedagogical knowledge* (pp. 19–34). Philadelphia: Falmer.

Beyer, L., Feinberg, W., Pagano, J., & Whitson, J. (1989). *Preparing teachers as professionals: The role of educational studies and other liberal disciplines.* New York: Teachers College Press.

Bigge, M. (1982). *Learning theories for teachers* (4th ed.). New York: Harper & Row.

Bloom, A. (1967). The crisis of liberal education. In R. Goldwin (Ed.), *Higher education and modern democracy: The crisis of the few and the many* (pp. 121–140). Chicago: University of Chicago Press.

Bloom, A. (1987). *The closing of the American mind.* New York: Simon & Schuster.

Blustein, D. (1989). The role of career exploration in career decision-making of college students. *Journal of College Student Development, 30,* 111–117.

Book, C., Freeman, D., & Brousseau, B. (1985). *Comparing academic backgrounds and career aspirations of education and noneducation majors* (Research and Evaluation in Teaching Education Program Evaluation Series No. 2). East Lansing: College of Education, Michigan State University. (ERIC Document Reproduction Service No. ED 256 755)

Borkow, N., & Jordan, K. (1983). *The teacher workforce.* Washington, DC: Congressional Research Service, Library of Congress.

Borrowman, M. (1956). *The liberal and technical in teacher education.* New York: Teachers College Press.

Boser, J., Wiley, P., & Pettibone, T. (1986). *A comparison of participants in traditional and alternative teacher preparation programs.* (ERIC Document Reproduction Service No. ED 278 648)

Braverman, H. (1974). *Labor and monopoly capital.* New York: Monthly Review Press.

Britzman, D. (1987). Cultural myths in the making of a teacher: Biography and social structure. *Harvard Educational Review, 56*(4), 442–456.

Brogdon, R., & Tincher, W. (1986). *Higher aptitude high school students' opinion of career choice.* (ERIC Document Reproduction Service No. ED 279 632)

Brookhart, S., & Loadman, W. (1992). School-university collaboration: Across cultures. *Teaching Education, 4*(2), 53–68.

Bruner, J. (1960). *The process of education.* New York: Vintage.

Burden, P.(1982). *Interviews with experienced teachers: A reality base for preservice teachers.* Paper presented at the Association of Teacher Educators Mid-America Mini-Clinic, Columbia, MO. (ERIC Document Reproduction Service Number ED 218 261)

Burden, P. (1990). Teacher development. In R. Houston (Ed.), *Handbook of research on teacher education* (pp. 311–328). New York: Macmillan.

Burruel, J. (1971). The simplicity of the liberal arts colleges and Mexican-American community needs. In D. Bigelow (Ed.), *The liberal arts and teacher education: A confrontation* (pp. 120–124). Lincoln: University of Nebraska Press.

Byers, J. (1984). *The prediction of commitment to the teaching profession.* (ERIC Document Reproduction Service Number ED 251 452)

Carnegie Foundation for the Advancement of Teaching. (1988). *The conditions of teaching: A state-by-state analysis.* Lawrenceville, NJ: Princeton University Press.

Carnegie Task Force on Teaching as a Profession. (1986). *A nation prepared: Teachers for the 21st century.* Washington, DC: Carnegie Forum on Education and the Economy.

Carter, K. (1990). Teachers knowledge and learning to teach. In R. Houston (Ed.), *Handbook of research in teacher education* (pp. 291–310). New York: Macmillan.

Cattell, J. (1932). Teaching as a profession. *School and Society, 36*(935), 697–698.

Changing course: A 50-state survey of reform measures. (1985, February 5). *Education Week,* pp. 11–30.

Chapman, D. (1982). Attrition from teaching careers. *American Educational Research Journal, 19*(1), 93–105.

Chapman, D. (1983). A model of the influences on teacher retention. *Journal of Teacher Education, 34*(5), 43–49.

Chapman, D. (1984). Teacher retention. *American Educational Research Journal, 21*(3), 645–658.

Chapman, D., & Green, M. (1986). Teacher retention: A further examination. *Journal of Educational Research, 79*(5), 273–279.

Charters, W., & Waples, D. (1929). *The commonwealth teacher training study.* Chicago: University of Chicago.

Christensen, J. (1985). Adult learning and teacher career stage development. In P. Burke & R. Heidman (Eds.), *Career-long teacher education* (pp. 158–180). Springfield, IL: Thomas.

Cohen, E. (1986). *Designing groupwork: Strategies for the heterogeneous classroom.* New York: Teachers College Press.

Cohen, M., Klink, B., & Grana, J. (1990). *Teacher retention: A longitudinal comparison of those who teach and those who don't.* Paper presented at the annual meeting of the American Educational Research Association, Boston, MA. (ERIC Document Reproduction Service No. ED 320 909)

Conant, J. (1963). *The education of American teachers.* New York: McGraw-Hill.

Cooper, W. (1932). *National survey of the education of teachers.* Washington, DC: Government Printing Office.

Cornbleth, C. (1986). Ritual and rationality in teacher education reform. *Educational Researcher, 15* (4), 5–14.

Cornbleth, C. (1989). Cries of crisis, calls for reform, and challenges of change. In L. Weis, P. Altbach, G. Kelly, H. Petrie, & S. Slaughter (Eds.), *Crisis in teaching.* Albany: SUNY Press.

Crites, J. O. (1978). *Career Maturity Inventory.* Monterey, CA: CTB/McGraw-Hill.

Cross, K. (1984). The rising tide of school reform reports. *Phi Delta Kappan, 66*(5), 167–172.

Cuban, L. (1987). *The managerial imperative and the practice of leadership in schools.* Albany, NY: SUNY Press.

Cuban, L. (1990). Reforming again, again, and again. *Educational Researcher, 19*(1), 3–13.

Dahlquist, J. (1990). Liberal arts colleges: The right crucibles for teacher education. In T. Warren (Ed.), *A view from the top: Liberal arts presidents on teacher education* (pp. 7–15). Lanham, MD: University Press of America.

Darling-Hammond, L. (1984). *Beyond the commission reports: The coming crisis in teaching* (Report No. R–3177-RC). Santa Monica, CA: Rand Corporation.

Darling-Hammond, L. (1990). Teachers and teaching: Signs of a changing profession. In R. Houston (Ed.), *Handbook of research on teacher education* (pp. 267–290). New York: Macmillan.

Darling-Hammond, L., & Snyder, J. (1992). Framing accountability: Creating learner-centered schools. In A. Lieberman (Ed.), *The changing contexts of teaching: Ninety-first yearbook of the National Society for the Study of Teaching* (pp. 11–36). Chicago: University of Chicago Press.

Defino, M., & Hoffman, J. (1984). *A status report and content analysis of state mandated teacher induction programs.* (ERIC Document Reproduction Service No. ED 251 438)

DeLong, T. (1984). Teachers and their careers. Why do they choose teaching? *Journal of Career Development, 112*(Winter), 118–125.

Densmore, K. (1987). Professionalism, proletarianization and teacher work. In T. Popkewitz (Ed.), *Critical studies in teacher education: Its folklore, theory and practice* (pp. 130–160). London: Falmer.

Denton, J., & Smith, N. (1983). *Alternative teacher preparation programs: A cost efficient comparison.* (ERIC Document Reproduction Service No. ED 237 569)

Derber, C. (Ed.). (1982). *Professionals as workers: Mental labor in advanced capitalism.* Boston: Hall.

DeYoung, A. (1986). Educational "excellence" versus teacher "professionalism": Toward some conceptual clarity. *Urban Review, 18*(1), 71–84.

Diegmueller, K. (1991, February 20). Like a major-league baseball scout, Dallas recruiter combs the country in search of raw teaching talent. *Education Week,* 6–7.

Dreeben, R. (1970). *The nature of teaching: Schools and the work of teachers.* Glenview, IL: Scott, Foresman.

Duke, D. (1984). *Teaching: The imperiled profession.* Albany, NY: SUNY Press.

Dunbar, J. (1981). Moving to a five-year teacher preparation program! The perspective of experience. *Journal of Teacher Education, 32*(1), 13–15.

Egbert, R. (1980). Excellence in education. *Journal of Teacher Education, 31*(2), 5–7.

Elbaz, F. (1983). *Teacher thinking: A study of practical knowledge.* London: Croom Helm.

Etzioni, A. (1969). *The semi-professions and their organization.* New York: Free Press.

Feiman-Nemser, S. (1990). Teacher preparation: Structural and conceptual alternatives. In R. Houston (Ed.), *Handbook of research on teacher education* (pp. 212–233). New York: Macmillan.

Feiman-Nemser, S., & Floden, R. (1986). The cultures of teaching. In M. Wittrock (Ed.), *Handbook of research on teaching* (pp. 505–526). New York: Macmillan.

Feiman-Nemser, S., & Parker, M. (1990). Making subject matter part of the conversation in learning to teach. *Journal of Teacher Education, 41*(3), 32–43.

Feinberg, W. (1987). The Holmes Group report and the professionalization of teaching. *Teachers College Record, 88*(3), 366–377.

Feistritzer, C. (1983). *The condition of teaching.* Princeton, NJ: Carnegie Foundation for the Advancement of Teaching. (ERIC Document Reproduction Service No. ED 238 869)

Fessler, R. (1985). A model for teacher professional growth. In P. Burke & R. Heidman (Eds.), *Career-long teacher education* (pp. 181–193). Springfield, IL: Thomas.

Finkelstein, B. (1984). Education and the retreat from democracy in the United States, 1979-198? *Teachers College Record, 86,* 275–282.

Fisher, R., & Feldman, M. (1985). Some answers about the quality of teacher education students. *Journal of Teacher Education, 36*(3), 37–40.

Florio-Ruane, S. (1989). Social organization of classes and schools. In M. Reynolds (Ed.), *Knowledge base for beginning teachers* (pp. 163–172). New York: Pergamon.

Flowers, J. (Ed.). (1948). *School and community laboratory experiences in teacher education.* Washington, DC: American Association of Teachers Colleges.

Folger, J., Astin, H., & Bayer, A. (1970). *Human resources and higher education.* New York: Sage.

Foucault, M. (1972). *Power/Knowledge: Selected interviews and other writings.* (G. Colin, Ed.). New York: Pantheon.

Fox, S., & Singletary, T. (1986). Deductions about supportive induction. *Journal of Teacher Education, 37*(1), 12–15.

Friedman, A. (1977). *Industry and labor: Class struggle at work and monopoly capitalism.* London: Macmillan.

Frymier, J. (1987). Bureaucracy and the neutering of teachers. *Phi Delta Kappan, 69,* 9–14.

Fullan, M. (1991). *The new meaning of educational change* (2nd ed.). New York: Teachers College Press.

Fullan, M., & Hargreaves, A. (1991). *What's worth fighting for in your schools?* Toronto, Canada: Ontario Public School Teachers' Federations. (ERIC Document Reproduction Service No. ED 342 128)

Fuller, F. (1969). Concerns of teachers: A developmental conceptualization. *American Educational Research Journal, 6*(2), 207–226.

Fuller, F., & Brown, O. (1975). Becoming a teacher. In K. Ryan (Ed.), *The 74th yearbook of the National Society for the Study of Education, part 2* (pp. 25–52). Chicago: University of Chicago Press.

Gardner, W. (1989). Preface. In M. Reynolds (Ed.), *Knowledge base for the beginning teacher* (pp. ix–xii). Oxford, England: Pergamon.

General education in a free society. (1945). Cambridge, MA: Harvard University Press.

Gideonese, H. (1984). State educational policy intransition. *Phi Delta Kappan, 66,* 205–208

Gideonese, H. (1989). *Relating knowledge to teacher education.* Washington, DC: American Association of Colleges for Teacher Education.

Ginsberg, M., & Clift, R. (1990). The hidden curriculum of preservice teacher education. In R. Houston (Ed.), *Handbook of research in teacher education* (pp. 450–465). New York: Macmillan.

Giroux, H. (1988). *Teachers as intellectuals: Toward a critical pedagogy of learning.* South Hadley, MA: Bergin & Garvey.

Giroux, H. (1992). *Border crossings: Cultural workers and the politics of education.* New York: Routledge.

Goertz, M., Ekstrom, R., & Coley, R. (1984). *The impact of state policy on entrance into the teaching profession.* Princeton, NJ: Educational Testing Service.

Goertz, M., & Pitchor, B. (1985). *The impact of NTE use by states on teacher selection.* Princeton, NJ: Educational Testing Service.

Goetz, J., & Le Compte, M. (1984). *Ethnography and qualitative design in educational research.* New York: Academic Press.

Goode, W. (1969). The theoretical limits of professionalization. In A. Etzioni (Ed.), *The semi-professions and their organization* (pp. 266–313). New York: Free Press.

Goodlad, J. (1984). *A place called school.* New York: McGraw-Hill.

Gordon, L. (1976). *Survey of interpersonal values.* Chicago: Science Research Associates.

Gordon, L. (1984). *Survey of personal values.* Chicago: Science Research Associates.

Grant, C., & Zeichner, K. (1981). Inservice support for first year teachers. *Journal of Research and Development in Education, 14*(2), 99–111.

Greene, M. (1984). Excellence and the basics. In C. Eisele (Ed.), *Current issues in education* (pp. 22–28). Normal, IL: John Dewey Society.

Greenwood, E. (1957). Attributes of a profession. *Social Work, 2*(3), 45–55.

Griffin, G. (1985). Teacher induction. *Journal of Teacher Education, 36*(1), 42–46.

Grossman, P., Wilson, S., & Shulman, L. (1989). Teachers of substance: Subject matter knowledge for teaching. In M. Reynolds (Ed.), *Knowledge base for beginning teachers* (pp. 23–36). New York: Pergamon.

Guyton, E., & McIntyre, J. (1990). Student teaching and school experiences. In R. Houston, (Ed.), *Handbook of research on teacher education* (pp. 514–534). New York: Macmillan.

Hall, G. (1982). Induction: The missing link. *Journal of Teacher Education, 33*(3), 53–55.

Harap, H. (1951). *Preparation of teachers in the area of curriculum and instruction* (National Society of College Teachers of Education Monograph No. 2). Austin: University of Texas.

Hargreaves, A., & Dawe, R. (1986). Paths of professional development: Contrived collegiality, collaborative culture, and the case of peer coaching. *Teaching and Teacher Education, 6,* 227–241.

Harper, C. (1939). *A century of public teacher education*. Washington, DC: National Education Association.

Harren, V. (1979). A model of career decision making for college students. *Journal of Vocational Behavior 14,* 119–133.

Hart, S. P., & Marshall, J. D. (1992). *The question of teacher professionalism.* (ERIC Document Reproduction Service No. ED 349 291)

Harvey, W., Madaus, G., & Kreitzer, A. (1987). Charms talismanic: Testing teachers for the improvement of American education. In E. Rothkoff (Ed.), *Review of research in education, 14* (pp. 169–238). Washington, DC: American Educational Research Association.

Hawk, P., & Robards, S. (1987). Statewide teacher induction programs. In D. Brooks (Ed.), *Teacher induction: A new beginning* (pp. 33–43). Reston, VA: Association of Teacher Educators.

Hodenfield, G., & Stinnett, T. (1961). *The education of teachers: Conflict and consensus.* Englewood Cliffs, NJ: Prentice-Hall.

Hoffman, J., Edwards, S., O'Neal, S., Barnes, S., & Paulissen, M. (1986). A study of state mandated beginning teacher programs and their effects. *Journal of Teacher Education, 37*(1), 16–21.

Holland, J. (1985). *The self-directed search: A guide to educational and vocational planning.* Odessa, FL: Psychological Assessment Resources.

Holmes Group. (1986). *Tomorrow's teachers.* East Lansing, MI: Author.

Holmes Group. (1990). *Tomorrow's schools.* East Lansing, MI: Author.

Hopfengardner, J., Lasley, J., & Joseph, E. (1983). Recruiting preservice teacher education students. *Journal of Teacher Education, 34*(4), 10–13.

Horton, B. (1944). Ten criteria of a genuine profession. *Science Monthly, 58,* 164.

Howey, K., & Strom, S. (1987). Teacher selection reconsidered. In G. Katz & J. Rath (Eds.), *Advances in teacher education, volume 3* (pp. 1–34). Norwood, NJ: Ablex.

Howsam, R., Corrigan, D., Denemark, G., & Nash, R. (1976). *Educating a profession.* Washington, DC: American Association for Colleges of Teacher Education.

Hoy, W., & Rees, R. (1977). The bureaucratic socialization of student teachers. *Journal of Teacher Education, 28*(1), 23–26.

Hoy, W., & Woolfolk, A. (1990). Socialization of student teachers. *American Journal of Education, 27*(2), 279–300.

Hughes, E. (1969). Professions. In K. Lyn (Ed.), *The professions in America* (pp. 1–14). Boston: Beacon.

Huling-Austin, L. (1990). Teaching induction programs and internships. In R. Houston, M. Haberman, & J. Sikula (Eds.), *Handbook of research in teacher education* (pp. 535–548). New York: Macmillan.

Huling-Austin, L. (1992). Research on learning to teach: Implications for teacher induction and mentoring programs. *Journal of Teacher Education, 43*(3), 173–180.

Hunt, D. (1968). Teacher induction: An opportunity and a responsibility. *NASSP Bulletin, 52* (330), 130–135.

Hutchins, R. (1953). *The conflict in education*. New York: Harper & Row.

Jackson, P. (1968). *Life in classrooms*. New York: Holt, Rinehart & Winston.

Jamar, D., & Ervay, S. (1983). The effect of teacher education on the career goals of women. *Phi Delta Kappan, 64*(8), 593–598.

Jerry, D. (1968). Teacher induction: An opportunity and a responsibility. *NASSP Bulletin, 52* (330), 117–122.

Johnson, D. (Ed.). (1982). *Class and social development: A new theory of the middle class*. Beverly Hills, CA: Sage.

Joseph, P., & Green, N. (1986). Perceptions on reasons for becoming teachers. *Journal of Teacher Education, 37*(6), 28–33.

Kagan, D. (1992). Professional growth among preservice and beginning teachers. *Review of Educational Research, 62*(2), 129–169.

Keith, M. (1987). We've heard this song . . . Or have we? *Journal of Teacher Education, 38*(3), 20–25.

Kellams, S. (1985). Current general and liberal education reform efforts: The cycle continues. *Educational Studies, 16*(2), 117–126.

Kennedy, M. (1989). *Challenging the myths about teacher preparation*. Paper presented to the Office for Educational Research and Improvement, Washington, DC.

Kennedy, M. (1990). *Trends and issues in: Teachers' subject matter knowledge*. (ERIC Document Reproduction Service Number ED 322 100)

Kester, R., & Marockie, M. (1987). Local induction programs. In D. Brooks (Ed.), *Teacher induction: A new beginning* (pp. 25–31). Reston, VA: Association of Teacher Educators.

Kimball, B. (1986). *Orators and philosophers*. New York: Teachers College Press.

King, A., & Brownell, J. (1966). *The curriculum and the disciplines of knowledge*. New York: Wiley.

Koerner, J. (1963). *The miseducation of American teachers*. Boston, MA: Houghton Mifflin.

Kottkamp, R., Provenzo, E., & Cohn, M. (1986). Stability and change in a profession: Two decades of teacher attitudes, 1964–1984. *Phi Delta Kappan, 67*(8), 559–567.

Laman, A., & Reeves, D. (1983). Admission to teacher education programs: The status and trends. *Journal of Teacher Education, 34*(1), 2–4.

Langford, G. (1978). *Teaching as a profession*. Manchester, England: Manchester University Press.

Lanier, J., & Little, J. (1986). Research on teacher education. In M. Wittrock (Ed.), *Handbook of research on teaching* (pp. 527–569). New York: Macmillan.

Larson, M. (1977). *The rise of professionalism*. Berkeley: University of California Press.

Lawson, H. (1992). Beyond the new conception of teacher induction. *Journal of Teacher Education, 43*(3), 163–172.

Learned, W., & Wood, B. (1938). *The student and his knowledge*. New York: Carnegie Foundation for the Advancement of Teaching.

LeFerve, C. (1967). Teacher characteristics and careers. *Review of Educational Research, 37*(4), 433–447.

Levine, M. (Ed.). (1992). *Professional practice schools: Linking teacher education and school reform.* New York: Teachers College Press.

Lewis, L., & Kingston, W. (1989). The best, the brightest, and the most affluent: Undergraduates at elite institutions. *Academe, 75*(6), 28–33.

Lichtenstein, G., McLaughlin, W., & Knudsen, J. (1992). Teacher empowerment and professional knowledge. In A. Lieberman (Ed.), *The changing context of teaching: Ninety-first yearbook of the National Society for the Study of Education* (pp. 37–58). Chicago: University of Chicago Press.

Lieberman, A. (1992). *The changing context of teaching: Ninety-first yearbook of the National Society for the Study of Education.* Chicago: University of Chicago Press.

Lieberman, A., & Miller, L. (1984). *Teachers, their world and their work: Implications for school improvement.* Alexandria, VA: Association for Supervision and Curriculum Development.

Lieberman, M. (1956). *Education as a profession.* Englewood Cliffs, NJ: Prentice-Hall.

Lightfoot, S. L. (1986). On goodness in schools: Themes of empowerment. *Peabody Journal of Education, 63,* 9–28.

Lincoln, Y., & Guba, E. (1985). *Naturalistic inquiry.* Beverly Hills, CA: Sage.

Little, J. (1987). Teachers as colleagues. In V. Richardson-Koehler (Ed.), *Educators' handbook* (pp. 491–518). White Plains, NY: Longman.

Little, J. (1990). The persistence of privacy: Autonomy and initiative in teachers' professional relations. *Teachers College Record, 91*(4), 509–536.

Livingston, C., & Borko, H. (1989). Expert-novice differences in teaching: A cognitive analysis and implications for teacher education. *Journal of Teacher Education, 40*(4), 36–42.

Lofquist, L., & Dawis, R. (1969). *Adjustment to work.* New York: Appleton-Century-Crofts.

Lortie, D. (1975). *Schoolteacher: A sociological study.* Chicago: University of Chicago Press.

Macklin, M. (1981). Teaching professionalism to the teaching profession. *The Australian Journal of Education, 25*(1), 24–36.

Maritain, J. (1943). *Education at the crossroads.* New Haven, CT: Yale University Press.

Marshall, J., Otis-Wilborn, A., & Sears, J. (1991). Leadership and pedagogy: Rethinking leadership in professional schools of education. *Peabody Journal of Education, 66*(3), 78–103.

Marshall, J., Sears, J., & Otis-Wilborn, A. (1987). *A longitudinal study of a demonstration project related to the recruitment, preparation and retention of highly qualified persons for the teaching profession: The [Bridenthal] interns — the second year.* (ERIC Document Reproduction Service No. 282 842)

Marso, R., & Pigge, F. (1987). Differences between self-perceived job expectations and job realities of beginning teachers. *Journal of Teacher Education, 38*(6), 53–56.

Mattingly, P. (1975). *The classless profession.* New York: New York University Press.

Mattingly, P. (1987). Workplace autonomy and the reforming of teacher education. In T. Popkewitz (Ed.), *Critical studies in teacher education: Its folklore, theory and practice* (pp. 35–56). London: Falmer.

McDiarmid, W., Ball, D., & Anderson, C. (1989). Why staying one chapter ahead doesn't really work: Subject specific pedagogy. In M. Reynolds (Ed.), *Knowledge base for beginning teachers* (pp. 193–206). New York: Pergamon.

McDonald, J. (1985). A career ladder and career alternatives for teachers. In P. Burke & R. Heidman (Eds.), *Career-long teacher education* (pp. 223–249). Springfield, IL: Thomas.

McDonald, J. (1992). *Teaching: Making sense of an uncertain craft.* New York: Teachers College Press.

McDonald, J., & Elias, P. (1980). *Study of induction programs for beginning teachers: A crisis in training* (vol. 1). Princeton, NJ: Educational Testing Service. (ERIC Document Reproduction Service No. ED 257 775)

McLaren, P. (1991). Critical pedagogy: Constructing an arch of social dreamng and a doorway to hope. *Journal of Education, 173*(1), 9–34.

McLaughlin, M., Pfeifer, R., Swanson-Owens, D., & Yee, S. (1986). Why teachers won't teach. *Phi Delta Kappan, 67*(6), 420–426.

Medley, D. (1982). *Teacher competency testing and the teacher educator.* Charlottesville: University of Virginia, Bureau of Educational Research.

Moore, W. (1970). *The professions.* New York: Sage.

Murray, F. (1986). Teacher education. *Change, 18*(6), 19–25.

National Commission on Excellence in Education. (1983). *A nation at risk: The imperative for educational reform.* Washington, DC: Government Printing Office.

National Commission for Excellence in Teacher Education. (1985). *A call for change in teacher education.* Washington, DC: American Association of Colleges for Teacher Education. (ERIC Document Reproduction Service No. ED 252 525)

National Education Association. (1986). *Estimates of school statistics 1985–1986.* West Haven, CT: Author.

National Society of College Teachers of Education. (1935). *Studies in education.* Chicago: University of Chicago Press.

Nelli, E. (1984). A research-based response to allegations that education students are academically inferior. *Action in Teacher Education, 6*(3), 73–80.

Nelson, B., & Wood, L. (1985). The competency dilemma. *Action in Teacher Education, 7*(1–2), 45–57.

Nelson, H. (1985). New perspectives on the teacher quality debate. *Journal of Education Research, 78*(31), 133–140.

Newman, J. (1959). *The idea of a university.* Garden City, NY: Doubleday.

Noddings, N. (1992). Gender and the curriculum. In P. Jackson (Ed.), *Handbook of research on curriculum* (pp. 669–684). New York: Macmillan.

Odden, A. (1986). Sources of funding for education reform. *Phi Delta Kappan, 67*(5), 335–340.

Odell, S. (1990). Support for new teachers. In T. Bey & C. Holmes (Eds.), *Mentoring: Developing successful new teachers* (pp. 3–23). Reston, VA: Association of Teacher Educators.

Oldendorf, W. (1989). Teacher education at Berea College: Building a rationale for uniqueness in a liberal arts setting. In J. DeVitis & P. Sola (Eds.), *Building bridges for educational reform: New approaches to teacher education* (pp. 204–219). Ames: Iowa State University Press.

Olson, L. (1988, December 14). Poll: Teacher job satisfaction co-exists with deep concerns. *Education Week,* pp. 5, 18.

Ornstein, A. (1979). Toward greater teacher professionalism. *Illinois School Journal, 59,* 3–4.

Ornstein, A. (1981). The trend toward increased professionalism for teachers. *Phi Delta Kappan, 63,* 196–198.

Ost, D. (1989). The culture of teaching: Stability and change. *The Educational Forum, 53,* 163–177.

Ost, D., & Ost, L. (1988). The culture of teaching: Implications for staff development. *Journal of Staff Development, 9*(3), 50–55.

Otis-Wilborn, A., Marshall, J., & Sears, J. (1989). *A longitudinal study of a demonstration project related to the recruitment, preparation and retention of highly qualified persons for the teaching profession: The [Bridenthal] interns — the third year.* Unpublished manuscript.

Otis-Wilborn, A., Marshall, J., & Sears, J. (1990). Commitment: A reflection of the quality of preservice teachers. *Peabody Journal of Education, 65*(Fall), 107–129.

Passow, A. (1984). *Reforming schools in the 1980's: A critical review of the national reports.* (ERIC Document Reproduction Service No. ED 242 850)

Phenix, P. (1962). The use of the disciplines as curriculum content. *Education Forum, 26*(3), 273–280.

Plank, D., & Ginsberg, R. (1990). Catch the wave: Reform commissions and school reform. In J. Murray (Ed.), *The educational reform movement of the 1980s* (pp. 121–142). Berkeley, CA: McCutchan.

Popkewitz, T. (1991). *A political sociology of educational reform.* New York: Teachers College Press.

Popkewitz, T., & Lind, K. (1989). Teacher incentives as reform: Implications for teachers' work and the changing control mechanism in education. *Teachers College Record, 90*(4), 575–594.

Popkewitz, T., & Pittman, A. (1986). The idea of progress and the legitimation of state agendas: American proposals for school reform. *Curriculum & Teacher, 1*(1–2), 11–24.

Powell, A. (1980). *The uncertain profession.* Cambridge, MA: Harvard University Press.

Pratte, R., & Rury, J. (1989). Professionalism, autonomy, and teachers. *Educational Policy, 2*(1), 71–89.

Pratte, R., & Rury, J. (1991). Teachers, professionalism, and craft. *Teachers College Record, 93*(1), 59–72.

Pullias, E. (1940). Teaching: A profession or a trade? *Educational Forum, 4,* 263–270.

Raizen, S. (1986). Strategies to increase teacher supply and quality. *Teacher Education Quarterly, 13*(4), 22–30.

Raywid, M. (1987). Excellence and choice: Friends or foes? *Urban Review, 19*(1), 35–47.

Rich, J. (1985). The role of professional ethics in teacher education. *Action in Teacher Education, 7*(3), 21–24.

Roberson, S., Keith, T., & Page, E. (1983). Now who aspires to teach? *Educational Researcher, 12*(6), 13–21.

Robinson, V. (1985). *Making do in the classroom: A report on the misassignment of teachers.* Washington, DC: Council for Basic Education and American Federation of Teachers.

Rosenholtz, S. (1987). Education reform strategies: Will they increase teacher commitment? *American Journal of Education, 95*(4), 534–562.

Rosenholtz, S. (1989). *Teachers' workplace: The social organization of schools.* New York: Longman.

Roth, R., & Pipho, C. (1990). Teacher education standards. In R. Houston, M. Haberman, & J. Sikula (Eds.), *Handbook of research in teacher education* (pp. 119–135). New York: Macmillan.

Rothman, E. (1977). *Troubled teachers.* New York: McKay.

Runyan, C. (1990). *No more isolated Cinderellas at the swimming hole: A call for needs-based developmental induction.* Paper presented at the 15th annual national conference of the National Council of the States, Orlando, FL.

Ryan, K., Newman, K., Mager, G., Applegate, J., Lasley, L., Flora, R., & Johnston, J. (1980). *Biting the apple: Accounts of first year teachers.* New York: Longman.

Sandefur, J. (1985). Competency assessment of teachers. *Action in Teacher Education, 7*(1–2), 1–12.

Sarason, S. (1971). *The culture of the school and the problem of change.* Boston: Allyn & Bacon.

Schlechty, P. (1990). *Reform in teacher education: A sociological view.* Washington, DC: American Association of Colleges for Teacher Education. (ERIC Reproduction Document No. ED 332 981)

Schlechty, P., & Vance, V. (1983). Recruitment, selection and retention: The shape of the teaching force. *The Elementary School Journal, 83*(4), 469–487.

Schmuck, R., & Schmuck, P. (1983). *Group processes in the classroom* (4th ed.). Dubuque, IA: Brown.

Schoenfeld, A. (1985). Metacognitive and epistemological issues in mathematical understanding. In E. Silver (Ed.). *Teaching and learning mathematical problem-solving* (pp. 177–188). Hillsdale, NJ: Erlbaum.

Schön, D. (1989). Professional knowledge and reflective practice. In T. Sergiovanni & J. Moore (Eds.), *Schooling for tomorrow* (pp. 188–206). Boston: Allyn & Bacon.

Sears, J. (1981, January). *Teaching and professionalism: Transcending the profes-*

sion-ocrat. Paper presented at the Henry Lester Smith Conference on Educational Research, Bloomington, IN.

Sears, J. (1984). *A critical ethnography of teacher education programs at [Founders] University: An inquiry into the perceptions of students and faculty regarding quality and effectiveness.* Unpublished doctoral dissertation, Indiana University.

Sears, J. (1990a). Institutionalizing change in teacher education: Indiana University, a retrospective study. *Peabody Journal of Education, 65*(Fall), 180–208.

Sears, J. (1990b). Recruiting minorities into teaching. *Teaching Education, 3*(1), 76–81.

Sears, J., Marshall, J., & Otis-Wilborn, A. (1988). *Teacher education policies and programs: Implementing reform proposals of the 1980s.* Chapel Hill, NC: Southeastern Educational Improvement Laboratory. (ERIC Document Reproduction Service No. 296 985)

Sears, J., Marshall, J., & Otis-Wilborn, A. (1989). The political economy of teacher training: Attracting high-ability persons into teaching, a critique. *Teacher Education Quarterly, 16*(4), 5–72.

Sears, J., Marshall, J., & Otis-Wilborn, A. (1990). Bringing some class to teaching: Following the pied pipers of teacher education reform. In W. Tierney (Ed.), *Culture and ideology in higher education* (pp. 151–186). New York: Praeger.

Sears, J., Moyer, P., & Marshall, J. (1986). *A longitudinal study of a demonstration project related to the recruitment, preparation and retention of highly qualified persons for the teaching profession: The [Bridenthal] interns — The first year.* (ERIC Document Reproduction Service No. 272 454)

Sewell, W. (1971). Inequality of opportunity in higher education. *American Sociological Review, 36*(5), 793–809.

Shaker, P., & Ullrich, W. (1987). Reconceptualizing the debate over the general education of teachers. *Journal of Teacher Education, 38*(1), 11–15.

Shanker, A. (1985). The making of a profession. *American Educator, 9*(3), 10–17, 46, 48.

Shaplin, J., & Powell, A. (1964). A comparison of internship programs. *Journal of Teacher Education, 15,* 175–183.

Shulman, L. (1987). Knowledge and teaching: Foundations of the new reform. *Harvard Educational Review, 57*(1), 1–22.

Silver, H., & Hanson, R. (1981). *Teaching style inventory.* Moorestown, NJ: Hanson Silver & Associates.

Sizer, T. (1984). *Horace's compromise: The dilemma of the American high school.* Boston, MA: Houghton-Mifflin.

Slaughter, J. (1990). The liberal arts college and the challenge of teacher education. In T. Warren (Ed.), *A view from the top: Liberal arts presidents on teacher education* (pp. 118–128). Lanham, MD: University Press of America.

Smith, A., Travers, P., & Yard, G. (1990). *Codes of ethics for selected fields of professional education.* St. Louis: University of Missouri School of Education. (ERIC Document and Reproduction Service No. ED 318 736)

Smith, E. (1962). *Teacher education: A reappraisal.* New York: Harper & Row.

Smith, R. (1986). *A study of the difference in the satisfaction with teaching work between high academic and low academic ability teachers.* Unpublished doctoral dissertation, University of Utah.

Smylie, M., & Denny, J. (1989). *Teacher leadership: Tensions and ambiguities in organizational perspective.* Paper presented at the annual meeting of the American Educational Research Association, San Francisco.

Sockett, H. (1989). Research, practice and professional aspiration within teaching. *Journal of Curriculum Studies, 21*(2), 97–112.

Sockett, H. (1990). Accountability, trust, and ethical codes of practice. In J. Goodlad, R. Soder, & K. Sirotnick (Eds.), *The moral dimensions of teaching* (pp. 224–250). San Francisco: Jossey-Bass.

Sockett, H. (1993). *The moral base for teacher professionalism.* New York: Teachers College Press.

Soder, R. (1990). The rhetoric of teacher professionalization. In J. Goodlad, R. Soder, & K. Sirotnik (Eds.), *The moral dimensions of teaching* (pp. 35–86). San Francisco: Jossey-Bass.

Spero, J. (1986). *The use of student financial aid to attract prospective teachers: A survey of state efforts.* (ERIC Document Reproduction No. ED 267 687)

Spring, J. (1985). *American education: An introduction to social and political aspects.* White Plains, NY: Longman.

Sprinthall, N., & Thies-Sprinthall, N. (1983). The teacher as an adult learner: A cognitive-developmental view. In G. Griffin (Ed.), *Staff development: Eighty-second yearbook of the National Society for the Study of Education, part 2* (pp. 13–33). Chicago: University of Chicago Press.

Stinnett, T. (1955). *Teacher education: The decade ahead.* Washington, DC: National Education Association.

Stodolosky, S. (1985). Teacher evaluation: The limits of looking. *Educational Research, 13*(9), 11–18.

Stoltzfus, V. (1990). Small is beautiful: Teacher education in the liberal arts setting. In T. Warren (Ed.), *A view from the top: Liberal arts presidents on teacher education* (pp. 44–55). Lanham, MD: University Press of America.

Stone, J. (1968). *Breakthrough in teacher education.* San Francisco: Jossey-Bass.

Strike, K. (1990a). The legal and moral responsibility of teachers. In J. Goodlad, R. Soder, & K. Sirotnik (Eds.), *The moral dimensions of teaching* (pp. 188–223). San Francisco: Jossey-Bass.

Strike, K. (1990b). Teaching ethics to teachers: What the curriculum should be about. *Teaching and Teacher Education, 6*(1), 47–53.

Strom, S. (1989). The ethical dimension of teaching. In M. Reynolds (Ed.), *Knowledge base for beginning teachers* (pp. 267–276). New York: Pergamon.

Sullivan, J. (1981). *Women's career aspirations: A national survey of traditional and nontraditional aspirations of college freshmen.* Unpublished doctoral dissertation, Florida State University.

Super, D. (1957). *The psychology of careers.* New York: Harper.

Super, D. (1980). A life-span life-space approach to career development. *Journal of Vocational Behavior, 16,* 282–298.

Super, D. (1990). A life span, life-space approach to career development. In D. Brown, L. Brooks, & Associates (Eds.), *Career choice and development* (pp. 192–261). San Francisco: Jossey-Bass.

Super, D., & Hall, D. (1978). Career development: Exploration and planning. *Annual Review of Psychology, 29,* 43–49.

Swanson, P. (1968). A time to teach—And a time to learn. *NASSP Bulletin, 52* (330), 74–84.

Sykes, G. (1983). Public policy and the problem of teacher quality: The need for screens and magnets. In L. Shulman (Ed.), *Handbook of teaching and policy* (pp. 97–125). New York: Longman.

Tabachnick, B., & Zeichner, K. (1984). The impact of the student teaching experience on the development of teacher perspectives. *Journal of Teacher Education, 35,* 28–36.

Talbert, J. (1986). The staging of teachers' careers: An institutional perspective. *Work and Occupations, 13*(3), 421–443.

Tamir, P. (1988). Subject matter and related pedagogical knowledge in teacher education. *Teaching & Teacher Education, 4,* 99–110.

Taylor, F. (1911). *The principles of scientific management.* New York: Harper.

Taylor, H. (1969). *Students without teachers.* New York: McGraw-Hill.

Tom, A. (1987). Replacing pedagogical knowledge with pedagogical questions. In J. Smyth (Ed.), *Educating teachers: Changing the nature of pedagogical knowledge* (pp. 9–18). Philadelphia: Falmer.

Tom, A., & Valli, L. (1990). Professional knowledge for teachers. In M. Wittrock (Ed.), *Handbook of research on teaching* (pp. 373–392). New York: Macmillan.

Tymitz-Wolf, B. (1984). The new vocationalism and teacher education. *Journal of Teacher Education, 35*(1), 21–25.

Vaughn, J. (1979). Government investments in research and development on inservice: NIE's role. *Journal of Teacher Education, 30,* 33–35.

Veenman, S. (1984). Perceived problems of beginning teachers. *Review of Educational Research, 54*(2), 143–178.

Villeme, M., & Hall, B. (1985). Higher ability teachers: How do they differ from lower ability teachers in their use of selected teaching practices? *Action in Teacher Education, 20*(3), 27–30.

Waller, W. (1932). *The sociology of teaching.* New York: Wiley.

Warren, T. (Ed). (1990). *A view from the top: Liberal arts presidents on teacher education.* Lanham, MD: University Press of America.

Watts, D. (1987). Student teaching. In M. Haberman & M. Backus (Eds.), *Advances in teacher education, volume 36* (pp. 151–167). Norwood, NJ: Ablex.

Weaver, W. (1979). In search of quality: The need for talent in teaching. *Phi Delta Kappan, 61*(1), 29–32.

Weaver, W. (1981). The talent pool in teacher education. *Journal of Teacher Education, 32*(2), 32–36.

Weaver, W. (1984). Solving the problem of teacher quality, part I. *Phi Delta Kappan, 66*(2), 108–115.

Weil, P., & Weil, M. (1971). Professionalism: A study of attitudes and values. *The Journal of Teacher Education, 22*(3), 314–318.

Weinrach, S., & Srebalus, D. (1990). Hollands' theories of careers. In D. Brown, L. Brooks, & Associates (Eds.), *Career choice and development* (pp. 37–67). San Francisco: Jossey-Bass.

Weiss, L. (1985). Excellence and student class, race, and gender cultures. In P. Altbach, G. Kelly, & L. Weiss (Eds.), *Excellence in education* (pp. 217–232). Albany: SUNY Press.

White, R. (1983). *Teachers as state workers and the politics of professionalism.* Unpublished doctoral dissertation, Australian National University.

Williams, J. (1988). To teach or not to teach: A question for women. *Free inquiry in creative sociology, 16*(2), 209–216.

Wilson, S., Shulman, L., & Richert, A. (1987). "150 different ways" of knowing: Representations of knowledge in teaching. In J. Calderhead (Ed.), *Exploring teachers' thinking* (pp. 104–124). London: Cassell.

Wise, A. (1989). Professional teaching: A new paradigm for the management of education. In T. Sergiovanni & J. Moore (Eds.), *Schooling for tomorrow* (pp. 301–310). Needham Heights, MA: Allyn & Bacon.

Wise, A. (1990). Six steps to teacher professionalism. *Educational Leadership, 47,* 57–60.

Woodring, P. (1957). *New directions in teacher education.* New York: Fund for the Advancement of Education.

Yonemura, M. (1987). Reflections on teacher empowerment and teacher education. *Harvard Educational Review, 56*(4), 473–480.

Zeichner, K. (1987). The ecology of field experiences: Toward an understanding of the role of field experiences in teacher development. In M. Haberman & M. Backus (Eds.), *Advances in teacher education, volume 36* (pp. 94–117). Norwood, NJ: Ablex.

Zeichner, K. (1989). Learning from experience in graduate teacher education. In A. Woolfolk (Ed.), *Research perspectives in the graduate preparation of teachers* (pp. 12–29). Englewood Cliffs, NJ: Prentice-Hall.

Zeichner, K. (1991). Contradictions and tensions in the professionalization of teaching and the democratization of schools. *Teachers College Record, 92*(3), 363–379.

Zeichner, K., & Gore, J. (1990). Teacher socialization. In R. Houston, M. Haberman, & J. Sikula (Eds.), *Handbook of research in teacher education* (pp. 329–348). New York: Macmillan.

Zeichner, K., & Liston, D. (1990). Traditions of reform in U.S. teacher education. *Journal of Teacher Education, 41*(2), 3–20.

Zeichner, K., & Tabachnick, B. (1984, April). *Social strategies and institutional control in the socialization of teachers.* Paper presented at the annual meeting of the American Educational Research Association, New Orleans.

Zimpher, N. (1989). The RATE Project: A profile of teacher education students. *Journal of Teacher Education, 40*(6), 27–30.

Index

About the Authors

James T. Sears is a professor in the Department of Educational Leadership and Policies at the University of South Carolina and a teaching professor for the South Carolina Honors College. He is also a Visiting Scholar at the Center for Feminist Research at the University of Southern California and has served as a Senior Research Fellow at the South Carolina Educational Policy Center. Earning his baccalaureate summa cum laude in history at Southern Illinois University, Professor Sears earned his master's degree in political science at the University of Wisconsin–Madison, and a master's degree and doctorate in education at Indiana University. He has taught in elementary and secondary schools in the United States and overseas. Professor Sears specializes in cultural studies with a focus on curriculum and sexuality. He has written nearly 100 book chapters, articles, essays, and scholarly papers; has written, co-authored, or edited five books; and, along with J. Dan Marshall, serves as co-editor of *Teaching Education*.

J. Dan Marshall is an associate professor in the Department of Curriculum and Instruction at Pennsylvania State University. Working with Dr. Sears, he has co-edited *Teaching and Thinking About Curriculum: Critical Inquiries* (New York: Teachers College Press, 1990), as well as the past four years of the innovative journal, *Teaching Education*. Professor Marshall's scholarly articles have appeared in publications ranging from *Radical Teacher* and *JCT* to *Educational Leadership* and *Vitae Scholastica*. He is active at the state and national levels in organizations including the Association for Supervision and Curriculum Development and the American Educational Research Association and he is a recent factotum for the Professors of Curriculum Group.

Amy Otis-Wilborn is an associate professor in the Department of Exceptional Education at the University of Wisconsin–Milwaukee. She also is Director of the Center for Teacher Education in the School of Education coordinating reform efforts. Professor Otis-Wilborn earned her Bachelor of Science degree in elementary education and special education from the University of Kansas Medical Center. After teaching for ten years, she returned to complete her doctorate at the University of Kansas in special education, concentrating on legal issues and policy analysis. Professor Otis-Wilborn's research and writing have focused on teacher education as it relates to the fields of general and special education.